"This is not a typical introduction to the letters or his theology, nor a handbook for how to interpret the Pauline epistles, but something of a hybrid of the three. MaGee's clear writing attests his experience as a gifted teacher of undergraduates; his Christian commitments as he handles the Word of God make this book something that pastors can circulate in their churches with confidence. Highly recommended."

—D. A. Carson,
Research Professor of New Testament,
Trinity Evangelical Divinity School

"In this carefully crafted guide, Dr. MaGee provides a reliable introduction to the reading of Paul's letters through an informed discussion of a host of methodological issues. Demonstrating his skills as a seasoned teacher, Dr. MaGee provides helpful tools for both the appreciation and application of the gospel that Paul preaches. Beginning students will find this volume helpful in grasping the content of Paul's letters, while more advanced readers will benefit from the fair presentation of the current issues in Pauline studies."

—David W. Pao,
Professor of New Testament and Chair of the New Testament Department,
Trinity Evangelical Divinity School

"For MaGee, 'It takes wisdom to move from the original meaning of Paul's letter to faithful responses that capture the potential of Paul's teachings for transformed living in current context.' Thus, writing from his wealth of experience in the college classroom, he challenges students to engage in a rigorous and thorough analysis of Paul's writings in order to understand its original message, but always with an eye towards discovering Paul's relevancy for personal transformation. MaGee provides a wide perspective in which to hear various viewpoints about Paul, without diminishing the greater desire for his readers to take Paul's message to heart in practical Christian living."

—David Sparks,
president of Footstep Ministries
and author of *The Daily Insight Series on Paul*

"Forged in the fire of the college classroom, *Studying Paul's Letters with the Mind and Heart*, is an excellent, as well as accessible, introduction to the life and ministry of the apostle Paul. With precision and passion, Greg MaGee presents his readers with an up-to-date summary of Pauline studies while equipping them to thoughtfully read, carefully interpret, and meaningfully apply God's Word for themselves. MaGee's work is illustrated from Scripture as well as life, and his crisp footnotes nicely complement the text."

—Randall J. Gruendyke,
Pastor of Ministry Leadership,
Grace Evangelical Free Church, La Mirada, CA

"For a fresh, well-informed guide to understanding Paul's letters, Greg MaGee's new book is just what students and teachers need. It provides a wealth of valuable information about the first-century background of Paul and his readers, guidance on how to interpret and apply Paul's teachings for personal transformation, and a summary of Paul's central theological ideas—all in a lively, focused style that is well-suited for individual study or for a classroom setting. Chapters on authenticity of the letters, on Paul's use of the Old Testament, and on the New Perspective on Paul are particularly helpful. Highly recommended!"

—Buist M. Fanning,
Senior Professor Emeritus of New Testament Studies,
Dallas Theological Seminary

Studying Paul's Letters with the Mind and Heart

Gregory S. MaGee

Studying Paul's Letters with the Mind and Heart
© 2018 Gregory S. MaGee

Published by Kregel Publications, a division of Kregel, Inc., 2450 Oak Industrial Dr. NE, Grand Rapids, MI 49505–6020.

Maps of Paul's journeys were designed by Shawn Vander Lugt, Managing Editor for Academic and Ministry Books at Kregel Publications.

The Greek font, GraecaU, is available from www.linguistsoftware.com/lgku.htm, +1-425-775-1130.

ISBN 978–0–8254–4472–2

Printed in the United States of America

18 19 20 21 22 / 5 4 3 2 1

■ ■ ■

To my parents,
John and Ruby MaGee

■ ■ ■

CONTENTS

■ ■ ■

ACKNOWLEDGMENTS

Many people have contributed indirectly to this book. I was blessed to grow up in supportive family and church environments that helped shape my spiritual interests from a young age. In particular, my parents expressed a winsome, consistent, and deeply rooted faith through their lives and words. Friends and mentors with Cru (formerly Campus Crusade for Christ) shaped me in significant ways during my four years in college and ten years after graduation. During those years, I enjoyed serving on ministry teams in the US and East Asia that prioritized studying the Scriptures. Those team Bible studies helped fuel my interests in studying the Bible and teaching others how to do so as well. Professors at Dallas Theological Seminary and Trinity Divinity School influenced me through their spiritually edifying instruction and mentoring, and classmates brightened the journey as we sought to follow Christ together.

In recent years, the administration, faculty, and staff at Taylor University have helped create a great atmosphere for my teaching, scholarship, and friendships. Energetic and gifted Taylor students have kept me excited to return to teaching each semester and have given me inspiration for writing projects such as this book. Jerusalem University College (Israel), Tutku Tours (Turkey), and Footstep Ministries (Greece and Rome) guided me through many of the lands that were part of Paul's story. Upland Community Church has faithfully taught the Scriptures and provided many avenues for fellowship and service. In particular, I have enjoyed watching lively, but thoughtful, students respond to many passages in Acts and Paul's letters in the high school Sunday school class I teach.

Early on in my work with Cru, I married Emily, who has encouraged and sharpened me like no one else has. We have trusted God through life's challenges and opportunities, and we have raised three wonderful children together. Emily was so supportive when I returned to the academic world after our years with Cru. She was always a good sport when I returned home from classes and discussed my half-formed biblical and theological thoughts with her. She continues to listen patiently and offer wise feed-back when I look to her to help process teaching and writing ideas.

I also thank God for the people who have helped with this project directly. I am grateful for the team at Kregel, including Paul Hillman, Herb Bateman, Shawn Vander Lugt, Laura Bartlett, and Duncan Burns. Taylor University granted my sabbatical leave for the spring of 2017, which gave me focused time to research and write. Watching Taylor students in my Pauline Epistles classes interact with Paul's letters has given me insight into the way that Paul's letters impact lives in so many different ways. These students have also helped me refine material and assignments that are included in this book. I especially appreciate former students Ben Stuckey and Daniel Ford for offering their valuable feedback on various chapters in this book. Finally, my wife Emily has helped with proofreading and by providing encouragement and advice when I needed it the most.

—Greg MaGee
Upland, Indiana

■ ■ ■

ABBREVIATIONS

AB	Anchor Bible
BECNT	Baker Exegetical Commentary on the New Testament
BSac	*Bibliotheca Sacra*
CBQ	*Catholic Biblical Quarterly*
CNTUOT	*Commentary on the New Testament Use of the Old Testament*
CTR	*Criswell Theological Review*
DLNT	*Dictionary of the Later New Testament and Its Developments.* Edited by R. P. Martin and P. H. Davids. Downers Grove, IL: InterVarsity Press, 1997.
DNTB	*Dictionary of New Testament Background.* Edited by Craig A. Evans and Stanley E. Porter. Downers Grove, IL: InterVarsity Press, 2000.
DPL	*Dictionary of Paul and His Letters.* Edited by Gerald F. Hawthorne and Ralph P. Martin. Downers Grove, IL: InterVarsity Press, 1993.
EncJud	*Encyclopedia Judaica.* Edited by Fred Skolnik and Michael Berenbaum. 2nd ed. 22 vols. Detroit: Macmillan Reference USA, 2007.
ESV	English Standard Version
GNT	Good News Translation
HCSB	Holman Christian Standard Bible
HNTC	Harper's New Testament Commentaries
HTR	*Harvard Theological Review*
JBL	*Journal of Biblical Literature*
JETS	*Journal of the Evangelical Theological Society*
JSNT	*Journal for the Study of the New Testament*
JSNTSup	Journal for the Study of the New Testament Supplement Series
NASB	New American Standard Bible
NEB	New English Bible

NET	*NET Bible, New English Translation.* 1st ed. Dallas: Biblical Studies Press, 2005.
NICNT	New International Commentary on the New Testament
NIGTC	New International Greek Testament Commentary
NIV	New International Version
NKJV	New King James Version
NLT	New Living Translation
NRSV	New Revised Standard Version
NTS	*New Testament Studies*
ProEccl	*Pro Ecclesia*
SBLDS	Society of Biblical Literature Dissertation Series
SGBC	Story of God Bible Commentary
STR	*Southeastern Theological Review*
TNTC	Tyndale New Testament Commentaries
TynBul	*Tyndale Bulletin*
VE	*Vox Evangelica*
WBC	Word Biblical Commentary
WUNT	Wissenschaftliche Untersuchungen zum Neuen Testament
ZECNT	Zondervan Exegetical Commentary on the New Testament

■ ■ ■

CHAPTER ONE

INTRODUCTION

An inspiration for this book comes from one of my favorite verses in Paul's letters: "And we also thank God continually because, when you received the word of God, which you heard from us, you accepted it not as a human word, but as it actually is, the word of God, which is indeed at work in you who believe" (1 Thess. 2:13). This verse paints a picture of potent words, changed lives, and encounters with the God of the universe. Let's take a closer look at the verse and what it says about reading Paul's letters with the mind and heart.

GOD'S WORD WAS AT WORK IN THIS CHURCH

The Thessalonian church was a source of joy for Paul and his co-laborers, and Paul regularly thanks God for them in this letter (1:2–3; 2:19–20; 3:7–10). Paul had invested himself in these young believers, and he was thrilled that they were doing so well spiritually. In 1 Thessalonians 2:13, Paul highlights the reason for their initial growth—their hearts had been responsive to Paul's message and had recognized it as having a divine origin and authority. Paul had taught them the gospel in his own words, but they perceived that God's good, wise, and perfect mind shone through that message. Because they had received God's word with hearts of faith and obedience, the Thessalonians were experiencing the ongoing power of God's word in their lives: the word of God was "indeed at work in you who believe."

Let those final words of the verse sink in for a moment: God's word is *at work* in the lives of believers. Paul's teaching, which we encounter in his letters, is designed to penetrate our lives and carry out a reconstruction project in us. God's Spirit implants the word in the recesses of our lives so that the seed can sprout, grow, and "produce a crop—some thirty, some sixty, some a hundred times what was sown" (Mark 4:20). Reading Paul's letters, or any other book from the Bible, cannot be reduced to an exercise of understanding information or satisfying our intellectual curiosity. We fail to read God's Word as it is intended to be read when we leave no time and space for the intersection of God's words and our needs as his children.

At some point in our Christian experience, most of us can identify with the joy and power of meeting with God through the Bible and seeing his word at work in us. God's words of grace and truth expose us to his wisdom and beauty, the darkness of sin in our lives, the power of Christ, the compelling vision of being part of his people, the challenges of walking by faith and obedience rather than by sight and selfishness, and the hope of God's kingdom returning in full glory. God's Spirit applies rich words and messages to our lives at the right time for the right purposes. We see growth in our lives, and we feel motivated to share what we are learning with others.

But we can also likely identify with Bible study that becomes dry or merely academic. Seemingly endless processing of information doesn't appear to make much difference in our worship or service to the Lord. The word no longer seems to be at work in our lives.

All Christians go through seasons of vibrancy and dryness in their spiritual lives. Sometimes the stresses and distractions of life weigh us down and sap our motivation to dive into the Scriptures. But I suspect that flawed approaches to studying God's word are also to blame for lack of forward movement. Reading too skeptically or with a desire simply to amass knowledge of the letters' contents can quickly lead us astray. Or if we just passively wait for others to tell us what the letters really mean, we are never spurred on to wrestle with the letters on our own. In this book, I hope to provide guidance and direction for a more fruitful study of Paul's letters, even within an academic context. I want readers to experience the stirrings of anticipation and wonder when they open the pages of Paul's letters.

THE PURPOSE OF THIS BOOK

This book is not a traditional introduction, a handbook for interpretation, or a theology of Paul, but a hybrid of those three, with the goal of guiding readers in self-discovered learning. There is a danger of making introductions to Paul a bit dry and impractical. The focus of this book is both mind and heart. I want readers to have what they need to develop both the motivation and the ability to pursue transformational learning in the Pauline Epistles. A secondary source should not eclipse the primary source but should allow it to remain on the center stage. That is especially true when the primary source is the Bible. This book on Paul is designed to keep the spotlight on Paul's letters. I also hope that this book's focus on practical questions, skills in interpretation, and spiritual growth will appeal to a wide audience of readers both in university Bible classes and within churches that honor and study God's Word.

The chapter titles for *Studying Paul's Letters with the Mind and Heart* are in the form of questions. The book addresses questions readers typically ask (or need to ask) about the letters in order to fully engage with the material in a meaningful and life-changing way. Readers may feel embarrassed to voice some of these questions, out of fear that everyone else already knows the answer, or that it is somehow spiritually immature to have such questions in the first place. This book is an open invitation to ask and explore the answers to these questions. These questions and answers serve a greater purpose: to prepare us to plunge into Paul's letters and to "taste and see that the LORD is good" (Ps. 34:8).

THE PLAN OF THIS BOOK

Following this introduction, in **chapter two** we will answer the question, "Why listen to Paul?" In the chapter we will take an honest look at the theological and historical legitimacy of reading Paul's letters as God-breathed Scripture. Paul's authority is linked to his status as an apostle, so we will explore the significance of apostleship in early Christianity and the topic of why Paul was counted among the apostles. This important first step of receiving Paul's teaching as God's word made all of the difference for the Thessalonians, and I believe that this is an urgent topic for us as well. This will prompt us to open ourselves to God's work in us when we read his letters.

Chapter three analyzes where Paul's letters fit into his life and ministry. We will locate Paul's letters within the chronological, geographical, and missional settings of his church-planting ministry. We will also meet some of the cherished colleagues who assisted Paul along the way. Paul did not write from the comfort of his library or as part of an academic think-tank. He wrote in the midst of a grueling but rewarding life of ministry to churches throughout the Roman world.

Chapter four orients readers to Paul's world and background. Paul did not live in a vacuum but in a complex world of multiple cultures and fast-changing conditions. The chapter will examine the significance of Paul's background as a Pharisee and Roman citizen of Tarsus. The realities of travel, visiting influential cities, living under a Roman government, and enduring multiple imprisonments will be unfolded as well.

Chapter five tackles the issue of whether all thirteen letters were really written by Paul. This chapter looks at the claim that Paul did not actually write some of the letters bearing his name. This leaves us with the categories of the "disputed" and "undisputed" letters of Paul. There are actually a couple of known imitations of Paul's letters in circulation. We will look at some excerpts from 3 Corinthians and the Epistle to the Laodiceans in this chapter and see what so obviously marks them as pretenders. After that, we will examine and respond to some common arguments against the authenticity of some of Paul's canonical letters and consider the historical and theological implications of these debates.

In **chapters six and seven** I hand the keys of the car to the reader. The goal of these chapters is to prepare you to dive into Paul's letters on your own. The chapters will prepare and equip you for your own transformative reading of Paul's letters. I will walk you through a process of preparing a letter summary for any of Paul's letters. The whole point of this process is to foster self-discovered learning. I typically remember the things I have learned on my own (or as part of a small group Bible study) for a much longer time than things someone else has told me. We will look at how to study Paul's letters through observing, interpreting, and applying both the parts and the whole of each letter.

Chapter eight confronts a question that is increasingly becoming more of a debated topic: Are there such things as "correct" interpretations of Paul's letters? The chapter challenges readers to think about where meaning is found in Paul's letters, using concepts such as authorial intent, speech-act theory, and the distinction between interpretation and application as conversation-starters.

For the word to be at work in us, interpretation must lead to application. **Chapter nine** asks, "How can I wisely apply Paul's teachings?" This chapter builds off of the interpretation/application distinction from the previous chapter. The chapter will look at helpful principles for transferring Paul's teaching from one culture to another. Even Paul "contextualized" his message when he responded to specific problems in his churches. We can observe how Paul contextualized his teachings in his culture for guidance about how to do likewise in our settings.

Chapter ten looks at specific interpretive challenges in Paul's letters. Certain interpretive issues in each of Paul's letters require special attention. For instance, in 1 Corinthians, how do we identify and deal with the so-called Corinthian slogans that surface throughout the letter? Also, what relevance do "household codes" have to teachings on family life in Ephesians and Colossians? You will also be introduced to a process for deciding between competing interpretations for debated passages.

An intriguing question surfaces in **chapter eleven**: From where does Paul get his material? Topics in this chapter include the relationship between Paul's letters and Jesus's teachings, the significance of Paul's conversion for his message, the relevance of other revelations, and the prominent contribution of the Old Testament to Paul's thinking. Since the Old Testament plays such a major role in Paul's teaching, **chapter twelve** analyzes how Paul interacts with the Old Testament in both sweeping and specific ways.

Chapter thirteen looks at the question, "What are the experts saying about Paul these days?" The chapter serves as a springboard for further academic study of Paul's letters. Readers will learn about several areas of disagreement about how to understand Paul, which has led to schools of thought known as the Old Perspective, New Perspective, and Apocalyptic Perspective on Paul.

Building off of the previous chapter, **chapter fourteen** seeks to forge a common way forward from the various perspectives on Paul, asking,

"What ideas were especially important to Paul?" The chapter will iden-tify some of Paul's theological ideas that have the most explanatory power, such as the gospel, union with Christ, the arrival of God's eternal kingdom, and "imperatives" for Christian living that are built upon "indicative" theological truths.

A NOTE TO TEACHERS USING THIS BOOK AS A TEXTBOOK

Each year at Taylor University I teach undergraduate students from Paul's letters, in both a general New Testament Survey course and an upper-level Pauline Epistles class. I have watched students delve into challeng-ing discussions of Paul's letters during classroom sessions. Students also display what they are learning in reflection journals, letter summary assignments (see chapters six and seven), and validation papers (see chap-ter ten). In my office or over coffee I listen to the struggles some of the students face when they seek to understand, embrace, and apply Paul's letters. I also witness their excitement when they resonate with an idea from Paul's letters that they have never considered before. This book is the product of those conversations inside and outside the classroom.

I have written this book as a supplement to the primary sources of Paul's letters. Each chapter should help equip students to interact with Paul's letters in a more informed and substantive way. Additional read-ings—of other primary sources such as the Epistle to the Laodiceans or of articles or essays that go deeper into certain topics—can further facilitate the students' preparation. Feel free to adjust the order of the chapters when you assign them. Many of the chapters can be read as separate essays, though there are some chapters that are best read as pairs. Chapters six and seven work in tandem to orient students to the method of preparing a letter summary. The tasks and challenges of inter-pretation and application are treated together in chapters eight and nine. Chapters eleven and twelve broach the subject of Paul's sources in two parts. Finally, after chapter thirteen explores the competing "camps" in Pauline studies, chapter fourteen aims to identify commonly acknowl-edged central themes in Paul's teachings.

Using this book for course reading should free you up to lead students through specific passages and topics of interest during class time. I often consult students' letter summary assignments immediately after they turn them in, in order to know what questions they are asking about the letters. Sometimes I adapt my lesson plan, taking my cues from the questions they ask in their assignments, since that means that students already feel motivated to explore those topics. Ideally, you and the students will have your Bibles open with a sense of anticipation each class period. I sincerely hope that this book helps foster that type of atmosphere!

■ ■ ■

CHAPTER TWO

WHY SHOULD I LISTEN TO PAUL?

W hy should I listen to Paul? Some of you will read the title of this chapter and answer immediately, "Because it is in the Bible!" Many churches rightly emphasize the complete trustworthiness and divine authority of every book, chapter, and verse of the Bible. As a result, you have no doubt that everything written in Paul's letters is God's communication to us and profitable for our growth in Christ. This theological conviction about the Bible's truthfulness and authority shapes the way you engage with Paul's writings. You have the habit of reading, reflecting upon, and responding to Paul's writings as divinely inspired Scripture.

For others this posture towards Paul's writings does not come as naturally. In our educational environment we are taught to weigh the logic, value, and practicality of ideas we encounter. We read literature to both understand and evaluate the authors' points of view. We are ready to be stretched by what we read, but when we identify an idea that seems out of step with the world as we know it, we dismiss the idea as an obsolete relic from another era or a viewpoint that doesn't have universal validity. Some of my students throughout the years have approached Paul in this way. They are comfortable with embracing Jesus's teachings without equivocation, but they hold back a bit with Paul's writings. They tend to treat Paul like they do Augustine, C. S. Lewis, Elisabeth Elliot, or other admired Christian thinkers whose ideas are appreciated but not taken as gospel.

On one level, this approach makes sense. Paul's writings are certainly *nothing less* than authentic human discourse: Paul writes to churches and individuals with real concerns and points to convey. We should appreciate the human element that shines through in the letters. But we catch glimpses throughout Paul's letters that he carried deep within himself a profound self-awareness of a higher calling. Paul gives hints of this calling when he refers to himself as a servant, minister, ambassador, and prisoner of Jesus Christ. In using these labels Paul acknowledges his commissioning from God and his accountability to God for how he serves (1 Cor 4:1–2; 9:16–17; Gal. 1:10; 1 Thess. 2:4; 2 Tim. 2:4). But most overtly, in a number of places in his letters, Paul writes as an *apostle*. If we want to read and appreciate Paul's own perspective about what he wrote, we need to come to terms with this vital feature of his self-understanding.

PAUL'S USE OF "APOSTLE" TO DESCRIBE HIS MINISTRY

Paul is not shy about pointing out that he is an apostle. Paul highlights his calling as an apostle at the beginning of nine of his thirteen letters.[1] Paul identifies himself simply as an "apostle of Jesus Christ" in Titus 1:1. Other letters include this title but add "by the will of God" (2 Cor. 1:1; Eph. 1:1; Col. 1:1; 2 Tim. 1:1) or the similar "by command of God our Savior and of Christ Jesus" (1 Tim. 1:1). Romans 1:1 specifies that Paul was "called to be an apostle," and 1 Corinthians 1:1 relates this calling to the will of God. The most extensive articulation of Paul's apostleship in an opening greeting appears in Galatians 1:1, where Paul begins with "Paul, an apostle—sent not from men nor by a man, but by Jesus Christ and God the Father, who raised him from the dead." Paul thus associates his apostolic identity with God's will and God's choice to call Paul into this role. These are relatively brief descriptions of Paul's apostleship, but since Paul states his apostolic status up front in these letters he sets the tone for how he will relate to his readers in the rest of each letter.[2]

Additional treatment of Paul's apostleship surfaces in other parts of Paul's letters. In Romans 1:5 Paul speaks about having "received grace and apostleship" to carry out his ministry. In Romans 11:13 Paul specifies that he is "the apostle to the Gentiles" (and connects this calling to his right to instruct the Gentiles who are reading the letter).[3] Paul makes a similar claim about his apostleship and a Gentile-oriented ministry in 1 Timothy 2:7: "And for this purpose I was appointed a herald and an apostle—I am telling the truth, I am not lying—and a true and faithful teacher of the Gentiles." In both 1 Timothy 2:7 and 2 Timothy 1:11 ("And of this gospel I was appointed a herald and an apostle and a teacher"), Paul recalls being "appointed" to become an apostle (see also 1 Cor. 12:28), which echoes the concepts of "calling" and "the will of God" found in his opening greetings. Paul does not see his apostolic status as incidental. It was a gift and responsibility that God had bestowed upon him.

---

1. Later in this book we will support the plausibility of the view that Paul wrote all thirteen letters traditionally attributed to his name.
2. For a compact but quite thorough survey of how Paul presents his apostleship at the beginning of his letters, see Frank Matera, *God's Saving Grace: A Pauline Theology* (Grand Rapids: Eerdmans, 2012), 20–21.
3. Paul elaborates on this ministry to the Gentiles in Romans 15:15–19, as his explanation for why he has written them so boldly in the first place (verse 15). Paul's conviction about reaching the Gentiles seems to have been shaped by Isaiah 49:1–6, since he echoes language about being called "from the womb" (Gal. 1:15) to be a "light to the nations" (Acts 13:47) from that passage (see also F. F. Bruce, *Paul: Apostle of the Heart Set Free* [Grand Rapids: Eerdmans, 1981], 146).

Some biblical scholars use the label "apostolic apology" to describe a number of extended presentations of Paul's apostolic calling.[4] The purpose of these sections can be to defend the legitimacy of Paul's apostleship (Gal. 1:10–2:10), to remind readers of the way Paul initially carried out his apostolic ministry with them (1 Thess. 2:1–12), or to introduce the story of his apostolic calling to churches that had not experienced firsthand contact with Paul in the past (Eph. 3:1–13; Col. 1:23–2:5).[5] These sections of material provide helpful glimpses into the origins of Paul's apostleship and how Paul understood that calling. In Galatians 1:11–16, Paul talks about meeting face to face with the resurrected Christ and receiving a revelation and calling from him.[6] Paul had been entrusted (passive voice of πιστεύω) by God with the "grace" of proclaiming Christ's name among the Gentiles (Gal. 2:7, 9), so Paul felt a profound sense of accountability to serve God faithfully. Similarly, in 1 Thessalonians 2 Paul recalls being entrusted (also the passive voice of πιστεύω) by God with the gospel (2:4), which had freed up Paul to speak boldly and sincerely to the Thessalonians (2:2–5). Rather than using his apostolic authority in a self-seeking or domineering way, Paul had gently addressed the deepest needs of the Thessalonians (2:6–8). Finally, Paul cherishes being a steward of God's grace and revealed mystery (Eph. 3:2–9; Col. 1:23–27). Paul knows that God has generously allowed him to participate in the wonderful, eternal plans that were finally coming to fruition in Paul's day.

We will look at some other key passages about Paul's apostleship later in this chapter, but for now it is sufficient to note that Paul's apostleship was not an afterthought but a central feature of the way he understood his ministry. Paul's consciousness of his apostolic calling shaped the way he interacted with his churches, both in person and in his letters. He had been called into service by God to invest in churches with intentional goals in mind.

THE SIGNIFICANCE OF APOSTLESHIP IN CHRISTIANITY

Within early Christianity, it was no small thing to be called an apostle. To understand the exact relevance of Paul's apostolic calling to the letters he wrote, we will examine the significance of apostleship in the early church and for the church throughout history. Consider for a moment the historic Nicene Creed, which Christians have affirmed throughout most of church

---

4. Hendrikus Boers, "The Form Critical Study of Paul's Letters: 1 Thessalonians as a Case Study," *NTS* 22 (1975): 153; Gregory S. MaGee, *Portrait of an Apostle: A Case for Paul's Authorship of Colossians and Ephesians* (Eugene, OR: Pickwick, 2013), 82.
5. This assumes that Ephesians was written to churches in multiple cities, and that Paul had not personally visited some of these churches.
6. Galatians 1:16 can be translated as God revealed his Son "to me" (as with the ESV) or "in me" (NIV). The difference is not that significant, since Paul is using a common Greek preposition (ἐν) that is not intended to communicate an extremely precise nuance.

history.[7] Part of this creed states that "we believe in one, holy, catholic and *apostolic* church." The church that Christians believe in is the apostolic church, the church that emerged from the ministry of the apostles and follows the teaching of the apostles.

We can extend this to say that Christians believe in the *apostolic* Jesus. Let this idea sink in. You trust in Jesus, but which Jesus? How do you know the Jesus in whom you trust? Some second-century Gnostics professed belief in Jesus, but it was a Jesus they had shaped to fit into their own aberrant theological system. It was a Jesus made into their own image. It was not the apostolic Jesus.

Brushing aside the apostles' Jesus is still a temptation today. Some people worship Jesus as a great idea—the Jesus they want him to be—a Jesus that can be adapted to their goals and sensibilities. But Christians have historically affirmed a very specific Jesus while rejecting any departure from this Jesus.

Which Jesus do we worship, and how do we know this Jesus? We are dependent on the apostles' testimony about him. We have no direct access on our own to a substantive knowledge of Jesus.[8] We trust Jesus, but we trust in the apostles' account of Jesus, as opposed to some other version of Jesus. The Bible presents the apostles as the authoritative and definitive eyewitnesses to Jesus's life, ministry, teachings, death, and resurrection. This can be observed in various places in the New Testament.

Soon after Jesus ascended into heaven a fascinating scene unfolds, as recorded in Acts 1:12–26. Jesus's eleven remaining disciples, who are called apostles in verse 26, set out to replace Judas so that they can move forward as a complete unit of twelve once again (see Mark 3:14; Acts 1:2). As they consider the different candidates for the twelfth position, they specify the most important qualification, in verses 21–22: The candidate must have accompanied Jesus during the entire length of his public ministry (see also John 15:27). The finalist had to have been present beginning with Jesus's baptism, throughout all of Jesus's public and private ministry with his disciples, until Jesus had ascended to heaven (which had just occurred in the prior scene—Acts 1:9–11). This prerequisite for becoming an apostle was tied to the nature of the apostles' ministry: he "must become a witness with us of his (Jesus's) resurrection" (Acts 1:22). The apostles were witnesses, charged with the sacred task of proclaiming what they had experienced firsthand.[9]

7. The full version of the Nicene Creed was established at the Council of Constantinople in AD 381.

8. We can know Jesus experientially, by the Spirit (1 Cor. 2:11–16; 2 Cor. 3:17–18; Eph. 1:17; 3:16–19; Col. 1:9), but this communion *with* Jesus is meant to be anchored in truth that has been passed down *about* Jesus (Rom. 10:14–17; 1 Cor. 15:1–2; Gal. 1:9; 2 Thess. 2:15; 1 John 1:2–3; Jude 3). For the inherent compatibility in Paul's letters between divine knowledge received from apostolic teachings and truth experienced by the Spirit, see George Eldon Ladd, *A Theology of the New Testament* (Grand Rapids: Eerdmans, 1974), 388–91.

9. See Richard Bauckham, *Jesus and the Eyewitnesses: The Gospels as Eyewitness Testimony* (Grand Rapids: Eerdmans, 2006), 114–16.

The primary task of the apostles would be to testify to the reality of Jesus's resurrection. These witnesses would proclaim this truth and its significance within the context of Jesus's entire public ministry. They would be credible witnesses, since they had actually seen and heard what they were testifying about. John sheds light on the credibility of the apostles' testimony in 1 John 1:1: "That which was from the beginning, which we have heard, which we have seen with our eyes, which we have looked at and our hands have touched—this we proclaim concerning the Word of life." These same witnesses would be able to safeguard the story of Jesus against distorted accounts of his ministry. They spoke with Jesus's delegated authority (Matt. 28:18–20; see also Matt. 10:40), as those who had been chosen and appointed by Christ to carry out his mission (Mark 3:14; Acts 1:2).[10] As long as they were alive, they could correct those who proclaimed something about Jesus that simply was not true. As seen in the book of Acts, the early church proclaimed a highly public message about Jesus from the start. The existence of multiple eyewitnesses (beginning with the twelve but extending to "more than five hundred" other believers, according to 1 Cor. 15:6) helped ensure that an accurate and unified portrayal of Jesus would be passed down. The apostolic eyewitnesses shared with others all that Jesus had commanded them (Matt. 28:18–20), and this task included their writing or authorizing written accounts of Jesus's ministry so that future generations would also have access to the authentic Jesus.[11]

The apostles of the early church had a crucial task of proclaiming Jesus with the credibility of eyewitnesses and the authority of Jesus's chosen servants. For such a weighty responsibility, Jesus promised divine enablement. Jesus assured his disciples that the Holy Spirit would come to assist them in this mission: "But the Helper, the Holy Spirit, whom the Father will send in my name, he will teach you all things and bring to your remembrance all that I have said to you" (John 14:26; see also John 16:12–14; Eph. 3:5–9). It is for this reason that Jesus told his disciples to wait for the empowerment of the Holy Spirit before they began their ministry of testifying about Jesus (Acts 1:8).

Because of their presence with Jesus as eyewitnesses and the divine enablement of their teaching ministry, the apostles function as the authoritative sources for Jesus and his ministry. They were multiple eyewitnesses who preached publicly about Jesus, confirmed each other's testimony, and

---

10. Some scholars have proposed that the concept of the New Testament apostle arises from the rabbinic-Jewish idea of the *shaliach*, an authorized representative in legal affairs, since both the apostle and *shaliach* carry the authority of the ones who sent them. Others have pushed back against this parallel as being too narrow and unsupported by evidence predating the New Testament, and they tie apostles more generally to divinely commissioned spokespersons such as the prophets in the Old Testament. See Francis H. Agnew, "The Origin of the NT Apostle-Concept: A Review of Research," *JBL* 105 (1986): 75–96.

11. On the reliability of eyewitness memory, see Bauckham, *Jesus and the Eyewitnesses*, 330–55.

left generations to come with written accounts of what they proclaimed. Believers during the era of the early church and believers today know Jesus because the apostles carried out their task faithfully.

WHY IS PAUL COUNTED AMONG THE APOSTLES?

But what about Paul? He was not one of these twelve apostles. He had not followed Jesus during Jesus's earthly ministry. How could he be considered a credible source for knowing and understanding Jesus? Paul addresses this question in some of his letters, in which he explains that he is indeed a legitimate apostle, even though he was also "untimely born" (ESV) as an apostle (1 Cor 15:8). Let's explore the nature of Paul's apostleship in more detail.

Paul's apostleship resembles the apostleship of the original twelve in one important way: he saw the resurrected Jesus and thus could testify that Jesus was alive and undoubtedly the Messiah.[12] The apostles of Acts 1 recognized this as their primary responsibility, and it was Paul's as well. Paul refers to his dramatic encounter with the resurrected Jesus in Galatians 1:15–16: "But when God . . . was pleased to reveal his Son in me so that I might preach him among the Gentiles, my immediate response was not to consult any human being." This event on the road to Damascus is recounted in greater detail in Acts 9, 22, and 26.[13] The resurrected Jesus appeared to Paul and spoke to him, resulting in both Paul's conversion and his enlistment into ministry.[14]

At several points in 1 Corinthians Paul connects his apostleship to the fact that he had seen the risen Christ. In a string of rhetorical questions in 1 Corinthians 9:1, Paul follows "Am I not an apostle?" with "Have I not seen Jesus our Lord?" This implies that Paul associated the idea of apostleship with having seen the resurrected Christ. More explicitly, in 1 Corinthians 15:5–8 Paul lists the various witnesses to the resurrected Jesus, concluding the list with these words: "Last of all he appeared to me also, as to one abnormally born" (verse 8). This resurrection appearance qualifies Paul to be an apostle, even if the timing and manner of his appointment make him "abnormally born," and his prior track record of persecuting the church makes him "the least of the apostles" (1 Cor. 15:9). The wording "last of all" also suggests that Paul's apostleship contributes to

---

12. Even near the end of Paul's life, Paul still summarized his basic gospel message as the resurrection of the promised Messiah: "Remember Jesus Christ, raised from the dead, descended from David. This is my gospel" (2 Tim. 2:8).
13. In the Acts accounts, while the power of Paul's own experience stands out most overtly, Ananias's corroborating vision and the presence of Paul's traveling companions make the event more than simply a private vision.
14. Paul's experience on the road to Damascus can be characterized as a conversion as long as we avoid the idea of Paul leaving one religion (Judaism) for another (Christianity). This description would be misleading, since at this point "the Way" was not sharply differentiated from its Jewish roots.

a foundational ministry that was unique to the first generation of eyewitnesses to Jesus and his resurrection. Paul is not simply a minister in a general sense; he is part of the group of early witnesses to Jesus that has articulated the meaning and significance of Jesus's ministry in a definitive and conclusive way for the Christian church.[15]

Paul points to God's miraculous work through his ministry as supporting evidence for his authentic apostleship. Most directly, Paul describes these miraculous works as the "signs of a true apostle" (2 Cor. 12:12; see also Rom. 15:18–19). The early church saw the gospel advance through a twofold strategy of tell-and-show. According to Hebrews 2:3–4, after Jesus proclaimed salvation in his ministry, God continued to advance Jesus's message through both the testimony of the disciples who had heard Jesus first-hand and through the supernatural work of the Spirit through those disciples. Paul spread the news of salvation in the same way: God worked miraculously through him to confirm the truth of his message.[16]

Another point that adds to Paul's credibility is that he did not volunteer himself to become an apostle. Far from it. Christ stopped Paul in his tracks and commissioned him to be an apostle. Paul had been absolutely opposed to the claim that Jesus was the Messiah or that he had risen from the dead. He had intended to stamp out the early Christian movement through intimidation and force. The dramatic turnaround in Paul's life (and the apostolic calling that accompanied it) could be explained only by God's supernatural intervention (Gal. 1:13–16; 1 Tim. 1:13–14). This stood out even to some of Paul's contemporaries, who "glorified God" because of this shocking turn of events (Gal. 1:22–24). Paul was so cognizant of this grace and unsought ministry that he referred to his calling as an "obligation" (Rom. 1:14) and something that he was compelled to carry out (1 Cor. 9:16). God had acted freely and unilaterally in assigning Paul this noble task, so Paul felt that he had no other choice than to fulfill this calling.

Though the process took some time, other apostles and influential leaders in the early church acknowledged Paul's apostleship and observed the distinguishing mark of God's Spirit in Paul's ministry. Galatians

---

15. Authors of the New Testament refer to the apostles sometimes as a narrow group consisting of the original twelve (Mark 3:14), as a medium-sized group of all those who had seen the resurrected Lord and were commissioned to proclaim him (1 Cor. 15:3–11), or arguably as an even larger group of pioneering missionaries, which could include Silas and Timothy (1 Thess. 2:6), Barnabas (1 Cor. 9:5–6), and Andronicus and Junia (Rom. 16:7). This last group could overlap significantly with the second. Paul's case for his own apostleship is that it meets the criteria of that intermediate group, which puts him on equal footing with even the original twelve (see Gal. 1:1–2:10; 1 Cor. 9:1; 15:3–11). For the complexities of Paul's conception of apostleship, see the discussion in Andrew Clark, "Apostleship: Evidence from the New Testament and Early Christian Literature," *VE* 19 (1989): 49–65.

16. God's miraculous activity through Paul also resulted in spiritual transformation within Paul's hearers. Paul recognizes the fruitful work of the Spirit displayed in his churches (see 1 Cor. 9:2; 15:10; 2 Cor. 3:1–3).

1:10–2:10 gives snapshots of how this unfolded. Though Paul denies that his apostleship is in any way dependent upon or derived from the other apostles' authority (Gal. 1:11–20), he does recount an important meeting with Peter and other "pillars" of the early church in which some of the other apostles affirmed the legitimacy of Paul's apostleship. In that meeting the pillars "recognized that I had been entrusted with the task of preaching the gospel to the uncircumcised, just as Peter had been to the circumcised" (Gal. 2:7). Accordingly, the leaders who were present recognized that God was working equally through the apostolic ministries of Peter and Paul, validating Paul as "an apostle to the Gentiles" (Gal. 2:8). Paul notes that "James, Cephas [Peter] and John" all gave their blessing to Paul and Barnabas for their Gentile-focused ministry (Gal. 2:9). The Jerusalem Council recorded in Acts 15 paints a similar picture of unity and mutual respect between Paul and the other apostles.

Much of the rest of the book of Acts describes the ministry of Paul to various locations in the Gentile world, in keeping with his significance as an apostle to the Gentiles. As some early church writings were beginning to be identified as particularly authoritative and on par with the Hebrew Scriptures, Paul's letters were readily received into this collection.[17] This interest in Paul's apostolic ministry continues into the post-apostolic age. Two early church leaders in the generations that followed Paul reveal their evaluation of Paul. In approximately AD 96 the author of 1 Clement writes, "Take up the epistle of the blessed Paul the apostle" (47.1). Around AD 120 Ignatius of Antioch assured his readers, "I do not give you orders like Peter and Paul: they were apostles" (Ign. *Rom.* 4.3). Paul had won the confidence of his contemporaries, and the generations that followed continued to appreciate Paul's important contributions as an apostle in the early church.

THE REASON GOD CHOSE PAUL

One lingering question about Paul's apostleship remains: Why Paul? Why did God enlist Paul into apostolic ministry, alongside other apostles who had actually accompanied Jesus in his earthly ministry? Paul seems to have ruminated over this question, too. He gives a thoughtful answer to the question in 1 Timothy 1:12–17. The passage begins with a strong note of gratitude. Paul marvels at God's grace in the light of his offensive past as "a blasphemer and a persecutor and a violent man" (1 Tim. 1:13).[18] Elsewhere in Paul's letters, Paul likewise characterizes his ministry as a gift of

---

17. For an early glimpse into the beginning stages of this reception, see 2 Peter 3:15–16.
18. Similarly, Paul finds wonder in God's gracious choice of using a former persecutor as his emissary (Eph. 3:7–8).

grace from God—a gift he did not deserve.[19] Paul then proceeds to answer the question of "Why me?" very directly in 1 Timothy 1:15–16: "Christ Jesus came into the world to save sinners—of whom I am the worst. But for that very reason I was shown mercy so that in me, the worst of sinners, Christ Jesus might display his immense patience as an example to those who would believe in him and receive eternal life." Paul is convinced that the story of his undeserved reconciliation to God captures a central idea of the gospel message—that God saves sinners. Paul's personal experience reinforces the truth of the gospel message he proclaimed. God was using both Paul's life and his message to announce the life-changing grace that is found in Jesus Christ.[20]

There is a mosaic memorial of Paul in the town of Berea (in modern-day Greece), commemorating Paul's ministry to the people of that town nearly two thousand years ago (see Acts 17:10–12). Here is a picture of that memorial (see Figure 1).

We can spot in the mosaic many familiar features of how Paul has been portrayed artistically throughout church history. He carries a sword (recalling church tradition that Paul was beheaded) and scrolls. His hairline is receded and his nose is angular.[21] But what I like most about this memorial is Jesus's position above Paul. This highlights the main point of this chapter. We listen to Paul because he is Jesus's authorized representative to speak into our lives as believers. Paul is not an independent voice sharing interesting theories about Jesus. Like other apostles, he has been commissioned to bear witness about the life, death, resurrection, and future return of Christ to this world. He is an apostle by the will of God, appointed for ministry by the resurrected Jesus. This

Figure 1—Mosaic Memorial in Berea

19. Paul speaks of his ministry as flowing from God's grace in Romans 1:5; 12:3; 15:15–16; Galatians 1:15; 2:9; Ephesians 3:2, 7–8. Additionally, Paul attributes any ministry success to God's gracious work through him (1 Cor. 3:10; 15:10).

20. For further exploration of Paul's apostleship, see Matera, *God's Saving Grace*, 16–48.

21. The apocryphal Acts of Paul, from the second century, mentions these features of Paul, and they appear in most depictions of him. We can't be confident in the accuracy of this description, but it has shaped how Paul has been characterized ever since. See Acts of Paul 3.2.

memorial portrays an image that is consistent with the history that we read about in Paul's letters and the rest of the New Testament. It reminds us to follow in the footsteps of the young Thessalonian believers, who appraised Paul's message "as it actually is, the word of God, which is indeed at work in you who believe" (1 Thess. 2:13).

CONCLUSION

For the reader who was already convinced, theologically, that all of Paul's words carry the stamp of God's truthfulness and authority, I hope that this chapter has strengthened your conviction by showing you how and why Paul was invested with this authority. For the reader who struggles with submitting to Paul's words as divine communication, I hope that you will reconsider your hesitancy after observing that this was Paul's own conviction, that the early church embraced Paul's apostolic standing, and that Paul's message and his own experience heralds the wonders of the sacrificial grace and power of Jesus Christ for our lives. We have to wrestle with the apparent implication that Paul's letters consist of divine, life-changing discourse.[22] This divine revelation opens a window to truths that change us at our core. Are you ready to offer yourself to the Spirit's work in your life, as you hear him speak the words of God through the apostle Paul?

---

22.   For an exploration of the nature of divine discourse, see Nicholas Wolterstorff, *Divine Discourse: Philosophical Reflections on the Claim that God Speaks* (Cambridge: Cambridge University Press, 1995), 40–54.

■ ■ ■

CHAPTER THREE

HOW DO PAUL'S LETTERS FIT INTO HIS LIFE AND MINISTRY?

I n this chapter we dive into history. We'll learn how Paul's ministry unfolded and determine a rough chronology for Paul's travels and letters. We'll examine the missionary challenges and theological debates that loomed overhead as Paul wrote his letters. We'll even get to know some of Paul's coworkers. The goal is to develop a basic historical framework that will help us locate the individual letters within larger developments in the expansion of the early church.

Developing a timeline for Paul's ministry and writings is fraught with difficulties. Paul assumes that his original readers already know the backdrop of events he mentions. He does not need to be explicit about exact dates for events he refers to, because the dates and events are already familiar to the readers. Debates over the authorship of some of Paul's letters and the historical reliability of Acts further complicate matters. Some scholars would exclude Acts and Paul's disputed letters from the discussion because they believe that these works were written apart from first-hand knowledge about Paul's life. Even when we embrace all of Paul's letters and Acts as reliable, information from Paul's letters has to be matched carefully with what we learn from Acts, and that is not always an easy task. Luke and Paul pursued different objectives in their writings, and they selected only the events and details that advanced those objectives.

To get the ball rolling, we will need to make some starting assumptions. First, I do believe that Paul wrote all thirteen of the letters attributed to him. I also value Acts as historically reliable, especially according to the common standards of practice among historians in Luke's day.[1] For instance, Luke may have occasionally chosen to arrange

---

1. See Colin J. Hemer, *The Book of Acts in the Setting of Hellenistic History*, ed. Conrad H. Gempf, WUNT 49 (Tübingen: J. C. B. Mohr [Paul Siebeck], 1989), 43–49; Ben Witherington, III, *The*

material out of strict chronological sequence, for thematic purposes, while still communicating the facts of events in a trustworthy manner. In addition, Luke does not record every word of his characters' speeches but provides summaries that preserve the gist of the content. Overall, Luke demonstrates his credibility through his detailed knowledge of topics such as land and sea travel routes, and the cultural, religious, and political features of different geographical areas he wrote about.[2] Acts and disputed letters such as Colossians and 2 Timothy provide lots of detailed information on Paul's whereabouts and networks. These details align well with what we know from Paul's undisputed letters and can be used to round out our understanding of Paul's ministry.

HISTORY AND DATES

There are several historical points of reference that help match Paul's timeline to actual dates.[3] We begin with the date of Jesus's crucifixion and resurrection, which is calculated to be either AD 30 or 33. Second, Paul recalls being driven out of Damascus by the Nabatean ruler Aretas (2 Cor. 11:32; see also Acts 11:23–25), who probably had jurisdiction over Damascus from at least AD 37 to his death in 39 or 40.[4] Third, Josephus records that Herod Agrippa I (grandson of Herod the Great) died after he had reigned over all of Judea for three years, during the first three years of Emperor Claudius's rule, which corresponds to AD 44 (Josephus, *Ant.* 19.8.2).[5] In Acts 12:20–23 Luke places a similar account of Herod's death during the year before Paul and Barnabas left for their first missionary journey.[6] A fourth clue comes from Claudius's banishment of the Jews from Rome (Acts 18:2), which aligns with the Roman historian Suetonius's report of an edict estimated to have been

---

Acts of the Apostles: A Socio-Rhetorical Commentary (Grand Rapids: Eerdmansz; Carlisle: Paternoster, 1998), 87–88.

2. See examples in Hemer, *Book of Acts*, 107–58.

3. I am indebted to the summary and analysis of these sources in Hemer, *Book of Acts*, 251–70, and D. A. Carson and Douglas Moo, *An Introduction to the New Testament,* 2nd ed. (Grand Rapids: Zondervan, 2005), 366–70.

4. See Loveday C. A. Alexander, "Chronology of Paul," *DPL* 117. Supporting an earlier date for Paul's run-in with Aretas is Eckhard J. Schnabel, *Paul and the Early Church*, vol. 2 of *Early Christian Mission* (Downers Grove, IL: InterVarsity; Leicester: Apollos, 2004), 1037–38.

5. Hemer, *Book of Acts*, 165–66.

6. Luke does not seem to be too concerned about the exact sequence of events from the end of Acts 11 to the beginning of Acts 13, which is where Luke places the account of Herod's death. Luke introduces scenes with Herod with the words, "It was about this time . . ." (Acts 12:1). Josephus (*Ant.* 20.2.5) mentions a famine that can be dated in the AD 45–47 range, and this likely fits the famine prophesied about in Acts 11:27–30. Luke either rearranges material for thematic purposes (Carson and Moo, *Introduction to New Testament*, 367), or the prophecy preceded the event by a few years (Witherington, *Acts of the Apostles*, 79–80).

enacted in AD 49 (Suetonius, *Claud.* 25.4).[7] The fifth reference point is an inscription mentioning an official named Gallio, who was proconsul of Corinth during part of the time Paul ministered there (Acts 18:12). A museum at Dephi, Greece, preserves a stone that has a chronological list of rulers for Corinth, and Gallio shows up on that stone. His term as proconsul of Corinth can be dated to AD 51–52.[8] Sixth, the known reigns of Felix and Festus in the late 50s help us estimate the dates of Paul's imprisonments in Caesarea and Rome (Acts 23:23–26:32). Finally, church traditions associating Paul's final imprisonment and death with Nero's campaign of persecution against Christians offer some guidance.

Here is one possible timeline of the events of Paul's ministry and letters:

- Christ's resurrection: (30/33)
- Paul's Conversion: (34/35)
- Ministry in Arabia (35–37)
- Ministry in Syria and Cilicia (37–47)
- First missionary journey with Barnabas (and Mark) to Cyprus and southern Galatia (47–48)
- Time in Antioch (Acts 15:26–28; Gal. 2:11–14) (48–49)
  * Paul writes the letter to the Galatians
  * Paul and Barnabas participate in the Jerusalem Council
- Second missionary journey with Silas (and later, Timothy) to Syria, Cilicia, southern Galatia, Macedonia, and Achaia (49–52)
  * Paul writes 1 Thessalonians
  * Paul writes 2 Thessalonians
  * Paul returns to Jerusalem and Antioch
- Third missionary journey to southern Galatia, Asia, Macedonia, Achaia, Illyricum (52–57)
  * Paul writes 1 Corinthians
  * Paul visits Corinth
  * Paul writes the Corinthians a "severe" letter that is now lost
  * Paul writes Philippians
  * Paul writes 2 Corinthians
  * Paul writes Romans
- Paul brings a collection to Jerusalem, is arrested, held for two years in Caesarea, and transferred to Rome (57–60)
- Paul is under house arrest in Rome (60–62)
  * Paul writes Philemon
  * Paul writes Colossians
  * Paul writes Ephesians

---

7. The dating of Suetonius's report about the edict is somewhat uncertain, since it is based on the much later assessment (fifth century AD) of the historian Orosius (*Hist.* 7.6). See Hemer, *Book of Acts*, 167–68.
8. Ibid., 252–53..

- Additional ministry in Asia, Macedonia, and Crete (62–64)
    * Paul writes 1 Timothy
    * Paul writes Titus
- Paul's second Roman imprisonment and death (64–65 or beyond)
    * Paul writes 2 Timothy

EARLY YEARS: A PROMISING BUT CONTESTED START

From Acts 9 we read about the beginnings of Paul's (or Saul's) ministry as a follower of Christ.[9] Paul spends "many days" in Damascus immediately after his conversion (Acts 9:23). When Paul was stationed in Damascus, he also moved around throughout nearby Arabia (Gal. 1:17), home to the Nabatean kingdom, of which King Aretas was a ruler (2 Cor. 11:32). We can assume that Paul spent that time engaged primarily in ministry, because Acts mentions that he preached in the synagogues that Jesus was the Son of God, the Messiah (Acts 9:19–22), and he had to evade arrest in Damascus for similar activities (Acts 9:23–25; 2 Cor. 11:32–33).[10] Paul spent up to three years in the region (Gal. 1:18).[11]

From Damascus Paul proceeded to visit Jerusalem (Acts 9:26–29; Gal. 1:18) and Judea (Acts 26:20).[12] Acts is vague about the amount of time spent in Judea, but Galatians suggests that the stay in Jerusalem was quite brief (Gal. 1:18). Both accounts agree that Paul's interactions with early church leaders and other believers were limited (Acts 9:26–27; Gal. 1:18–19, 22), while Acts also adds that controversy was already erupting over Paul's ministry (Acts 9:29). Paul met briefly with Peter and James (the brother of Jesus and a rising leader in the early church) during Paul's stay in Jerusalem (Gal. 1:18–19).

After a quick stop in Caesarea (a major port north of Jerusalem) Paul settled down in Tarsus, a city in the province of Cilicia (Acts 9:30). Paul used his hometown as a base for his broader ministry endeavors, spending time throughout Cilicia and, eventually, the nearby province of Syria (Gal. 1:21).[13] As in Arabia and Jerusalem, Paul made his preaching ministry his

---

9. Luke refers to Paul as Saul in Acts 7:58–13:9, before using the name Paul after that. The Jewish name Saul fit most naturally when Paul's significant dealings were with the Jews. Once Paul embarked on his ministry to the Gentiles, the Roman name Paul was more suitable to that context.

10. See Schnabel, *Paul and the Early Church*, 1035–37.

11. "Three years" could be calculated either in terms of total months (somewhere around thirty-six months) or as parts of three calendar years (which could be anywhere from two to three years). Both ways of counting time were used in Paul's day. Note that in Acts 28:30 Luke states more specifically that Paul spent "two whole years" in Rome.

12. It is difficult to know the nature of Paul's pursuits in Judea. In Acts 26:20 he mentions preaching in "all Judea," but he must have been ministering independently from the churches there, since the (already present) churches didn't know him personally (Gal. 1:22).

13. Syria and the eastern section of Cilicia, including Tarsus, were governed together at that time in history, which is why the two provinces are grouped as a unit in Acts 15:23, 41; Gal. 1:21 (F. F. Bruce, *New Testament History* [New York: Doubleday, 1971], 245).

focus (Gal. 1:23). Some of the churches that sprouted up in that area (Acts 15:23) may have originated with Paul's ministry.[14]

Paul's time in Syrian Antioch, one of the most prominent cities in the Roman Empire, deserves special attention. A large number of people in Antioch had turned to Christ before Paul arrived there (Acts 11:20–21). The Jerusalem church leaders sent Barnabas to assist these new believers. Barnabas recruited Paul to help him, and the two of them spent a year with the believers in Antioch (Acts 11:22–26). This became the church that later commissioned Paul and Barnabas to venture out on their missionary journey. The believers of Antioch also sent Paul and Barnabas on a famine-relief visit to Judea during that year (Acts 11:27–30). This likely corresponds to the visit Paul recalls in Galatians 2:1–10.[15] By this time, it had been approximately fourteen years since Paul's conversion and eleven years since his move to Tarsus.[16]

Paul's early years as a follower of Christ were characterized by bold ministry in the face of heated opposition and other hardships. Paul encountered murderous schemes from Jews in Damascus (Acts 9:23) and Hellenistic Jews in Jerusalem (Acts 9:29). While Acts and Paul's letters do not recount specific threats or persecution covering Paul's time in Syria and Cilicia, some of the trials listed in 2 Corinthians 11:23–33 probably arose from that time period. Only a few of those incidents are accounted for elsewhere in Paul's previous letters or in Acts, so some could have occurred during Paul's outreaches in Syria and Cilicia. Paul also received his "thorn in [the] flesh" (and the heavenly visions that preceded it) during this time, which created ongoing difficulty for him but reminded him to rely upon the Lord (2 Cor. 12:6–10).[17]

Something about Paul's preaching throughout this period ignited intense opposition among the Jews. Perhaps it was a combination of his direct message, a bold style, and his past as an outspoken opponent of Jesus and his church. Paul focused on "proving" that Jesus was the Messiah, and he was effective in doing so (Acts 9:22). Luke also describes Paul's approach as "bold" or "fearless" on several occasions (Acts 9:27, 28; other times later in Acts). Paul's turnabout from foe to friend of Jesus and the church may have particularly frustrated the Jews (Acts 9:21). Paul's abrupt change of heart threatened to give more credence to this upstart sect they called "the Way."

Jewish believers in Christ appear to have had mixed feelings about Paul and his message as well. They were slow to fully trust that he was

---

14. John B. Polhill, *Paul and His Letters* (Nashville: Broadman & Holman, 1999), 67.

15. See Hemer, *Book of Acts*, 247–51; Schnabel, *Paul and the Early Church*, 987–91.

16. Assuming concurrent periods of time with the three- and fourteen-year references (Gal. 1:18; 2:1), Paul's second visit to Jerusalem occurred around AD 46 or 47, which falls within the time frame of the famine that struck Judea.

17. Paul speaks vaguely about the thorn, which is most likely a physical malady but could also represent persecution or some sort of recurring trial or temptation.

"one of them" (Acts 9:26–27), but they eventually praised God for his dramatic conversion and reversal (Gal. 1:23–24). Still, even leaders of the church were wary about Paul's message of freedom in Christ and the corollary of Gentile inclusion in the people of God. It is possible that James (the brother of Jesus) wrote the New Testament letter known by his name during Paul's time in Syria and Cilicia. The letter reflects concerns about the abuse of Paul's message in a licentious and self-centered direction.[18] Paul's subsequent meeting with James, Peter, and John (Gal. 2:1–10) helped get the leaders more on the same page. James, Peter, and John recognized that Paul and his team needed space to minister specifically to Gentiles. They realized that Paul's message to the Gentiles did not subvert the gospel that they preached to the Jews.

Paul seems to have established his own ministry orbit in his early years, before joining Barnabas in Antioch. But by the end of his stay in Antioch, his expanding network included Barnabas, the elders of the church at Antioch, and Titus (Gal. 2:1–3), with apostles in Jerusalem granting their blessing for his work. Paul's initial forays into ministry had set the stage for a wider influence for Christ, especially among the Gentiles.

PAUL'S FIRST MISSIONARY JOURNEY: FAST-PACED AND EVENTFUL OUTREACHES

Paul's first official missionary journey, with Barnabas, was a whirlwind tour with all sorts of obstacles and successes. During this journey and the ones that followed, Paul and his teams focused on church-planting, reflecting a pattern that can be summarized in the following steps:

1. Evangelism (starting in the synagogue, when there was one in a city)
2. Teaching and encouraging believers in their new identity and growth in Christ
3. Choosing elders for ongoing leadership at the local level
4. Providing spiritual support through prayer and letter writing, along with follow-up visits when possible

At each stage Paul and his coworkers faced opposition from both Jews and Gentiles. Paul's gospel message was perceived as threatening since it encroached on so many areas of life, affecting spiritual allegiances, social relationships, cultural practices, economic activity, and even political

---

18. Many scholars place the book of James at a later date, but it seems to fit best at a time before the Jerusalem Council and before any of Paul's letters were in circulation. Paul and James appeared to forge more common ground as time went on. The Jerusalem Council gave official blessing to the main thrust of Paul's teachings, and James led those proceedings. Also, Paul's letters signal his own awareness that his teachings could be distorted and misapplied to promote sinning (see Rom. 6:1–2, 15; Gal. 5:13–6:10), which echoed some of James's concerns in his letter.

loyalties. Paul's ministry soon developed the reputation of "turning the world upside down" (Acts 17:6, NRSV).

Paul and Barnabas's sending church seemed to recognize the great potential and serious challenges of such a ministry. The church leaders in Antioch commissioned Paul and Barnabas for missionary service, after earnestly seeking God's direction and spending extensive time in prayer and fasting (Acts 13:1–3). They sent Paul and Barnabas to conduct a challenging series of outreaches in Cyprus, Pisidian Antioch, Iconium, Lystra, and Derbe (see Map 1). John Mark also traveled with them to Cyprus, before returning prematurely to Jerusalem.

Map 1—Paul's First Missionary Journey

Divine miracles often accompanied Paul's preaching, and the combination of a persuasive message and powerful signs made an immediate impact at each location. Residents in the southern part of the Roman province of Galatia (Pisidian Antioch, Iconium, Lystra, and Derbe) were particularly receptive (Acts 13:48; 14:1, 21). At the same time, Jews in several places forcefully opposed the work. This hostile and unstable environment seems to have contributed to the relatively short duration of each visit. But after their first pass through each location, Paul and Barnabas returned to many of the cities to further encourage the new believers and designate elders for the ongoing governance of each new church (Acts 14:23).

Then Paul and Barnabas returned to Antioch, where they gave their sending church a full report of their activities and the encouraging results they had seen. Luke's summary statement includes a description that is too easily skimmed over. Paul and Barnabas celebrated that God "had opened a door of faith to the Gentiles" (Acts 14:27). This represented a crucial turning point in the church, but not everyone would be happy about that.

DEVELOPMENTS IN ANTIOCH: TENSIONS OVER A PARADIGM SHIFT

Coming off of an exhilarating first missionary journey, Paul and Barnabas settled down in their home base of Antioch for a number of months. During their time in Antioch, storm clouds continued to develop over the question of the Gentiles' integration into God's family. The church was in the midst of a massive paradigm shift over the idea of cleanliness in God's sight. Throughout God's history with Israel, he had taught his people to distinguish between the clean and the unclean (Lev. 10:10; Ezek. 22:26; 44:23). As God's chosen and set-apart people, the Jews avoided entanglements with the Gentiles and their unclean practices. But now, God communicated a new message: Gentiles could be clean "as is," because through Christ and by the Spirit, God had made them clean.

Paul was an early adopter of this new paradigm, and he understood the full implications of it. He proclaimed that the Gentiles did not need to be circumcised or otherwise follow the Jewish law, because they were now completely clean in Christ, through faith. Paul had been given a green light to continue his work with the Gentiles and introduce them to the freedom they could have in Christ (Gal. 2:1–10). Imagine his alarm, then, when Gentile believers from churches in Syrian Antioch and southern Galatia were being persuaded that they were not actually spiritually clean after all. Teachers from Judea were trying to convince Gentile converts to become circumcised and begin abiding by the Mosaic laws (Acts 15:1; Gal. 1:6–7; 6:12). Even Peter (also known by his Aramaic name Cephas), after having treated the believing Gentiles in Antioch as spiritual equals, began to withdraw from them when he felt the pressure to conform again to the old paradigm (Gal. 2:11–14). Paul responded vehemently to these developments and defended the full place of uncircumcised Gentile believers in the family of God. He debated with the so-called Judaizers in person in Antioch (Acts 15:2), and he confronted Peter over his duplicity (Gal. 2:14–21).

In the wake of these events Paul also took the time to write his letter to the churches of Galatia. These were most likely the same churches he and Barnabas had established just months before.[19] Paul could not stand to see

---

19. This assumes two things about the letter to the Galatians. One, it addresses the churches in the Roman province of Galatia (in a view known as the southern Galatian theory), rather than the ethnic region of Galatia (northern Galatian theory). These were some of the cities that Paul and Barnabas visited on their first missionary journey. Second, Paul wrote the letter *before* the Jeru-

them so confused about their status and growth in Christ, so he wrote a sharp letter rebuking them for abandoning full dependence on Christ for righteousness and spiritual freedom.

Paul and Barnabas then traveled to Jerusalem to participate in a gathering of church leaders commonly known as the Jerusalem Council. With James presiding over the meetings, Peter, Barnabas, and Paul were given opportunities to share how God had been at work so evidently among the Gentiles. The matter was settled. James led a decision of the whole church (Acts 15:22) to write a letter expressing the church's official position: the Gentiles were complete in Christ and should be accepted as equals in God's family.[20] This decree was then communicated to the church in Antioch, which had been at the center of the controversy (Acts 15:30–31).

PAUL'S SECOND MISSIONARY JOURNEY: NEW OPEN DOORS AND A NEW TEAM

The church's consensus to embrace the new paradigm that welcomed Gentiles into the family of God set the stage for increasingly ambitious missionary projects. But first, a conflict erupted within Paul's original ministry team. Barnabas wanted to take Mark along again for another missionary journey, but Mark's prior abandonment of the team had left a bad taste in Paul's mouth.[21] So Barnabas and Mark returned to Cyprus while Paul called upon Silas to join him on a new journey (see map 2). Previously Silas had been tapped to accompany Paul and others to Antioch to communicate the results of the Jerusalem Council (Acts 15:22, 32). This implies that Silas was a Jewish Christian who was both trusted by the Jerusalem church and sympathetic to Paul's vision for the Gentiles.

Paul and Silas returned to some of Paul's old stomping grounds to strengthen the young believers in those cities and share the outcome of the Jerusalem Council (Acts 15:41; 16:4–5). Along the way, they recruited a believer from Lystra named Timothy to accompany them in their ministry travels (Acts 16:1–3). When they arrived in Troas, Luke may have joined them for a trip to Philippi, if that is how we are to understand the switch

---

salem Council of Acts 15. This view is contested, but Galatians makes more sense as being written before the Council, reflecting a period of uncertainty in which even Peter seems confused about the best way to handle fellowship between Jewish and Gentile believers.

20. The letter freed Gentile believers from the requirements of circumcision and other rituals of Jewish life but did not eradicate God's stipulations for moral living (see Jesus's own distinction between ritual and moral defilement in Mark 7:14–23). The letter also gave guidance on how Gentiles should live sensitively among the Jews around them (Acts 15:20–21). Paul himself advocated that approach in a later letter (1 Cor. 9:19–24).

21. The disagreement over personnel perhaps aggravated the subtle strain that had developed from Barnabas's equivocation over showing public solidarity with Gentile believers (Gal. 2:13). See Bruce, *Apostle of the Heart Set Free*, 212.

to first person ("we") at that point in the narrative (Acts 16:10).[22] The team ventured out together to the provinces of Macedonia and Achaia. In Macedonian cities such as Philippi, Thessalonica, and Berea they found fertile spiritual soil but also met with energetic opposition from Jews and Gentiles.

First Paul, and then Silas and Timothy, traveled to Athens and conversed with the philosophically minded inhabitants of that city (Acts 17:14–15; 1 Thess. 3:1). A handful of people responded positively to the gospel (Acts 17:34–35), but there are no traces of a church that formed from Paul's ministry in Athens. After Timothy had revisited the Thessalonians, and Silas had traveled back to Macedonia, the three eventually met again in Corinth.[23] In Corinth Paul preached and taught about Christ for a year and a half while he worked as a tentmaker (Acts 18:2–3, 11). He also formed a friendship with two married tentmakers, Priscilla and Aquila, who became Paul's valuable allies for Christ in the years that followed.

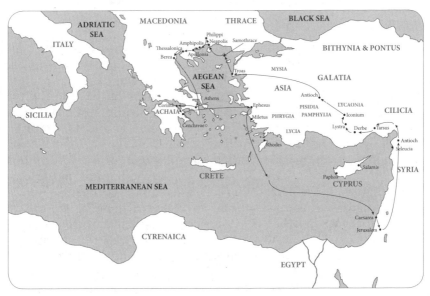

Map 2—Paul's Second Missionary Journey

Paul, with the assistance of Silas and Timothy, wrote 1 Thessalonians and probably 2 Thessalonians during his time in Corinth. The Thessalonian believers had gotten off to a promising start in their faith, but Paul's

---

22. The theory that Luke wrote as a participant in the action in the "we" passages is the best explanation for the author's use of first person plural in certain sections (Acts 16:10–17; 20:5–15; 21:1–18; 27:1–28:16).

23. The movements of Silas and Timothy are determined from a harmonization of Acts 17:14–18:5 with 1 Thessalonians 3:1–6 (see F. F. Bruce, *The Book of Acts*, rev. ed., NICNT [Grand Rapids: Eerdmans, 1988], 328).

time with them had been relatively short (Acts 17:2–4; 1 Thess. 1:6–10). After Timothy had returned from seeing how the Thessalonian believers were doing (1 Thess. 3:1–6), Paul wrote the first letter to further reinforce the reality of their new identity in Christ and assure them of Christ's future victory in the world. Paul wrote 2 Thessalonians soon after, to further clarify how to live actively for Christ in the midst of evil until Christ returns to bring ultimate justice to the world.

After eighteen months Paul, Priscilla, and Aquila all traveled to Ephesus. Paul stayed there briefly and promised to return, while Priscilla and Aquila remained in Ephesus for a longer time. Paul sailed to Caesarea, visited Jerusalem, and then went back to Antioch (Acts 18:22). His second missionary journey had ended, after he had accomplished several impor- tant goals. First, he had strengthened existing churches. Second, he had started new churches that he would continue to invest in, such as churches in Philippi, Thessalonica, and Corinth. Third, he had broadened his network of devoted co-laborers, forging partnerships with Timothy, Priscilla, and Aquila in particular.

PAUL'S THIRD MISSIONARY JOURNEY: ENERGETIC MINISTRY AND PRODUCTIVE WRITING

Luke records that Paul remained in Antioch for an indeterminate period of time before resuming missionary outreach (Acts 18:23). Paul once again made special visits to encourage churches that he had established during his first missionary journey (see map 3). Then, he fulfilled a prom- ise by returning to Ephesus, which he made a home base for ministry for up to three years (Acts 20:31). Paul's work touched the province of Asia as a whole during that time (Acts 19:10, 22). The region had the reputation for incidents of overt manifestations of spiritual activity and general inter- est in spiritual phenomena. Such dynamics can be observed in Acts 19, where Jewish exorcists made an appearance, and crowds who witnessed the exorcists' humiliation repudiated their sorcery and reliance on magi- cal incantations (Acts 19:13–19). The people of Ephesus also took pride in being caretakers of the goddess Artemis's temple and honor, and Paul's gospel interfered with the spiritual, cultural, and economic influence of Artemis in the region of Asia (Acts 19:23–41).

Paul collaborated with trusted colleagues such as Priscilla, Aquila, Timothy, and Titus during this season of ministry. But many other minis- ters from multiple locales were being drawn into Paul's orbit as part of a united effort to bless the believers in Jerusalem and Judea with a financial gift (Rom. 15:25–32; 1 Cor. 16:1–4; 2 Cor. 8:18–19; Acts 24:17). Paul sent Timothy and Erastus to Macedonia and Achaia, ostensibly to gather some of these disciples to be part of a delegation that would travel to Jerusalem together (Acts 19:21–22). Paul soon followed, after a brief stop in Troas (2 Cor. 2:12–13). He traveled throughout Macedonia (Acts 20:2) and neighboring Illyricum (see Rom. 15:19) for a long time (see his explanations about his delayed visit to Corinth in 2 Cor. 1:15–24). Local church leaders such as Aristarchus of Thessalonica and Tychicus and Trophimus of Asia joined Paul and Timothy as they made their way through Greece, Macedonia (where they likely picked up Luke in Philippi), and back to Troas (Acts 20:2–6), before returning to Jerusalem (Acts 21:17).

Paul wrote three or four of his letters during his third missionary journey. Paul composed 1 Corinthians to address a church he had devoted eighteen months to during his previous journey. Paul wrote 1 Corinthians from Ephesus in the midst of a fruitful but contested ministry (1 Cor. 16:8).[24] The church in Corinth was struggling with immaturity, selfishness, immorality, and division, but spiritually sensitive people from within the church had reached out to Paul for input (see 1 Cor. 1:11; 7:1; 8:1; 12:1). Paul followed up his letter with a painful visit (2 Cor. 2:1) and another more pointed and urgent letter to them (2 Cor. 2:2–4, 9; 7:8–9, 12). This so-called "severe" letter has long since disappeared.[25]

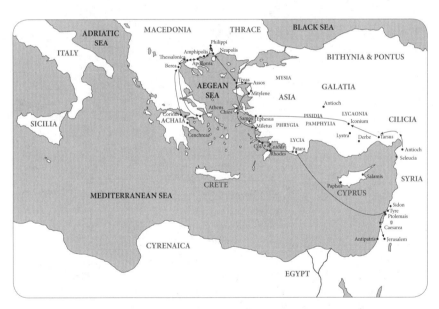

Map 3—Paul's Third Missionary Journey

In the midst of Paul's correspondence with the Corinthians, the hostility in Asia intensified (2 Cor. 1:8–11), perhaps even resulting in a

---

24. Paul had already written to the Corinthians previously (1 Cor. 5:9) in a letter that is now lost, so 1 Corinthians is at least his second letter to them.
25. Some people speculate that 2 Corinthians 10–13 is actually part of that severe letter. That debate will be discussed further in a later chapter.

brief but arduous imprisonment. I suspect that Paul wrote Philippians while he was incarcerated in Ephesus during this time.[26] Paul's teachings in Philippians on strength through suffering have much in common with what is found in 2 Corinthians.[27] Paul assured the Philippians that he was seeing God open new doors in his ministry, even in the midst of his undesirable circumstances.

The hardships Paul had endured in Asia were still fresh on his mind when he wrote 2 Corinthians (2 Cor. 1:8–11). He had moved on from Asia to Macedonia (1 Cor. 16:5; 2 Cor. 2:12–13), where he encountered another turbulent stretch of ministry (2 Cor. 7:5). Titus had returned from a visit to the Corinthians with an encouraging report about their progress (2 Cor. 7:6–7, 13–16). Paul wrote 2 Corinthians in response to Titus's update, and he sent Titus to deliver the letter and collect a financial gift for the Judean churches (2 Cor. 8:17–24; 12:18). Paul also prepared them for his anticipated visit to them (2 Cor. 12:14, 20–21; 13:1, 10).

After visiting Macedonia (Acts 20:1–2) and Illyricum (Rom. 15:19), and during his three month stay in Greece/Achaia (Acts 20:2–3), Paul most likely wrote Romans from Corinth and sent the letter with Phoebe, a minister who hailed from the nearby church in Cenchreae (see Rom. 16:1).[28] Paul planned on visiting the Roman churches in person but first wrote them the letter. In Romans, Paul introduces his gospel, which offers salvation for both Jews and Gentiles. Though Paul did not have a history with the Roman churches as a whole, he still greets many people who were part of his expanding web of Christian acquaintances (Rom. 16:3–16).[29]

JERUSALEM TO ROME: PAUL UNDER FIRE AND IN CHAINS

Paul and his team successfully arrived in Jerusalem to deliver their contributions to the churches of Judea. They also shared a ministry update with church leaders there (Acts 21:17–19). There were many Jews in the area,

---

26. Luke may not mention this imprisonment to avoid complicating Paul's defense against his Jewish accusers (the topic of the final eight chapters of Acts), since the Jews of Asia were the main instigators of bringing charges against Paul (Acts 21:27–28; 24:18–19).

27. Hints of Paul's precarious status and taxing conditions (Phil. 1:19–24, 30; 2:17, 25–30; 4:14) also do not match well with a later Roman house arrest described at the end of Acts. Though the mention of the palace guard (Phil. 1:13) and Caesar's household (4:22) create some doubts about the Ephesian imprisonment view, they are not fatal problems to what is otherwise an attractive view. Some scholars opt for a later date for Philippians, corresponding to Paul's first Roman imprisonment.

28. Phoebe's title, διάκονος, could be translated as either "minister" or "deacon(ess)." While in many of his letters Paul uses διάκονος generally ("minister"), in 1 Timothy and Titus it seems to denote a more specific office within a local church.

29. Some scholars have speculated that the list of greetings in Romans 16 was originally part of a letter to the Ephesians (especially given the known association of Priscilla and Aquila with the Ephesian church). But it is more probable that Paul is simply trying to build further bonds with the church by mentioning names already in his network.

however, who harbored animosity towards Paul, and after a chaotic scene at the temple, Paul spoke to the mob there. Paul's claim that God had called him to reach the Gentiles enraged the listeners, who demanded his death. Paul's status as a Roman citizen permitted him a temporary reprieve and a hearing before the Jewish Sanhedrin. But after a tense and heated exchange Paul was confined in the military barracks (Acts 23:10) at the corner of the temple. The barracks were known as the citadel of Antonia (Josephus, *Ant.* 15.11.4; 18.4.3).

After plots to kill Paul were discovered, he was transferred to Caesarea and kept under guard in Herod's palace (Acts 23:35; 24:23). The governor Felix, who had jurisdiction over both Tarsus (Paul's hometown) and Judea (where Paul was seized), heard Paul's case. Though Felix heard no strong reason to convict Paul, he wanted to stay on the Jews' good side and so held Paul for two years in Caesarea (Acts 24:27). The new governor Festus began his term in AD 59 and proceeded to examine Paul. He even brought in Herod Agrippa II (ruler of Galilee) to interrogate Paul. Neither of them saw grounds for charging Paul, but they decided to send Paul to Rome, since Paul had appealed to be tried before Emperor Nero (Acts 26:31–32).[30]

A harrowing journey by sea from the autumn of AD 59 (Acts 27:9) to the spring of AD 60 (Acts 28:11) brought Paul, Aristarchus, and Luke (Acts 27:2) to Italy and then Rome. Assured by divine visions of his safe arrival (Acts 23:11; 27:23–25), Paul endured a storm, shipwreck, and venomous snake bite before reaching Rome (see map 4).

Map 4—Paul's Journey to Rome

---

30. This was during Nero's stable years, while he was still guided by wise advisers.

FIRST ROMAN IMPRISONMENT: WAITING AND WRITING

The account in Acts 28 describes Paul's imprisonment as a house arrest (28:16, 20), which allowed Paul relative freedom to interact with both Jews and Gentiles over a period of two years (28:30–31). Acts does not report any resolution to Paul's case—just waiting.[31]

Paul took advantage of this time to do more letter writing. A slave named Onesimus arrived in Rome and sought out Paul.[32] Paul knew his master Philemon and composed the letter of that name from Rome. Paul likely wrote Colossians and Ephesians around that same time. Many of the same names surface in Philemon and Colossians, including Aristarchus, Luke, Mark, and Epaphras, who had planted the church in Colossae. Tychicus is mentioned as the letter carrier for both Colossians (4:7) and Ephesians (6:21), and the content of those two letters is quite similar. Paul probably wrote the letters early in his imprisonment, since the Lycus Valley (home of Colossae, Laodicea, and Hierapolis) may have suffered from a devastating earthquake as early as AD 60 or 61 (Tacitus, *Ann.* 14.27), and Paul does not indicate any knowledge of this tragedy in his letters.[33]

RELEASE AND CONTINUED MINISTRY

At some point the Romans released Paul, and he was free to minister once again. Since we are beyond the timeline of Acts at this point, it is more difficult to trace Paul's exact travels. Locations such as Macedonia (1 Tim. 1:3), Ephesus (1 Tim. 1:3; see also 2 Tim. 1:18), Crete (Titus 1:5), and the city of Nicopolis (Titus 3:12) surface as destinations. Though Paul had hoped to reach Spain (Rom. 15:24, 28), and later tradition (1 Clem. 5:7, from around AD 96) may indicate that he did,[34] his original plans may have been frustrated by his lengthy confinement in Rome. Coworkers in Paul's greater network during this period include Tychicus and Apollos (Titus 3:12–13), but our focus turns to two of Paul's most longstanding and trusted associates, Timothy and Titus.

Paul wrote 1 Timothy after he had left Timothy in Ephesus and traveled to Macedonia (1 Tim. 1:3). Ephesus had become a significant hub of

---

31. It is puzzling that Acts ends as it does. Does this suggest that Luke wrote Acts before Paul's fate was settled? Or was Luke protecting Paul from potential harm, knowing that Paul had been released but was still at risk of being turned over to his enemies? Or did Luke conclude where he did because the gospel had reached Rome, which meant that "to the ends of the earth" (Acts 1:8) was becoming a reality? See the discussion in Hemer, *Book of Acts*, 383–87, 406–8.

32. The exact circumstances that brought Onesimus to Paul are debated, but most likely Onesimus sought out Paul intentionally.

33. See Polhill, *Paul and His Letters*, 330.

34. *First Clement* does not actually mention that Paul reached Spain, but that he traveled to the limits of the west, which could denote either Spain or Rome (see Hemer, *Book of Acts*, 400).

ministry ever since Paul's third missionary journey. Probably shortly after, Paul wrote his letter to Titus, who was stationed in Crete. The content of both letters gravitates towards practical guidance for leading and organizing the churches in Ephesus and Crete. More and more, Paul had begun entrusting his work into the hands of capable associates.

SECOND ROMAN IMPRISONMENT: FINAL WORDS BEFORE PAUL'S DEATH

Paul apparently landed in prison a second time in Rome, and this time the outlook was much bleaker. The only information we have comes from 2 Timothy, a very personal letter that reads as Paul's final reflections and charge to his faithful colleague Timothy. Paul lingers under physical strain (2 Tim. 1:12; 2:8) in a Roman prison that was difficult to find (1:17), in stark contrast to his first confinement in Rome. He suffers and feels alone, having been abandoned by the previously reliable Demas (2 Tim. 4:10; Col. 4:14; Philem. 24), and having dispatched Titus and Tychicus to other cities (2 Tim. 4:10, 12). Priscilla, Aquila, Erastus, and Trophimus are stationed elsewhere (4:19–20) as well. Paul does take comfort in the presence of Luke and the prospect that Mark and Timothy might soon arrive (4:11). The approaching winter creates a sense of urgency, suggesting that Paul's well-being is at stake (4:9, 21). Paul sees the end in sight (4:6–8; 4:18), but he gratefully completes his leg of the race and passes the baton to Timothy (2:1–2; 4:1–5).

According to church tradition, Paul was beheaded in Rome, during the persecutions inflamed (!) by Emperor Nero in the wake of a fire that swept through Rome.[35] Paul's punishment would have fit his status as a citizen. He was spared the crucifixion that Jesus and (reportedly) Peter had suffered. Paul's life and ministry came to an end, but the effects of his ministry have continued even to today.

PAUL'S COWORKERS: A PANORAMIC VIEW

Far from being the lone ranger that he is often depicted to be, Paul served alongside many other devout followers of Christ. Paul valued his colleagues' presence with him but also delegated important tasks for them to carry out on their own. There are several interesting things to observe about these coworkers from the accounts in Acts and Paul's letters.

First, Paul's impressive network included both men and women. The men often receive more press, but note for a moment the women who stood out in his missionary circles. In Corinth Priscilla and her husband Aquila helped Paul plant a church, which they hosted for a time (1 Cor.

---

35. See the evaluation of the development of this tradition in Bruce, *Apostle of the Heart Set Free*, 441–42, 446–50.

16:9). They also taught Apollos and other believers in Ephesus (Acts 18:19, 24–26). Later they directed a house fellowship in Rome (Rom. 16:3–5). Phoebe received commendation as a minister or deacon of the church in Cenchreae, and Paul trusted her to deliver his letter to the Romans (Rom. 16:1–2). Quite possibly, Paul considered Junia (and her husband) an apostle (Rom. 16:7).[36] Four prophesying daughters of Philip the evangelist helped their father host Paul in Caesarea (Acts 21:8–9). Other female ministers or disciples referred to are Paul's coworkers Euodia and Syntyche (Phil. 4:2–3), the influential Philippian believer Lydia (Acts 16:13–15, 40), Laodicean house-church host Nympha (Col. 4:15), Colossian house-church host Apphia (Philem. 2), prominent Corinthian church member Chloe (1 Cor. 1:11), Timothy's godly grandmother and mother Lois and Eunice (2 Tim. 1:5), Roman ministers Mary, Tryphena, Tryphosa, and Persis (Rom. 16:6, 12), and Roman church participants such as Rufus's mother, Julia, Nereus's sister, and Claudia (Rom. 16:13, 15; 2 Tim. 4:21).

Second, some of Paul's coworkers function like Paul's delegates, carrying out work under his direction. Others seem to operate more independently. In the first category are ministers such as Timothy and Titus, who earlier in Paul's ministry take instructions or money to and from Paul's churches. Later, Paul sends Timothy to Ephesus and Titus to Crete to help teach the churches and install leaders. In the second category are Priscilla, Aquila, and Apollos. Priscilla and Aquila intersect with Paul in some cities but also pursue their own itinerary while continuing to stay in communication with Paul. Apollos is such a gifted speaker (Acts 18:24) that he attracts a following in Corinth (1 Cor. 1:12; 3:4). He rarely settles down in the same location that Paul does.[37]

Third, certain colleagues join Paul for a season, while others are with him for longer periods. In the first category, Barnabas works with Paul in Antioch and travels with him on Paul's first missionary journey. Silas (Silvanus) accompanies Paul on his second missionary journey. John Mark assists Paul and Barnabas in Cyprus and then later resurfaces toward the end of Paul's ministry. In the second category, other coworkers remain with Paul for the long haul. Priscilla and Aquila's association with Paul spans the time from his original visit to Corinth to Paul's second imprisonment in Rome (2 Tim. 4:19). Titus is part of Paul's team from at least Paul's famine visit to Jerusalem (Gal. 2:1) to the end of his life (2 Tim. 4:9). Timothy joins Paul early in his second missionary journey and receives Paul's final known letter.[38]

---

36. The Greek of Romans 16:7 is somewhat ambiguous. Andronicus and Junia are either "outstanding among the apostles" (NIV, NASB, NRSV) or "well-known to the apostles" (ESV, NET, HCSB). I favor the first reading, since the pair's familiarity to the apostles seems too incidental to highlight, and the second reading would differ somewhat from Paul's perspective in Galatians 2:6.

37. See E. Earle Ellis, "Coworkers, Paul and His," *DPL* 183.

38. Ibid.

Fourth, Paul's helpers include writing assistants (*amanuenses*) such as Tertius (Rom. 16:22) and Luke (2 Tim. 4:11), letter carriers such as Tychicus (Col. 4:7; Eph. 6:21) and Phoebe (Rom. 16:1–2),[39] and prison companions such as Epaphroditus (Phil. 2:25–30), Onesiphorus (2 Tim. 1:16–18), and Aristarchus. Aristarchus is a personal favorite of mine, since he is always in the thick of the action. He gets caught up in a riot in Ephesus (Acts 19:29), survives a shipwreck with Paul on the way to Rome (Acts 27:2), and perseveres with Paul during his first incarceration in Rome (Col. 4:10).

Fifth, Paul gathers associates from among both the Jews and the Gentiles. Barnabas and Silas have great credibility within the early Jewish church, but they take the risk of collaborating with Paul when Paul still has many detractors among the Jewish disciples. Paul's partnership with the Gentile Trophimus leaves Paul open to inaccurate accusations about defiling God's temple (Acts 21:27–29). Once again, Titus and Timothy deserve special inspection, since they exemplify the diversity of Paul's team but also illustrate his missional flexibility. Paul refuses to have Titus, a Gentile, succumb to circumcision, since it would have violated the truth of the gospel that Paul proclaimed (Gal. 2:1–5). Later, though, Paul takes the initiative to have Timothy circumcised (Acts 16:1–3), since Timothy has a Jewish mother but a Greek father (which is why he hasn't yet been circumcised). Since Timothy has a Jewish heritage, this step does not involve a compromise with the idea of freedom in Christ but is instead a strategic preparation for outreach among Jewish populations. This different treatment depending on the situation captures wonderfully Paul's determination "to be all things to all people" (1 Cor. 9:19–23).

USING THIS INFORMATION

Paul's missionary aims color his letters. We can't fully appreciate his letters without remembering Paul's missionary heart and knowing the basic progression of his travels. Use the maps in this chapter to locate the names of the cities and regions Paul visited as you read his letters. Consult the timeline of Paul's ministry to pinpoint where each letter fits. Look for the contributions of his various associates and notice how Paul values them and relies on them. Watch for how Paul navigates the turbulent waters that swirled around the acceptance of Gentiles into the church. There is much to observe and much to discover. I hope that you are getting excited about the journey!

---

39. A number of Greek manuscripts include scribal additions (comments added by copyists after Paul wrote the letter) at the end of Romans that explicitly note that Phoebe carried the letter to the Romans (Daniel B. Wallace, "Medieval Manuscripts and Modern Evangelicals: Lessons from the Past, Guidance for the Future," *JETS* 60 [2017]: 15–16).

■ ■ ■

CHAPTER FOUR

HOW DID PAUL'S WORLD AND BACKGROUND SHAPE HIS WRITINGS?

D oes Paul ever strike you as a disembodied mind, a convenient conduit for deep thoughts about God? We can tend to forget that Paul was a living and breathing first-century Jew who had to navigate the many challenges of living as a finite human being in a vast and complex Roman Empire. The more we learn about the world Paul lived in, the more we can picture in living color how Paul suffered, coped, and thrived within a setting that was expansive in its possibilities, though often messy in its realities.

Consider, for example, the inevitability of getting sick. Paul refers to his own illness when he visited the Galatians (Gal. 4:13–14). Epaphroditus, who attended to Paul in prison, was so sick that he almost died (Phil. 2:16–30). Paul's assistant Trophimus was too sick to travel (2 Tim. 4:20), and Paul's protégé Timothy struggled with frequent stomach ailments (1 Tim. 5:23). From this one small topic we see glimpses of the demanding world Paul and his coworkers inhabited. It was in these circumstances that Paul and his associates displayed the glory of Christ through their fragile humanity (2 Cor. 4:7).

Within the pages of the New Testament we can appreciate Paul as an historical figure who lived in a specific time and place. The book of Acts and Paul's letters give snapshots of Paul's formative influences and his intersections with the broader world beyond his missionary work and the churches he planted. We know that Paul was a citizen of Tarsus and Rome but was also affiliated with the Pharisees. Various places recount Paul's land and sea travels and his visits to different cities. In Acts in particular the looming presence of the Roman Empire can be felt. We can even read about Paul's imprisonments at the hands of the Romans.

Perhaps more than any other passage, 2 Corinthians 11:22–28 offers an extended look into the gritty realities of Paul's background and experiences as a Jewish Christ-follower in a Roman world. Paul speaks of frequent imprisonments, rigorous travels, inhospitable cities, and opposition from his fellow Jews. It is clear from the passage that the features of Paul's world were not just incidental stage props to the "real" action under the spotlight. Paul had to negotiate the physical, logistical, cultural, political, and religious challenges that the world presented him.

Plenty of other sources outside the Bible supplement what we know about Paul's world and help us gain more familiarity with that world. Information about Paul's background and setting won't dramatically change the meaning of passages as we read them, but it may help us fathom more deeply the weight and significance of his words. In the sections that follow, I will summarize and/or illustrate what we know about certain important areas of Paul's world and background.

TARSUS

Tarsus was the home city of Paul's family, and Paul spent considerable time in the city and its surrounding area in the years after his encounter with the resurrected Christ. Tarsus was situated in the Roman province of Cilicia, near the Mediterranean Sea, and it lies in the southeast corner of modern Turkey. Tarsus stood on the edge of a far-reaching Roman world that caught the attention of this "apostle to the Gentiles" (Rom. 11:13). Paul would have felt comfortable migrating from his respected, multicultural hometown to a similar neighboring city (Syrian Antioch), which then became the gateway for him to many other dynamic cities to the west.

Tarsus was known as a significant educational center in the Roman world. Strabo (*Geogr.* 14.5.13–15), writing decades before the time of Paul, characterizes the city's inhabitants as eager learners and points to famous native Tarsians who gained wider influence in Rome. By the time of Paul, however, some observers felt that the city's academic reputation had suffered as a result of declining morals and loss of intellectual focus (Dio, *Or.* 33.29, 48; Philostratus, *Vit. Apoll.* 1.7). Still, Paul readily affirmed his hometown as "no ordinary city" (Acts 21:39),[1] which suggests that even in his day Tarsus's image as a respectable city was still intact. It is impossible to know how much this intellectual atmosphere affected Paul, but his letters display an educated mind that could communicate effectively in a learned environment such as the one at Tarsus.

Like many cities in the Roman world, Tarsus had mixed religious loyalties. Eastern, Greek, and local gods were numbered among the city's favorites.[2] There are not many excavated ruins in Tarsus, but from coins and other records one can infer the existence of thirteen temples to gods

---

1. Dio Chrysostom, despite expressing disapproval for downward trends in Tarsus, still commended the city as "the greatest of all the cities in Cilicia" (Dio, *Or.* 34.7).
2. David W. J. Gill, "Behind the Classical Façade: Local Religions of the Roman Empire," in *One God, One Lord in a World of Religious Pluralism*, eds. Andrew D. Clarke and Bruce W. Winter (Cambridge: Tyndale House, 1991), 82–83.

and goddesses.[3] Paul would have grown up surrounded by reminders of a world beyond Judaism, a world that did not know Yahweh as the one true God but paid homage to many other gods and goddesses instead.

A sizeable Jewish community also existed in Tarsus at the time of Paul. It is possible that the Syrian ruler Antiochus Epiphanes IV brought Jews into Tarsus when he relaunched the city under its own government in 171 BC.[4] Paul's family would have lived near other Jews in the Jewish section of the city, and they may have congregated regularly at a synagogue in the city.[5] Synagogues functioned as meeting halls for worship as well as community centers for other social, educational, and religious activities. Paul regularly began his ministry to new cities in the synagogues.

Tarsus was outside of the land of Israel; in other words, it was a city of the Jewish diaspora, or dispersion. In the wake of the Babylonian invasion of Judea and the transport of many Jews away from their homeland in the sixth century BC, Jews gradually spread out to various places in the Roman Empire. Paul's identification with a city of the diaspora distinguished him from the original disciples, who hailed from the villages of Galilee. Although Paul may have moved to Jerusalem at a young age (see Acts 22:3; 26:4), he still identified Tarsus as his hometown. His parents would have handed down to him a broader perspective on the world. This prepared him to become "all things to all people" in his outreach to both Jews and Gentiles (1 Cor. 9:19–23).

Tarsus likely served as a training ground for Paul as a young minister. He appears to have settled down in Tarsus not long after Jesus called him into service (Acts 9:30; 11:25). Paul evidently spent much of his time in ministry for Christ in Tarsus and the surrounding areas during those years (Gal. 1:21–24).[6] As we have seen from this section, Tarsus offered an educationally rich atmosphere for Paul's intellectual stimulation, a Jewish community for his religious formation, and a religiously mixed launching pad for his forays into ministry outreach to both Jews and Gentiles.

CITIZENSHIP

Paul took pride in being born a Roman citizen (Acts 22:28), which meant that his family had attained the status of citizenship before he was born. Paul's parents may have become citizens when they were freed from slavery, when they were being recognized for service or generosity to the empire, or when the Romans sought to strategically incorporate the Jews of Tarsus into the Roman system.[7]

---

3. Schnabel, *Paul and the Early Church*, 1057.
4. William M. Ramsay, *The Cities of St. Paul: Their Influence on His Life and Thought* (London: Hodder & Stoughton, 1907), 180.
5. Ibid., 175–80.
6. Schnabel estimates that Paul was in or near Tarsus for nearly ten years (Schnabel, *Paul and the Early Church*, 1056).
7. Brian M. Rapske, "Citizenship, Roman," *DNTB*, 216.

Approximately 8 to 14 percent of residents in the Roman Empire were Roman citizens.[8] Citizens enjoyed special legal rights, including opportunities to appeal verdicts or request alternate locations for trials (see Acts 25:11; 26:32), and being spared certain punishments such as crucifixion or flogging (see Acts 22:25–29).[9] Local rulers did not always automatically recognize these rights, though.[10] Official registration records and punishments for false claims of citizenship helped safeguard the privileges of citizenship, so Paul may have kept his proof of citizenship with him when he traveled.[11]

In addition to being a Roman citizen, Paul was also a citizen of Tarsus (Acts 21:39). Philostratus draws attention to the presence of Jews among Tarsian citizens at a public assembly just a few decades after Paul's lifetime (*Vit. Apoll.* 6.34).[12] Rulers of cities granted citizenship in return for demonstrated loyalty or donations to the city's infrastructure projects.[13] Dual citizenship was quite common during Paul's day.[14]

Paul's status as a citizen of Rome, and less so of Tarsus, opened up advantages in his legal entanglements, but even more, gave him a respectable place in society. Still, Paul never aspired to be respectable, and when he weighed the consequences of following and serving Christ wholeheartedly, he apparently was never lulled into choosing the easier and more comfortable life of a respectable citizen. Instead, Paul was happy to claim his heavenly citizenship, and he treasured that citizenship as his ultimate joy and hope (Phil. 3:20–21).

TRAINING AS A PHARISEE

Paul's Roman roots and credentials stand alongside his religious tutelage under the Pharisees. Though scholars are not certain how old Paul was when he moved to Jerusalem to receive training as a Pharisee, Acts 22:3 and 26:4 suggest that Paul came to Jerusalem at an early age. There, he received an intensive training in the Jewish Law under a respected leader of the Pharisees named Gamaliel (Acts 22:3; see Acts 5:34). That training from "the strictest sect of our religion" (Acts 26:5) supplemented the introduction his parents and elders would have given him in Tarsus. In Paul's own descriptions of his upbringing, his Jewish identity and affiliation with the Pharisees looms large (Acts 21:39; 22:3; 23:6; 26:5; Rom. 9:3; 2 Cor. 11:22; Gal. 1:14; Phil. 3:5).

8. Eckhard J. Schnabel, *Jesus and the Twelve*, vol. 1 of *Early Christian Mission* (Downers Grove, IL: InterVarsity; Leicester: Apollos, 2004), 558.
9. Mark Reasoner, "Citizenship, Roman and Heavenly," *DPL*, 140; Polhill, *Paul and His Letters*, 15–16.
10. Rapske, "Citizenship, Roman," 217.
11. Bruce, *Apostle of the Heart Set Free*, 39–40.
12. As noted by Schnabel, *Paul and the Early Church*, 1058.
13. Ibid., 924.
14. Rapske, "Citizenship, Roman," 215.

We learn a lot about the Pharisees from the four canonical Gospels. The Pharisees were publicly visible religious leaders known for their piety (Matt. 9:14; 23:2). They often questioned or criticized Jesus and his disciples for their seemingly irregular religious practices (Matt. 12:24; Mark 2:15–24; 7:5; Luke 7:39; 19:39). Jesus denounced them for maintaining an outward religiosity that was simultaneously too severe yet ineffective at cultivating genuine spiritual growth (Matt. 23:3–13, 23–28). They conspired with the chief priests to oppose Jesus and hand him over to the Romans (Matt. 12:14; John 7:32; 11:45–57; 18:3).

The writings of Josephus supplement the picture we glean from the Gospels. Josephus describes the Pharisees as overtly religious but cordial and respected by the common people (*J.W.* 1.5.2; 2.8.14; *Ant.* 13.10.5–6; 18.1.3). The Pharisees' positive interactions within the Jewish community clarifies their role in the New Testament Gospels. Their opposition to Jesus arose not from general orneriness but from the perceived threat of Jesus being a subversive religious figure.

Josephus confirms the Gospels' picture of the Pharisees being very concerned about faithful interpretation of the Torah, or the Jewish, Mosaic Law (*J.W.* 1.5.2; 2.8.14). The Pharisees insisted on the direct relevance of the Mosaic Law, supported by additional commentary, or oral law, that sought to explicate and apply the law to various contexts for the Jews of their day.[15] The Pharisees recognized that widespread observance of the Torah would help the Israelites maintain their distinct identity as a holy nation within a broader world. They promoted fidelity to the law as an essential strategy for preserving the Jewish religious/cultural DNA.

As a Pharisee Paul had immersed himself in the study of the law (Phil. 3:5) and its traditional accumulated interpretations (Gal. 1:14). Upon encountering Christ, though, Paul began to view the law from a salvation-historical context. The law fit into a specific covenant—the Mosaic covenant—that was part of a progressing series of covenants that reached fulfillment in Christ.[16] For Paul the law was no longer directly binding on believers living in the new covenant era. Paul maintains that the law no longer defines what it means to be set apart as God's chosen people. Christ now occupies that pride of place, so that a believer's identity, and any cause to "boast," is found in Christ alone (see Gal. 2:20; 6:14–15).

According to Josephus, the Pharisees promoted a "third way" on the question of fate (or providence) and free will. While the Essenes gave great credit to fate in the course of human events, the Sadducees emphasized the ability of people to chart their own paths in life. The Pharisees forged

---

15.   See the helpful summary in Everett Ferguson, *Backgrounds of Early Christianity*, 3rd ed. (Grand Rapids: Eerdmans, 2003), 516, 542–43.

16.   Paul puts this chronologically sensitive view of the Law on full display in Galatians 3:10–4:7 (G. K. Beale and D. A. Carson, eds., *Commentary on the New Testament Use of the Old Testament* [Grand Rapids: Baker; Nottingham: Apollos, 2007], xxvi–xxvii).

a middle way between these two poles, allowing space for providence and free will to rest comfortably beside one another while still valuing providence as the more determinative category (*J. W.* 2.8.14; *Ant.* 13.5.9; 18.1.3). The Pharisees' endorsement of free will meant that they also upheld a doctrine of future rewards and judgments based upon human choices in this life.[17] We can see in Paul a similar preference for providence without the elimination of appeals to human action. Paul readily expounds on ideas such as election and predestination (see Eph. 1:3–14 and Rom. 8:28–30) while still extending genuine calls to respond to God in faith and obedience (Rom. 10:12–13; 2 Cor. 6:1–2). Paul also concurs with the Pharisees that God will one day judge all of humanity (Rom. 2:5–6; 1 Cor. 4:5; 2 Cor. 5:10), but Paul departs from them by proclaiming that Christ's substitutionary sacrifice means that those who are in Christ are spared condemnation and eternal judgment (Rom. 5:16; 8:1; 14:4; 2 Cor. 5:17–19).

In Josephus's portrayal of the Pharisees' view of life after death, he describes something resembling the immortality of the soul in one place (*J. W.* 2.8.14) while acknowledging the Pharisees' belief in bodily resurrection elsewhere (*Ant.* 18.1.3). Acts 23:9 agrees most closely with the latter passage from Josephus when it depicts the Pharisees' belief in bodily resurrection as standing in contrast to the Sadducees' denial of that doctrine (see also Mark 12:18 and parallels; Luke 14:1, 12–14; Acts 4:1–2). Paul's defense in Acts 23:6 is that he is still a Pharisee on this point, since he shares the Pharisees' "hope of the resurrection of the dead." Paul thus agrees strongly with the Pharisees on the resurrection, and this is verified when he spends much of 1 Corinthians 15 defending the believer's resurrection.

Paul started his theological training with a methodical exposure to the Hebrew Scriptures under the Pharisees' tutelage, but he reformulated his theology once he realized that the Scriptures pointed to Jesus as the Christ. In a later chapter we will examine more closely how indebted Paul was to the Old Testament in his letters, even as he adapted the shape of the story in response to Christ's revelation of himself to Paul. Paul was conversant with the Torah in all of its detail, but he knew that its bearing on life must now be subordinated to the reality of Christ's saving reign. In this he departed from his teachers, but he retained the basic Jewish worldview of God as creator, Yahweh, and the redeemer of Israel, as well as the specific doctrines of the Pharisees related to the resurrection of the dead and God's providential governance over human affairs. Paul's teachings thus amounted to a renewed and clarified way forward for God's people rather than a wholesale repudiation of the Pharisees' teachings.[18]

---

17. Menahem Mansoor, "Pharisees," *EncJud* 16:31.

18. It is telling that in Acts 23:6–9, Paul presents himself as a Pharisee who is still within the broader community of the Israelites, rather than as an outsider to the community.

TRAVEL

Paul's ministry as we know it wouldn't have been possible apart from his ability to travel around the Roman Empire. Paul traveled extensively during his missionary endeavors. His coworkers also traveled with and without him to plant and assist churches and to help deliver financial gifts to believers in need (Acts 12:30; Rom. 15:24–31; 1 Cor. 16:1–4). Trusted messengers even delivered letters back and forth from Paul and his churches. Travel allowed early Christians to bond not only locally, within individual house churches, but also as part of a broader multi-church community across the empire.[19]

Paul and his associates traveled by both land and sea, taking advantage of the relative ease of movement within the Roman Empire, while also facing dangers and hardships that accompanied both types of journeys. Paul's three missionary journeys and his transport to Rome are chronicled in Acts, but Paul mentions some of his travel experiences and plans in his letters as well. Both Paul and his coworkers were ready to invest time, expense, and effort to visit existing churches and establish new ones.

The Roman road system attests to the organizational competency of the Roman Empire. Military goals drove the construction of the 50,000 miles of roads, but the rest of the empire certainly benefitted as well.[20] The world in Paul's day became much smaller and more accessible because of this impressive network of roads the Romans built. The remnants of these roads are found even today inside and outside of cities such as ancient Philippi and Tarsus (see figure 2). Archaeological sites and museums preserve mile markers that demonstrate the careful planning and layout of these roads (see figure 3).

Since Paul was not a particularly wealthy man, he traveled by foot on his land journeys. Documents showing requirements for appearing in court reveal that people could typically walk the equivalent of eighteen miles per

Figure 2—Roman Road in Philippi

19.   See Wayne A. Meeks, *The First Urban Christians: The Social World of the Apostle Paul* (New Haven, CT: Yale University Press, 1983), 190.

20.   Polhill, *Paul and His Letters*, 21.

day.[21] Schnabel describes some of the risks inherent to land travel: "Travelers on land were in danger from highwaymen, robbers and innkeepers. . . . Depending on the region (mountains, deserts, swamps) and the season (summer, winter), storms, heat and cold created dangerous situations for the traveler. Illness and accidents could not be ruled out either, of course, nor the problem of running out of money."[22] Paul himself mentions bandits, hazardous rivers, dangerous cities and rural areas, and exposure to the elements in 2 Corinthians 11:26–27. These considerable obstacles meant that travelers had to hold their plans loosely. Paul sometimes apologized for last-minute alterations to traveling plans or recognized that any plans he made remained tentative.[23]

Though travelers had access to public lodging during their journeys, the inns and guest houses had poor reputations for quality and safety.[24] The strong early Christian emphasis on hospitality gave rise to better options for Paul and his team. Paul instructed Roman believers to welcome Phoebe, who delivered Paul's letter to them (Rom. 16:1–2; see also 1 Cor. 16:10; Col. 4:10). He also applauded Gaius's hospitality, which suggests that Paul had stayed with Gaius while he was in Corinth (Rom. 16:23). Paul expected Philemon to be ready to host him (Philem. 22).[25] Acts also shows examples of generous believers opening up their homes to Paul and his colleagues (Acts 16:15; 17:7; 21:8, 16; 28:14).

Figure 3—Roman Mile Marker, Archaeological Museum of Thessaloniki

Sea travel required securing passage on a ship that was traveling for trade or other commercial purposes (see the mention of cargo in Acts 21:3 and 27:10, 18), but it was still quite common to travel by sea.[26] Effective Roman governance neutralized threats from piracy, which is why that concern never surfaces in Acts or Paul's letters.[27] Boats traveled either close to the shore (see Acts

---

21. Schnabel, *Jesus and the Twelve*, 635.
22. Ibid., 636–37.
23. See Paul Trebilco, "Itineraries, Travel Plans, Journeys, Apostolic Parousia," *DPL* 450.
24. Brian M. Rapske, "Travel and Trade," *DNTB* 1246.
25. This request could also be a way of letting Philemon know that Paul will check up on him at some point, to see whether he had acted upon Paul's appeal for Onesimus.
26. Schnabel, *Jesus and the Twelve*, 634.
27. Ferguson, *Backgrounds of Early Christianity*, 88; Polhill, *Paul and His Letters*, 21.

27:1, 13) or on the open seas.[28] Shipwrecks were always a possibility (divers continue to find remains of ancient sunken ships in the Mediterranean and Aegean seas even today). Paul recalls his ordeals involving treacherous seas and shipwrecks in 2 Corinthians 11:25–26.

As winter approached, both sea and land travel became more precarious. Before the shipwreck on Paul's sea voyage to Rome, he warned the crew of unsafe sea conditions because they were entering the dangerous winter season after the Day of Atonement (Acts 27:9–10). Sea travel was typically put on hold during the winter months of early November to early March.[29] Land travel was similarly avoided during those months.[30] As a result, travelers often settled into a city over the winter (see Acts 28:11; 1 Cor. 16:6; Titus 3:12). In 2 Timothy 4:21 Paul asked Timothy to visit him (and bring important supplies—2 Tim. 4:13) before winter. Paul was concerned that the window of opportunity for safe travel would soon close.

From our perspective, travel in the Roman Empire sounds inconvenient and hazardous. But Paul would have undoubtedly thanked God for the opportunity to travel so freely. His ancestors had not experienced anything like the mobility he enjoyed. His ease of travel had made possible a ministry that spanned "from Jerusalem all the way around to Illyricum" (Rom. 15:19).

CITIES

To appreciate Paul's travels and his destination cities, be sure to read Paul's letters with a map in hand. We risk obscuring the humanity of Paul and his readers when we divorce these individuals from their historical settings. Conversely, we see more of the rich texture of Paul's letters when we can connect the geographical details in a passage to actual places on a map.

While Jesus and his disciples concentrated their itinerant ministry in the villages of Galilee, Paul spent time primarily in larger cities. Ambitious people and impressive buildings filled the cities of the Roman world. Building projects were funded by taxes and were often built with forced labor, using materials taken from local quarries or even stone from faraway islands in the Aegean Sea. The cities were centers of economic, political, social, and religious life. These areas of life were often tightly intertwined, so when Paul and his team arrived in a city and began to share the gospel, their ministry disrupted multiple aspects of a city's existence (see, for instance, Philippi in Acts 16:16–24 and Ephesus in Acts 19:21–41).

Among the categories of cities in the empire, Roman colonies and free cities are most relevant for studying Paul's letters. As Ferguson explains, Roman colonies, including Corinth, Philippi, and Troas, were equivalent to Rome in status and prestige. Roman colonies were populated by Roman

---

28. Ferguson, *Backgrounds of Early Christianity*, 87.
29. Schnabel, *Jesus and the Twelve*, 635.
30. Rapske, "Travel and Trade," 1245.

citizens, including many retired soldiers. Free cities such as Ephesus, Tarsus, and Syrian Antioch enjoyed a measure of independence but were subject to higher taxes and fewer privileges than the colonies were.[31]

Roman cities featured a central square, the (Greek) agora or (Roman) forum, lined by governmental buildings (such as basilicas), commercial shops, covered walkways (stoas), and pagan religious temples. The spaces and buildings displayed appealing architecture and art, and they were adorned with statues honoring powerful rulers, along with inscriptions paying tribute to benefactors or noteworthy public officials.[32] Other common structures in or around cities included *insulae* (adjoined groups of homes or apartments), *bouleuteria* (for governmental assemblies), *odea* (for concerts or speeches), gymnasiums, stadiums, theaters and amphitheaters, libraries, fountains (see figure 4), baths, and the city walls and gates. Many cities erected a temple on an acropolis that overlooked the city, and the acropolis provided a safe haven against potential attacks. Aqueducts transported water to residents of the city, and some coastal cities had ports or harbors (see figure 5).[33]

Figure 4—Fountain System in Corinth

31. See Ferguson, *Backgrounds of Early Christianity*, 41.
32. An inscription found in the ruins of Corinth describes the donation of a public official named Erastus, with detail that corresponds well to the Erastus who sends his greetings from Corinth in Romans 16:23.
33. For helpful overviews on ancient cities, see Schnabel, *Jesus and the Twelve*, 584–98; Duane F. Watson, "Cities, Greco-Roman," *DNTB* 212–15.

Figure 5—Road to the Harbor of Ancient Ephesus

If you visit the ruins of many ancient Roman cities today you will see reconstructed pagan temples all around (see figure 6). The inhabitants of the region used these temples for religious ceremonies but also for communal meals in which participants consumed food that previously had been sacrificed to honor the god or goddess of the temple. Meat sacrificed at temples also found its way into the local food markets. In this way idolatry was woven into the fabric of life in the cities, and early Christians had to learn how to cope with this unpleasant reality.[34] In both 1 Corinthians and Romans Paul offers counsel to believers who have different convictions about eating meat previously sacrificed to false gods. Paul's guidance carefully considers the various settings in which believers would have encountered sacrificed meat and then weighs competing concerns of freedom in Christ, individual conscience, and interpersonal harmony.

SLAVERY

The economic system in Paul's world relied heavily on slave labor, and households incorporated slaves into the family structure. In fact, Paul likely referred to slaves as a part of households when he acknowledged (with variation in the Greek wording) the households of Aristobulus (Rom. 16:10), Narcissus (Rom. 16:11), Chloe (1 Cor. 1:11), and Stephanas

---

34. Ferguson, *Backgrounds of Early Christianity*, 147, 190.

(1 Cor. 1:16; 16:15).[35] Along with victims of the slave trade (see Paul's negative reference to slave trading in 1 Tim. 1:10), prisoners of war, criminals, children of slaves, and debtors (and debtors' family members) could all become slaves. Slaves labored in the mines, fields, and households (overseeing financial matters, carrying out tasks to keep the household running smoothly, or caring for children).

Figure 6—Gateway to Aphrodite's Temple, Aphrodisias (modern Turkey)

Slaves sometimes attained freedom through a process known as manumission, either during the master's lifetime or upon the master's death, as instructed in the master's will. In a practice known as sacral manumission, slaves could pay for their freedom in the presence of gods in temples across the empire.[36] In Delphi, for instance, visitors can see a stone wall covered with inscriptions describing the slaves' emancipation from slavery as witnessed by Apollo, whose temple towers over the wall (see figure 7). When the slave was freed the master–slave relationship sometimes morphed into a patron–client relationship, with an ongoing dynamic of power imbalance between the two parties.

Paul does not attack the institution of slavery head-on but instead advises slaves and masters on how to conduct relationships with one

---

35.   Arthur A. Rupprecht, "Slave, Slavery," *DPL* 881.
36.   Ferguson, *Backgrounds of Early Christianity*, 60–61.

Figure 7—Temple of Apollo at Delphi

another in Christ-centered ways (Eph. 6:5–9; Col. 3:22–4:1; 1 Tim. 6:1–2; Titus 2:9–10). Paul's missionary goals seem to supersede any concerns about overturning the practice altogether, though even if he had wanted to, Paul and other Christians lacked the clout to bring about that type of wholesale change in law. The early believers were too much of a vulnerable minority group on the margins of society at that time. Besides, Paul's sense of calling began with summoning individuals to be reconciled to God and then helping them become integrated into churches marked by spiritual equality and unity in Christ (Gal. 3:28; Col. 3:11). Paul sustained a disciplined focus on this calling and never wavered from it.

In two places Paul does seem to support slaves gaining their freedom in certain circumstances. In 1 Corinthians 7:21 Paul encourages slaves to embrace freedom when it is made available to them.[37] And in Philemon, he may even pressure Philemon to release his slave Onesimus, though this interpretation is disputed by some scholars. At the very least, Paul calls for a radical reworking of the master-slave relationship around the shared, reconciled life that believers enjoy in Christ. Because the saving work and

---

37. Because Paul's compact language in the verse creates some ambiguity, the NRSV advances the opposite idea—that slaves should make the most of their slavery even if presented with an opportunity for freedom. A translation that conveys taking advantage of a chance to be freed from slavery (NIV, ESV, NASB, HCSB, NET, NKJV) is preferred. See David E. Garland, *1 Corinthians*, BECNT (Grand Rapids: Baker, 2003), 308–11.

indwelling presence of Christ levels the playing field for all believers, the master Philemon must view his slave Onesimus as his brother.

Paul's transformative gospel continued to inspire later generations of believers in the area of slavery. Although Paul's gospel initially prioritized bringing new life to individuals and spiritual vitality to churches, the gospel could not be contained within those arenas. When later Christians gained more of a platform to influence the broader culture, they applied this same gospel to confront the injustice of slavery in their day.

ROMAN GOVERNANCE AND THE IMPERIAL CULT

The countries we live in, along with the leaders that govern them, affect our lives in many big and small ways. We are bound to our country's laws, we benefit or suffer from wise or foolish leadership, and we appeal to common reference points—stories, constitutions, flags, symbols, anthems, and mottos—to make sense of our shared identities as residents of that country. Paul and his readers were similarly shaped by the Roman Empire, its leaders, and ideals.

The Roman Empire of Paul's time aspired to and partially arrived at what is known as the *Pax Romana*, a relatively peaceful environment across the empire brought about by Roman governance. This peace was dependent upon political stability and the successful integration of diverse indigenous people groups into the broader society. Though the Roman Empire was a melting pot of peoples with different traditions and cultures, the people lived under a larger empire that sought to give them a collective identity as well.

Most countries work hard to preserve the unity and stability of their territories, and Rome was no different. The Roman Empire promoted unity and loyalty through the strategic propagation of an elevated political ideology known as the imperial cult, or the emperor cult.[38] The imperial cult consisted of, among other things, visible expressions of gratitude and devotion to leaders past and present in the form of statues, busts, and images on coins, as well as temples dedicated to Rome and its leaders (see figure 8).[39] These vivid displays of love for Rome did not eclipse tributes to pagan gods and goddesses but stood alongside them.[40] The people had a sense that the gods had uniquely blessed Rome and its leaders, so at

---

38. Most narrowly, the imperial cult denotes "the ritual worship of living or dead emperors, most commonly in the form of animal sacrifice" (Colin Miller, "The Imperial Cult in the Pauline Cities of Asia Minor and Greece," *CBQ* 72 [2010]: 317). In a broader sense, however, it encompasses a host of practices and symbols meant to instill a sense of reverence for and allegiance to Rome and its rulers.

39. Richard A. Horsley, "Introduction: The Gospel of Imperial Salvation," in *Paul and Empire: Religion and Power in Roman Imperial Society*, ed. Richard A. Horsley (Harrisburg, PA: Trinity Press International, 1997), 11.

40. Miller, "Imperial Cult," 319–21.

Figure 8—Statue of Emperor Augustus, Archaeological Museum of Ancient Corinth

festivals and the games they offered thanks and sacrifices to deities for bestowing such a strong system and such gifted leaders on the world.[41]

A Greek inscription found in Priene, Asia Minor, provides a striking example of how the people used lofty language to venerate their leaders.[42] The people of Asia Minor wished to honor Augustus by highlighting the touch of the divine they saw in his leadership. They credit "Providence" with sending the gifted and virtuous Augustus to the world. They magnify Augustus as a "savior," "benefactor," and "god." They claim that his exploits have brought about peace and a wonderful new state of affairs for the world. They call his birth and presence in the world "good tidings" (from the Greek word for gospel—εὐαγγέλιον).

When we speak of the imperial cult we are referring to a way of honoring Rome that spilled over into this type of religious devotion. The worship was not as blatant as directly addressing the emperors as gods. Schnabel notes that prayers and sacrifices were offered "not *to* the emperor but *for* the emperor."[43] Still, Roman emperors allowed the people, especially those outside of Rome itself, to associate the emperors with the gods and the divine glory of Rome.[44] We see this quite vividly in the inscription from Priene, mentioned above. More direct veneration of dead Roman emperors occurred starting with Julius Caesar's death, since people believed that he was now counted among the gods.[45] Later emperors such as Caligula, Nero, and Domitian blurred the lines by seeking the glories of being treated as divine, in one way or another, during their lifetimes.

41.   Horsley, "Gospel of Imperial Salvation," 20–23. Miller, however, cautions that during Paul's time direct acts of sacrifice and worship were not yet that widespread (Miller, "Imperial Cult," 315–19).

42.   See A. D. Nock's English translation of the inscription in Ferguson, *Backgrounds of Early Christianity*, 46.

43.   Schnabel, *Jesus and the Twelve*, 619.

44.   Ferguson, *Backgrounds of Early Christianity*, 208.

45.   Ibid.

Respectable Roman senators strongly objected to emperors who sought such overt and excessive adulation, but across the empire there was a surprising appetite for elevating a deified Rome and its leaders.

The imperial cult created great problems for Jews and Christians. The Jews worshiped Yahweh as the one true God of the whole world, and they knew God's prohibitions against worshiping any other gods or their images. Christians held similar convictions about God and also recognized Jesus Christ as God's appointed King of kings and Lord of lords. Their most basic confession affirmed that "Jesus is Lord." Jews and Christians could not join the crowds in pledging supreme allegiance to Rome and its rulers.

Though a number of clashes with Roman power surface in the book of Acts, there are few direct objections to State power in Paul's letters. Still, while the denials of the legitimacy of Roman authority are absent, the simple affirmations of Christ's authority and his kingdom relegate Rome's authority to second place as a consequence of wholehearted commitment to Christ. Paul never watered down the reality of God's sovereignty or the promise of the full arrival of the comprehensive kingdom of God to this world (see 1 Cor. 15:24–28; Eph. 1:20–23; Col. 1:15–20). Paul does, however, seek to guide believers in living winsomely and constructively in the midst of their detractors (Rom. 12:14–21; 13:1–7; Col. 4:5–6; Titus 3:1–2).

IMPRISONMENT

Paul frequently ran afoul of agents of Rome, who along with Paul's enemies among the Jewish leaders had Paul seized and imprisoned a number of times.[46] Paul wrote five of his letters from prison—Ephesians, Philippians, Colossians, 2 Timothy, and Philemon. In 2 Corinthians, before Paul had written most or all of those prison letters, he recalls multiple incarcerations (see also the mention of his fellow prisoners in Romans 16:7), one of which is included in Acts (Acts 16:16–24). After writing 2 Corinthians, Paul spends extended time being detained in Jerusalem, the port city of Caesarea, and Rome (on two different occasions).

Confinement in the Roman Empire served as a temporary measure before prisoners were either exonerated or given their actual punishment.[47] This is the case for all of Paul's recorded imprisonments as well. The severity of conditions under Roman custody varied across the empire and according to the time period. Paul discovered this diversity of conditions as he spent time in military barracks (Acts 21–23), under house

---

46. Of course, Paul himself had been complicit in imprisoning many believers before Christ intervened in his life (Acts 8:3; 22:4; 26:10).

47. *The Digest of Justinian*, vol. 4, eds. Theodor Mommsen and Paul Krueger, trans. Alan Watson, (Philadelphia: University of Pennsylvania, 1985), 48.19.8. The *Digest* is a collection of opinions from leading jurists of the Roman Empire from multiple centuries leading up to the sixth century AD.

arrest (Acts 28:16, 30, which likely corresponds to his location when writing Ephesians, Colossians, and Philemon), and in the more grueling environments implied in descriptions from Philippians and 2 Timothy.[48] Despite the range of experiences a prisoner might encounter, scholars can still identify a general picture of prison life from the sources of that time.

Prison hardships fall into the two major categories of physical stresses and emotional strain.[49] Prisons were not designed with prisoners' comfort in mind, and they weren't even intended to support long-term health or survival, since the prisoners were not to be stationed there indefinitely. Substandard conditions included lack of sunlight, foul air, extremes in temperatures, only hard surfaces for rest, and insufficient food (see Lucian, *Tox.* 29). Heavy chains limited movement and created discomfort and pain to prisoners' limbs. These rigorous conditions threatened to cause a prisoner's health to spiral downward quickly, especially if beatings or other mistreatment had preceded the imprisonment (see Acts 16:22; 21:30–32; 2 Cor. 6:4–5; 11:23). Prisoners needed support from outside friends and family members to help sustain them physically, not to mention emotionally (as shown in Josephus, *Ant.* 18.202–204).

Relationships were strained for prisoners because of the honor–shame contours of ancient Mediterranean cultures. Being branded a criminal by the state brought shame to the prisoner and threatened to mar the good names of friends and associates of the prisoner. Reports suggest that acquaintances often abandoned prisoners upon their removal from respectable society (Lucian, *Tox.* 28; Livy 38.57.3; Seneca, *Ep.* 9.8–9). The added torments of loneliness and despair exacerbated the emotional state of prisoners.

Even Paul's milder confinements involved being chained (Acts 21:33; 26:29; 28:20; Eph. 6:20; Col. 4:18). These chains restricted Paul's freedom and visually reminded him and others that he was an accused man in the eyes of the law. In Philippians (and arguably 2 Corinthians 1 as well), Paul alludes to a more strenuous physical and emotional ordeal during his imprisonment, which may have occurred while he was in Ephesus (see the mention of "the province of Asia" in 2 Corinthians 1:8). Paul's deliberation between wanting to die and see Christ and continue in fruitful ministry in Philippians 1:19–26 hints at the agonizing nature of his detainment. His helper Epaphroditus apparently succumbs to the rigors of prison conditions and nearly dies while assisting Paul (Phil. 2:27, 30). If Paul had just emerged from this same imprisonment when he wrote 2 Corinthians, the first chapter of that letter may provide additional disturbing details of the intensity of the

---

48. Local officials were given some leeway in determining the best course of action for confining prisoners awaiting trial (*The Digest of Justinian* 48.3.1).

49. Comprehensive overviews of the Roman prison system can be found in Brian M. Rapske, *The Book of Acts and Paul in Roman Custody* (Grand Rapids: Eerdmans, 1994) and Richard J. Cassidy, *Paul in Chains: Roman Imprisonment and the Letters of Saint Paul* (New York: Herder & Herder, 2001).

imprisonment he had endured when he wrote Philippians. Paul recounts "despair[ing] of life" and feeling "the sentence of death" during that confinement (2 Cor. 1:8–9). He characterizes his imprisonment as "troubles" (1:8) and "deadly peril" (1:10).

Paul's struggle in prison seems nowhere more severe than in 2 Timothy. At the start of the letter he highlights both the physical and emotional toll of his imprisonment, using the words "suffering" and "shame" (1:8, 12). He then laments the hurt of desertion, contrasted with his appreciation for the loyal service of Onesiphorus (1:15–18), who may have died while staying with Paul in prison (note how Paul speaks about Onesiphorus in the past tense and mentions his family in 1:16 and 4:19). Language of hardship surfaces again in the letter (2:3), with Paul's further depiction of "suffering even to the point of being chained like a criminal" (2:9). Paul even begins to speak of impending death when he compares his life to a drink offering that is being poured out (see the similar language in Philippians 2:17) and predicts that his "departure is near" (2 Tim. 4:6). Paul shares his feelings of being abandoned by his colleague Demas (4:10) as well as by unnamed believers during his first legal defense hearing (4:16). He also expresses urgency when he asks Timothy to come quickly to assist him (4:9, 21) and to send Mark as well (4:11). Timothy and Mark would provide the practical and emotional support that a prisoner such as Paul would need, and Timothy would also bring a crucial item for Paul's survival—a cloak to keep him warm during the winter (4:13, 21).[50] As with the other details of Paul's world unfolded in this chapter, knowledge of the realities of incarceration in the Roman world heightens the humanity of Paul and keeps him securely anchored in his vivid historical setting.

CONCLUSION

Paul lived at the intersection of many shaping influences, including but not limited to the topics discussed in this chapter. Paul makes a fascinating historical figure, even if that is not the primary reason we read his letters. He is authentically human but carries out a divine calling to communicate God's revelation to the churches. Still, the world and background of Paul helps us take his letters even more seriously. His persuasive argumentation and theological mind emerges from a man thoroughly integrated into a Jewish and Greco-Roman setting and deeply rooted in an eventful and multifaceted past. This chapter gives a glimpse of that world and past so that we can read Paul more accurately and appreciate how the truth of God he proclaimed also worked itself out in his experiences.

---

50. Plutarch (*Phil..* 20.2) describes a prisoner resting with his soldier's coat on, apparently for the purpose of keeping warm.

■ ■ ■

CHAPTER FIVE

WERE ALL THIRTEEN LETTERS REALLY WRITTEN BY PAUL?

W hen we commence a serious study of the Pauline Epistles, a lingering question moves to the forefront: did Paul actually write the letters that bear his name? Many generations of Christians have answered that question in the affirmative, following in the footsteps of believers who lived in the first few centuries after Christ. The Muratorian Canon from the late second century credits Paul with writing the thirteen letters now included in our Bibles,[1] and some early New Testament manuscripts contain all thirteen letters as well.[2] In addition, numerous references or allusions to the letters in writings from church leaders in the second century attest to the early and widespread acceptance of all thirteen letters as Scripture.[3] But in the last several hundred years, scholars in the wake of the Enlightenment have voiced their skepticism that Paul wrote some of the letters. Is there any substance to these doubts? How should we evaluate the question?

Critical scholars today divide Paul's letters into the "undisputed" and "disputed" letters. Almost all specialists in Pauline studies affirm that Paul wrote the undisputed letters. On the other hand, great debate surrounds the disputed letters. The seven undisputed letters consist of Romans, 1 and 2 Corinthians, Galatians, Philippians, 1 Thessalonians, and Philemon.

---

1. Some opt for a fourth-century date for the Muratorian Canon's composition, but the arguments for a late second-century date are more convincing and seem to be winning the day (see the overview of research in Eckhard J. Schnabel, "The Muratorian Fragment: The State of Research," *JETS* 57 [2014]: 239–53).
2. One exception is $\mathfrak{P}^{46}$, the earliest surviving manuscript of Paul's collected letters (AD 200). The manuscript appears to omit the Pastoral Epistles, Philemon, and 2 Thessalonians, though a couple of these letters (but not all) would fit in the missing leaves from the back of the codex. As with many other early manuscripts, $\mathfrak{P}^{46}$ groups Hebrews with Paul's letters.
3. The letters of Paul became widely accepted as Scripture well before the final stabilization of the twenty-seven books of the New Testament canon toward the end of the fourth century.

The first four of these as a group are known as the *Hauptbriefe*, which in German means the "chief letters." Scholars start with these four letters to establish their sense of how Paul wrote and what his ideas were. They are confident that these four letters, with their lively style and groundbreaking theological ideas, represent the true voice of Paul. The latter three are deemed to concur with the substance and style of the *Hauptbriefe* and thus are also considered undisputed. That leaves six disputed letters, which are, in the rough order of least disputed to most disputed, 2 Thessalonians, Colossians, Ephesians, 2 Timothy, 1 Timothy, and Titus.

In this chapter we will examine why some specialists dismiss Paul's authorship of the disputed letters and respond to their reasons for doing so. First, we will consider the strange cases of two letters you have probably never heard of. They are two letters, written in Paul's name, that have been exposed as forgeries. Then we will spend time contemplating the theological objections raised against the disputed letters, along with arguments arising from stylistic patterns observed in those letters. Finally, we will explore the historical and canonical implications of rejecting Paul's authorship of one or more of his letters. Today, many readers become exposed to the charge that Paul didn't write some of his letters through Bart Ehrman's writings. We will focus our attention on arguments from his popular-level book, *Forged: Writing in the Name of God*, and his more detailed and comprehensive book, *Forgery and Counterforgery*.[4]

TWO KNOWN FORGERIES

Forgers hoping to write in Paul's name face a fundamental problem. They have something they want to say, but they need to say it like Paul would. Why take the time to write in the first place, if you don't have a message to get across? But the more it sounds like *your* message (in style or content), the more skeptical people will be that Paul wrote it. But when you try to mimic Paul's style and content, you'll feel hesitant to stray from wording and points that are familiar from Paul's writings, leaving you little room to articulate your own convictions. There are two second-century forgeries that run up against these formidable obstacles.

We will start by examining a rather dull letter known as the Epistle to the Laodiceans. This letter is preserved only in a number of Latin manuscripts, but there are good indications that someone originally wrote it in Greek.[5] The opening words of the letter present Paul, an apostle, as the

4.   Bart D. Ehrman, *Forged Writing in the Name of God—Why the Bible's Authors Are Not Who We Think They Are* (New York: HarperOne, 2011); Ehrman, *Forgery and Counterforgery: The Use of Literary Deceit in Early Christian Polemics* (Oxford: Oxford University Press, 2013).

5.   J. K. Elliott, *The Apocryphal New Testament: A Collection of Apocryphal Christian Literature in an English Translation* (Oxford: Clarendon, 1993), 544; J. B. Lightfoot, *St. Paul's Epistles to the Colossians and to Philemon* (London: Macmillan, 1892), 291–92.

author. Paul's name is the only individual name mentioned in the letter, apart from references to the Persons of the Godhead.

The first thing that stands out about the letter is its brevity—twenty verses in all. Even the canonical Philemon is longer, at twenty-five verses. Second, the letter contains words, phrases, and sentences that sound familiar from Paul's letters. It has a couple of verses that resemble excerpts from Galatians, and there are quite a few verses that bear a striking similarity to wording throughout Philippians. But since the verses are extracted from Galatians and Philippians without the greater context of those letters in mind, they take on a different, watered-down meaning in the Epistle to the Laodiceans. Paul's theological brilliance becomes the imitator's trite platitudes. Similarly, Paul's vivid style and well-developed thinking is reduced to the imitator's flat and superficial discourse, littered with abrupt changes of topic.

The search for an occasion, or something that would have prompted the historical Paul to write to the Laodiceans in the first place, turns up empty. There are no hints about the church's needs, concerns, or specific problems they were facing. Sure, the author mentions something vague about false teaching (Ep. Lao. 4), but he doesn't carefully engage the false teaching, so it seems unlikely that false teaching was the main reason the author decided to write.[6] The purpose for writing is likewise elusive. The author doesn't place emphasis on any given topic or reveal any type of thesis statement. By the time we reach the end of the letter, we still don't have a firm opinion about its main point. The argument of the letter is almost nonexistent. The author jumps from thought to thought very quickly but never develops his ideas. There is no coherent argument that could be outlined or summarized.

A second known forgery, 3 Corinthians, fares only slightly better under careful examination. Also originating in the second century, the letter is often found, in its surviving copies, inserted into a work known as the Acts of Paul. Most likely, though, the letter existed independently from the Acts of Paul when it was first written.[7] Unlike the case with the Epistle to the Laodiceans, 3 Corinthians has an occasion, purpose, and argument. The imitator hopes to counter specific false teachings that denied the goodness of physical creation and bodily resurrection.[8] The author writes to defend

---

6.   The final verse instructs the Laodiceans to read Paul's letter to the Colossians and share their letter with the Colossian church. Colossians 4:16 delivers the same directives, just in reverse order. This betrays the true occasion of the letter: the letter mentioned in Colossians was never found, and a forger wanted to supply us with it.

7.   The letter is accompanied by a prior letter from the Corinthians to Paul. These two letters were likely circulated together, but they were independent of the Acts of Paul (see Vahan Hovhanessian, *Third Corinthians: Reclaiming Paul for Christian Orthodoxy*, Studies in Biblical Literature 18 [New York: Lang, 2000], 48–53).

8.   The author makes the occasion overt by adding an introductory letter, from the Corinthians to Paul, in which the church's concerns about specific false teachings are presented directly.

these ideas and does so with a sustained argument drawing upon Israel's history, the incarnation and resurrection of Christ, and examples of new birth in nature and Scripture. The theology is compatible with Paul's but is more systematized, and reflects theological debates that arose only after Paul's lifetime.

Third Corinthians has "Paul" speaking about his ministry and imprisonment at the beginning and near the end of the letter in order to create some sense of connection to the historical Paul. The picture produced, however, doesn't tie into the rest of the letter's contents or quite fit with the canonical portrait of Paul. For example, the letter draws attention to Paul's imprisonment (3 Cor. 3:1, 33) and hardships (3 Cor. 3:2) without any apparent purpose in the letter.[9] Even more problematic is the language in 3 Corinthians 3:4: "I delivered to you in the beginning what I received from the apostles who were before me, who at all times were together with the Lord Jesus Christ."[10] In this verse the author uses a conflation of three canonical verses (1 Cor. 11:23; 15:3; Gal. 1:17) to depict his relationship to the apostles and their teaching, but in their new context, the combined verses subordinate Paul to the other apostles in a way that is unprecedented.[11] The real Paul struck a careful balance between pointing out his direct calling from Christ and his alignment with the other apostles' message.

Careful inspection also reveals a few curious omissions in the letter. The author rushes past the opportunity to give any meaningful blessing or thanks for his readers, which departs from Paul's typical practice.[12] The writer also neglects to mention Paul's colleagues, details of his travels, or individuals in the Corinthian church.

The Epistle to the Laodiceans and 3 Corinthians expose themselves as fakes in two different ways. The Epistle to the Laodiceans tries to stay so close to Paul's established script that it avoids saying anything meaningful. Its collection of familiar Pauline snippets loses its force apart from any greater purpose. Though 3 Corinthians says something important, it dives into an historical setting that corresponds to the second rather than first century. Its unremarkable comments about Paul at the beginning and end of the letter subtly diminish Paul's authority and aren't even relevant to the body of the letter, in which Paul disappears. Both letters shy away from

---

9. MaGee, *Portrait of an Apostle*, 77.

10. Translation (and verse numbering) from Wilhelm Schneemelcher, "The Acts of Paul," in *New Testament Apocrypha: Revised Edition of the Collection initiated by Edward Hennecke*, ed. Wilhelm Schneemelcher, trans. R. McL. Wilson (Louisville: Westminster John Knox, 1991–1992), 255.

11. MaGee, *Portrait of an Apostle*, 75–76.

12. Paul included blessings in all thirteen canonical letters, and thanksgiving sections in ten of the thirteen letters. The exceptions for thanksgivings are Galatians, in which Paul moves straight to a rebuke of his readers, and 1 Timothy and Titus, letters of practical instruction. Many of the thanksgivings also previewed themes Paul would develop more thoroughly later in the letter (1 Cor. 1:4–9; 2 Cor. 1:3–7; Phil. 1:3–6; Col.. 1:3–12; 1 Thess. 1:2–10; 2 Thess. 1:3–4; Philem. 4–7).

specific details about Paul's whereabouts, his coworkers' movements, or his personal contacts with individuals in the recipients' church.

What we can glean from the construction of these letters is that it is difficult to pull off a forgery that avoids discovery. And we would be surprised if earlier alleged forgeries in Christian history (such as 1 Timothy, for instance) were that much more sophisticated than later ones. They would have to do many things well in order to fool so many discerning believers, including those who lived only a generation or two after Paul's era (during the time the canonical forgeries supposedly surfaced). Imitators would have to construct a credible historical occasion that fit Paul's lifetime and context but also had some bearing on the issues in their own settings. Any personal details they dared to add would also need to conform to what we already know about Paul (which might be why the authors of the two known forgeries refrained from the effort). They would need to use language that sounded enough like Paul's, but not simply in a cut-and-paste manner. The theology would need to be consistent with Paul's as well.[13]

Let's return now to the disputed letters of Paul. Could forgers have created the illusion of Paul's authorship so successfully that the church was fooled for seventeen centuries? Did they manufacture sophisticated forgeries that were embraced for generations but whose façade nonetheless finally crumbled under more detailed scrutiny? Or do they still stand up to close investigation and vindicate themselves as originating from the same insightful mind as the author of Paul's undisputed letters?

SECOND THESSALONIANS

We begin with 2 Thessalonians, which receives a split verdict from the scholarly community. In his case against the authenticity of 2 Thessalonians Ehrman focuses his attention on 2 Thessalonians 2:1–2. First, he says that the author planted a warning in the verses about fake letters from Paul in order to boost the credibility of his own forgery.[14] Second, Ehrman claims that in verse 2 the author seeks to undercut the doctrine that the return of Christ is imminent and replace a sudden return with a return foreshadowed by a series of conspicuous signs (2 Thess. 2:3–12), which would contradict Paul's teachings elsewhere.[15]

In 2 Thessalonians 2:1–2 the author does caution his readers to beware of people speaking or writing in Paul's name. Is there a reasonable explanation for this that corresponds to the view that Paul wrote the letter? We

---

13. Many of these challenges recede for pseudepigraphal works in other genres, which is why pseude-pigraphal narratives and apocalypses were more widespread in Jewish and Christian circles (Montague Rhodes James, *The Apocryphal New Testament* [Oxford: Clarendon, 1924], 476).

14. Ehrman, *Forged*, 19–20; Ehrman, *Forgery and Counterforgery*, 24–25.

15. Ehrman, *Forged*, 106–7.

can surmise that Paul had learned that some of the Thessalonians thought
he had endorsed a view about the return of Christ that he did not actually
hold. Paul does not identify a specific person or letter that had spread this
theological confusion. He refers more generally to the ways that someone
might try to pass off their own teaching as Paul's—by relating a "spirit" or
"word" that Paul allegedly spoke, or by presenting a letter purported to
have come from Paul. Paul views any such unauthorized use of his name
as deception (2 Thess. 2:3). He seeks to guard against any future occurrence of this trickery by drawing attention to his own handwritten authen-
tication of each letter (2 Thess. 3:17).[16] The most we can say about these
comments is that Paul wants to clear up confusion about what the Thessalonians think that he is promoting.[17] As we know from Paul's letters and
elsewhere in the New Testament, false teaching was a critical problem in
the early church. This letter reflects that same milieu. Paul tries to defuse
the problem of heterodox teaching in the Thessalonian church before it
gets worse.

Contrary to Ehrman's interpretations and doubtful translations of 2
Thessalonians 2:2 ("the day of the Lord is almost here" or "the day of the
Lord is at hand"),[18] the letter does *not* combat the idea of the imminent
return of Christ. Rather, the author refutes the allegation that the day of
the Lord was already here. The day of the Lord consists of both salvation
for believers and judgment for unbelievers. After a primary emphasis on
salvation in 1 Thessalonians, the topic of judgment takes center stage in
2 Thessalonians. The believers in Thessalonica were enduring distressing
persecution at the hand of their opponents (2 Thess. 1:4). They longed for
the day of God's judgment against their oppressors, as an expression of
God's care and concern for them (2 Thess. 1:5–8). If that day had already
arrived, as false teachers were insinuating, that would mean that God was
already dispensing judgment, but in some diminished way that did not
bring true vindication for the readers. In 2 Thessalonians 2:1–2 the author
reassures his readers that God has not neglected their plight with some
sort of halfhearted intervention (2 Thess. 2:2).[19] Christ will still return,

---

16. Ehrman sees this as another deceptive device inserted to convince unsuspecting readers of the
authenticity of the letter (*Forged*, 107–8). Ehrman protests that Paul does not sign his letters in
most other cases (apart from 1 Cor 16:21, Gal. 6:11, Philem. 19, and Col. 4:18, which he considers a forgery), but more precisely, he does not *talk about* his signature in other letters. He may
very well have signed all of his original letters. We can't know anymore, because we have only
scribes' copies of those letters at our disposal.

17. See the similarly cautious conclusion in Paul Foster, "Who Wrote 2 Thessalonians? A Fresh Look
at an Old Problem," *JSNT* 35 (2012): 157–58.

18. Ehrman, *Forged*, 19, 107; Ehrman, *Forgery and Counterforgery*, 24, 163–65. Major English translations are split on the best translation of the phrase. The NIV, ESV, NASB, and HCSB support
"has (already) come." NRSV, NET prefer "is already here." KJV adopts "is at hand." No translation
proposes "is almost here," as Ehrman does in the one instance.

19. Perhaps some teachers in Thessalonica were over-spiritualizing the final judgment, just as some
would soon over-spiritualize resurrection in Corinth.

both to enact judgment on God's enemies and to gather his people to himself. Anyone who has told them a different story is deceiving them.

But is there a theological discrepancy between an imminent return (from Paul's typical teachings) and signs preceding that return (signs that are recounted cryptically in 2 Thessalonians 2:3–12), as Ehrman claims?[20] Not unless Jesus's own teachings are considered contradictory. In his teachings on the Mount of Olives, Jesus unfolds signs that will precede the end of the age (Matt. 24:3–35), just like Paul does in 2 Thessalonians 2. But Jesus also urges his disciples to be in a state of constant readiness, since his return will come like a thief in the night (Matt. 24:36–51).[21] This corresponds to Paul's main emphasis in 1 Thessalonians 5:1–11. In fact, to stress the relevance of signs preceding Christ's return, both Jesus and Paul draw upon concepts and language from Daniel (Matt. 24:15, 21, 30; 2 Thess. 2:3) and foretell the prevalence of lawlessness (Matt. 24:12; 2 Thess. 2:3–8) and deceptive signs and wonders (Matt. 24:23–26; 2 Thess. 2:9–11) during that period of buildup. On the flip side, to promote preparing for the unexpected arrival of God's kingdom Jesus and Paul use the same imagery of being alert for a thief (Matt. 24:42–44; 1 Thess. 5:2–4) and staying awake at night (Matt. 24:42–43; 1 Thess. 5:6–8). Ehrman exaggerates differences between 1 Thessalonians and 2 Thessalonians when in reality, the mix of teachings in the letters resembles the close juxtaposition of those same teachings in the Gospels.

Beyond Ehrman's two arguments from 2 Thessalonians 2:2 and 2:1–12, there are allegations that the content and wording of 1 Thessalonians and 2 Thessalonians are more closely related than what we find with most other pairs of Paul's letters. But this would not be too surprising if two things were true. First, if Paul wrote the two letters in close succession, we might expect him to resort to wording that was already fresh in his mind. Second, the fundamental needs of the church had not changed. The believers still needed encouragement to continue in faith, love, and perseverance (1 Thess. 1:3; 2 Thess. 1:3–4). They needed to live actively for Christ and represent him well until he returned, following the example of Paul and his associates (1 Thess. 2:9; 2 Thess. 3:8). Beyond these points of agreement, however, 2 Thessalonians bypasses much of what is found in 1 Thessalonians, contributing fresh insights to topics from the first letter that needed clarification (eschatology) or elaboration (eschewing idleness).

COLOSSIANS AND EPHESIANS

Colossians and Ephesians are usually treated together, since they have overlapping sections of material. Many people contend that the author of Ephesians used Colossians as a template for his own letter. Some

---

20. Ehrman, *Forged*, 107; Ehrman, *Forgery and Counterforgery*, 165–66.
21. See the similar point in Carson and Moo, *Introduction to the New Testament*, 540–41.

scholars affirm that Paul wrote Colossians, but other scholars they think that one forger (the author of Ephesians) borrowed from another forger's letter (Colossians).[22]

A common objection to Paul's authorship of both letters is that the letters promote an over-realized eschatology. In other words, these two letters advance a view that believers are already saved and have already been raised to be with Christ. Ehrman calls this eschatological teaching "anti-Pauline."[23] He insists that this perspective is incompatible with Paul's future-oriented salvation and resurrection of believers in his authentic letters.[24] Without the eagerly anticipated return of Christ to give them focus, the recipients of Colossians and Ephesians should settle for more comfortable and stable lives in their families (Eph. 5:22–6:9; Col. 3:18–4:1), which departs from the wholehearted devotion called for in the undisputed letters (see 1 Cor. 7).[25]

Once again, Ehrman simplifies what both the undisputed and disputed letters teach about salvation, overstating the resulting divergence in viewpoints. He also neglects accounting for the occasional nature of the letters. Paul wrote letters in response to actual needs on the ground, not as theoretical treatises in the air. He shifts his focus to whatever topics need most attention. So, in some letters Paul points believers to their eschatological hope in Christ (1 Thessalonians). They will see their salvation brought to fruition and experience the resurrection of their bodies when Christ returns. Others need to be chastened in their triumphant outlook on life, with reminders that a life of sacrificial service comes before ultimate glory (1 and 2 Corinthians). But in the midst of the spiritually confused environment of western Asia Minor, believers needed encouragement to stand tall in the saving work that Christ had already accomplished for them (Colossians and Ephesians). Because of their union with Christ, they could draw upon Christ's current spiritual authority for their own struggles against spiritual powers. The teachings in these various letters all fit cohesively within the New Testament vision of the kingdom of God, which has broken into our world through Christ but will fully manifest itself only when Christ returns. At times believers need to embrace the current implications of being united with Christ (Colossians and Ephesians), while other times they need to "groan" for the consummation of their salvation (Rom. 8:18–25).

---

22.   One argument against Ephesians being genuinely from Paul is that Paul would not have used a forgery as a source (Ehrman, *Forgery and Counterforgery*, 184). But if the spuriousness of Colossians rests on weak arguments, this argument against Ephesians is even weaker. Ehrman enlists this same shaky "domino-effect" argument when he further discredits 2 Timothy and Titus because they show knowledge of the supposedly unauthentic Ephesians (217).

23.   Ehrman, *Forgery and Counterforgery*, 177 n. 42, 182.

24.   Ehrman, *Forged*, 110–14.

25.   Ehrman, *Forgery and Counterforgery*, 178, 186.

While different occasions elicit different emphases, be careful not to miss the "already" language of salvation in Paul's undisputed letters (language that resembles a strong emphasis in Colossians and Ephesians). In Christ, God extends the full blessings of Abraham to believers (Gal. 3:7–9, 14). They "were saved," as the first part of a work that will be completed in the future (Rom. 8:24). Believers have already entered into a new creation mode of being (2 Cor. 5:17) and strive to live consistently with being alive already in Christ (Rom. 6:13). The very believers who were foreknown, predestined, called, and justified were also glorified by God (Rom. 8:30). Paul draws upon Christ's resurrection power in the midst of his sufferings for Christ (Phil. 3:10; 4:13). The resurrected life of Jesus flows through Paul as he puts himself on the line for his churches (2 Cor. 4:7–11). Apart from these specific examples of the already-experienced components of salvation and resurrected life are the key theological underpinnings to a current realization of God's blessings. The fact that believers are already united with Christ and have already received his eschatological Spirit means that they already have access to the benefits of being God's children. These doctrines of union with Christ and the reception of the Spirit are well-attested in the undisputed letters.

In the reverse, there are multiple "not yet" reminders in Colossians and Ephesians (which echoes a significant perspective from the undisputed letters). Paul directs believers' gazes to their heavenly hope (Col. 1:5, 27; Eph. 1:18), future inheritance (Col. 1:12; 3:24; Eph. 1:18; 5:5), a future bodily resurrection (Col. 1:18), and a future blessed existence with God (Eph. 2:7). Paul explains that believers' current union with the resurrected Christ guarantees their future glorification with Christ (Col. 3:3–4).[26] The Spirit who currently dwells in them is a down payment of their future redemption (Eph. 1:13–14; 4:30). Colossians and Ephesians do not perpetuate any simplistic idea that the benefits of resurrection and salvation have been completely attained in this life, with no future reserve to be enjoyed.

The tidy separation between eschatological urgency in the undisputed letters and long-term stability in Colossians and Ephesians also breaks down under closer investigation. The focus on the imminent return of Christ in 1 Thessalonians does not preclude Paul from prescribing a conventional life: "[M]ake it your ambition to lead a quiet life: You should mind your own business and work with your hands, just as we told you, so that your daily life may win the respect of outsiders and so that you will not be dependent on anybody" (1 Thess. 4:11–12). Paul also counsels believers to live peacefully and respectfully under human governments

---

26. Notably, believers' glorification is future in Colossians 3:3–4, whereas believers are already glorified according to Romans 8:30. This upends the simplistic eschatological dichotomy skeptics tend to impose on the undisputed and disputed letters of Paul.

(Rom. 13:1–7). On the flip side, Colossians and Ephesians call for moral vigilance and focus in preparation for a coming day of judgment and reward (Col. 3:4, 6; 4:5; Eph. 5:6, 15–16).

What about the significant sections of common material in Colossians and Ephesians? Does this indicate the literary dependence of Ephesians on Colossians? Two pairs of passages have striking similarities: Paul's dispatching of Tychichus to give the readers updates (Col. 4:7–8; Eph. 6:21–22), and instructions on how household members should relate to one another (Col. 3:18–4:1; Eph. 5:22–6:10). Otherwise, the wording in the two letters aligns less closely but supports common topics. The best explanation for these matching sections is that Paul wrote the two letters during the same time period (his first Roman imprisonment) to similar audiences (believers in the Roman province of Asia).

Though the common sections in the letters stand out, there are still numerous unique contributions in each letter. For example, Colossians refutes more false teaching, while Ephesians develops more of a theology of the Spirit. The one, consistent difference throughout even the corresponding topics is that Ephesians expands material that in Colossians focuses more narrowly on believers' union with Christ. Ephesians sees the logical application of union with Christ in believers' relationships with one another, especially between Jews and Gentiles.[27] Quite significantly, both letters stand powerfully on their own as coherent, insightful, and well-developed works. Assuming that Colossians was written first, a later imitator would have had an extremely difficult time pulling off a forgery that drew heavily upon Colossians, echoed passages from many of Paul's other letters, and yet was still so internally consistent.[28] There is certainly no hint of the patchwork compilation product that we see in the Epistle to the Laodiceans or the theological treatise from another era with some references to Paul tacked on at the beginning and end (3 Corinthians).

THE PASTORAL EPISTLES

The Pastoral Epistles consist of 1 Timothy, Titus, and 2 Timothy. Scholars routinely dismiss the authenticity of these letters addressed to Paul's well-known delegates. Most of these specialists believe that one author wrote all three letters, but that the author was not Paul. A number of distinctive elements tie the three letters together: the use of "here is a trustworthy saying" (1 Tim. 1:15; 3:1; 4:9; 2 Tim. 2:11; Titus 3:8), the prominence of

---

27. This idea is still present in Colossians (Col. 3:11), as well as in undisputed letters (Rom. 10:12; 1 Cor. 12:13; Gal. 3:28). It is just less extensively developed.

28. Material in Ephesians corresponds not only to passages and wording from Colossians but also to multiple verses in Romans, 1 Corinthians, and 2 Corinthians. There are also scattered connections to Philippians and 1 Thessalonians.

godliness (εὐσέβεια, in all three letters), the troubles caused by Alexander (1 Tim. 1:12; 2 Tim. 4:14), concern for the qualifications of church leadership (1 Tim. 3:1–13; Titus 1:6–9), and an emphasis on believers' consciences (1 Tim. 1:5, 19; 3:9; 2 Tim. 1:3).

Scholars regularly protest about inconsistencies in content between the Pastoral Epistles and Paul's undisputed letters. Ehrman alleges that in the undisputed letters, leaderless churches lived in expectation of Christ's return at any moment.[29] According to him, the Pastoral Epistles call for too much leadership and organization for the long haul, losing sight of the imminent return of Christ. This is another instance of creating artificial differences between two positions and amplifying the extent of those differences. Paul greets and commends church leaders in earlier letters (Phil. 1:1; 1 Thess. 5:12–13) and even instructs believers to submit to leaders on one occasion (1 Cor. 16:15–16). In the Pastoral Epistles, Paul continues to set his sights on the hope of Christ's return (1 Tim. 6:14–15; 2 Tim. 1:12, 18; 4:1, 8; Titus 2:13). Undisputed and disputed letters both suggest that Paul saw no contradiction between eagerly awaiting Christ's return and planning for the future. Though verses such as 1 Timothy 6:14–15 indicate that the author had reckoned with the possibility that the return of Christ could come at a time later than he expected, this does not rule out Paul as the author but perhaps implies a progression in his thinking about the topic over time. After all, Christ did *not* return as soon as the early Christians had anticipated. As thoughtful followers of Jesus, believers such as Paul would have processed that reality through prayer and would have reconciled themselves to God's freedom to work according to his own timetable.

Ehrman also lobs the charge that all three letters contain what he deems to be the classic pseudepigraphal device of verisimilitudes, which are seemingly unprompted details about people, past events, and even relatively inconsequential matters that pseudepigraphers add to letters to create the illusion of authenticity.[30] Examples for Ehrman include Paul's request for his cloak and parchments (2 Tim. 4:13), Paul's counsel to Timothy to drink wine for his stomach (1 Tim. 5:23), and Paul's disclosure of his travel plans (Titus 3:12).[31] The problem with this argument is that while forged letters include such details, authentic letters do as well! Paul regularly includes all sorts of names and detailed travel plans in his undisputed letters. And couldn't Galatians 4:13 ("As you know, it was because of an illness that I first preached the gospel to you") be viewed suspiciously? What about 1 Thessalonians 5:27 ("I charge you before the Lord to have this letter read to all the brothers and sisters")? And Philemon 22 ("And one thing more: Prepare a guest room for me, because I hope to be restored

---

29.   Ehrman, *Forged*, 100–102.
30.   Ehrman, *Forgeries and Counterforgeries*, 122–23, 212.
31.   Ibid., 122, 206, 210.

to you in answer to your prayers")? One person's verisimilitude is another person's authentic detail.[32]

Specific and personal details are especially prominent in 2 Timothy, with Paul revealing the strain of his imprisonment while trying to coordinate his assistants' travel and ministry plans from a distance. Ehrman acknowledges a possibility, which he once entertained but then discarded, that 2 Timothy could be considered genuinely from Paul, while 1 Timothy and Titus were forgeries.[33] But because of Ehrman's suspicions about the authenticity of 1 Timothy and Titus, along with the aforementioned links between the three Pastoral Epistles, Ehrman has become convinced that all three were written by the same author, who was a later admirer of Paul.[34] But why not move in the opposite direction? Since 2 Timothy resonates with Paul's personality and outlook, why not start with 2 Timothy, evaluate its legitimacy, and then move on to 1 Timothy and Titus?[35] After all, if 2 Timothy is deemed to be genuine, then its affinities with the other two letters could be strong points in their favor.

In summary, many of Ehrman's theological arguments against the disputed letters of Paul rest on overstated or premature interpretations of passages. Ehrman simplifies Paul's teachings by removing nuance and flexibility in his perspectives, adopts unlikely interpretations of passages without considering better options, and exaggerates differences between Paul's undisputed and disputed letters.[36] This spotlights the flaws of bypassing the careful work of exegetical imagination and persistence while resorting too readily to the charge of forgery.

STYLE AND VOCABULARY IN THE DISPUTED LETTERS

As I have tried to demonstrate briefly above, the theological incompatibilities between the undisputed and disputed letters of Paul that are appealed to as evidence against Paul's authorship of the disputed letters are overblown concerns. But what about arguments that these six letters contain language and stylistic constructions that depart from Paul's normal patterns? These arguments rely on technical discussions of statistical procedure and the Greek language and thus are more difficult for nonspecialists to assess. While statistical analyses seek to inject a note of objectivity in discussions of authorship, researchers still have to decide on

---

32. See also 1 Corinthians 16:5–9 and Galatians 6:17.
33. Ehrman, *Forged*, 97.
34. Ibid., 102.
35. See similar thoughts in N. T. Wright, *Paul and the Faithfulness of God* (Minneapolis: Fortress, 2013), 61.
36. Two examples on one page are that 1 Corinthians 5:5 consists of a "death curse" without any hope for repentance (the correct interpretation is likely just the opposite), and that 1 Timothy 2:15 upholds childbearing as an actual vehicle for salvation, which overlooks much better options for interpreting that verse in context (Ehrman, *Forgery and Counterforgery*, 207).

sample sizes and appropriate inputs (what verbal patterns and grammatical constructions will be measured in the first place). Different experts also frame the observations and results in different ways. A further complication arises with the possible stylistic contribution of Paul's coauthors.[37] The best studies recognize the limitations of statistical assessments of style and their implications for authorship.[38] At the very least, readers should consult these studies with caution, being aware of the complexities of these methods and the potential pitfalls of employing them.

Given these caveats, most scholars still detect some divergence of vocabulary and style between Paul's undisputed and disputed letters. Interpreters point to sentence length and complexity of syntactical structure for 2 Thessalonians, Colossians, and Ephesians, though some rigorous tests show that 2 Thessalonians aligns more closely to the *Hauptbriefe* than 1 Thessalonians does.[39] In Ephesians the divergence from the so-called Pauline norm is strongest in the early chapters,[40] perhaps owing in part to the high concentration of blessings and prayers there. Various studies reach different conclusions about whether the style of given letters are authentically Pauline. Some more recent statistical studies have refrained from dismissing the authenticity of 2 Thessalonians, Colossians, and Ephesians on stylistic grounds or have even found reasons for supporting the authenticity of those works.[41]

The Pastoral Epistles stand out in particular as possessing their own distinct style, so let's look at some possible reasons for this phenomenon. First, a later author could have written the Pastoral Epistles in Paul's name. Many scholars favor this view, but it is not the only possibility. Second, the specific occasions of the Pastoral Epistles could have elicited a different style of writing from Paul himself. Unlike in his other letters, Paul writes the Pastoral Epistles to trusted associates who were organizational insiders. They needed practical advice for running churches

---

37. Other names appear as co-authors, or at least co-senders, in 1 and 2 Corinthians, Philippians, Colossians, 1 and 2 Thessalonians, and Philemon. Richards notes that there must be some significance to the fact that those listed at the beginning of the letter did not include all believers or even all coworkers who were present when Paul wrote the letter (E. Randolph Richards, *Paul and First-Century Letter Writing: Secretaries, Composition, and Collection* [Downers Grove, IL: InterVarsity, 2004], 34–36, 105). See also Jerome Murphy-O'Connor, *Paul the Letter-Writer: His World, His Options, His Skills*, Good News Studies 41 (Collegeville, MN: Liturgical Press, 1995), 16–35.

38. See for example Kenneth J. Neumann, *The Authenticity of the Pauline Epistles in Light of Stylo-statistical Analysis*, SBLDS 120 (Atlanta: Scholars Press, 1990); D. L. Mealand, "The Extent of the Pauline Corpus: A Multivariate Approach," *JSNT* 59 (1995): 61–92.

39. Gerard Ledger, "An Exploration of Differences in the Pauline Epistles Using Multivariate Statistical Analysis," *Literary and Linguistic Computing* 10 (1995): 85–97; Mealand, "The Extent of the Pauline Corpus," 86.

40. Mealand, "The Extent of the Pauline Corpus," 86.

41. For the former, see Neumann, *Authenticity of the Pauline Epistles*. For the latter, see Anthony Kenny, *A Stylometric Study of the New Testament* (Oxford: Clarendon, 1996), 80–100; George K. Barr, *Scalometry and the Pauline Epistles*, JSNTSup 261 (London: Clark, 2004).

rather than general theological orientation to life in Christ. The more concrete problems confronted in the Pastoral Letters may have influenced the vocabulary and style.[42] Third, a writing secretary (amanuensis) might have assisted Paul when he wrote the Pastoral Epistles. Paul certainly used amanuenses in most, if not all, of his letters. Tertius identifies himself as Paul's secretary in Romans 16:22, and the attention Paul draws to his signature in some of his letters implies that an amanuensis wrote down the rest of each letter (1 Cor. 16:21; Gal. 6:11; Philem. 19; see also Col. 4:18; 2 Thess. 3:17). What we don't know for sure is how much latitude a secretary would have been given to write the Pastoral Epistles with his own style.[43] Though some scholars doubt that amanuenses would have left their own stylistic marks on Paul's writings, that possibility could explain why there is a difference of style in the Pastoral Epistles. Fourth, related to the amanuensis theory, letters could have been composed in significantly different ways. Some assistants could have recorded Paul's spoken words more directly, while Paul and his assistants may have taken more time to write several drafts of certain letters. Paul and his team may have relied more or less on preformed material in various letters, and they may have integrated that material more or less seamlessly.[44] The Pastoral Epistles could have been drafted in their own distinct way, thus explaining some of the variance from earlier letters.[45]

More studies on the styles of the thirteen letters in the Pauline corpus are sure to come. These discussions can play a helpful supplementary role to determinations about theological agreement among letters. In the end, though, if the theology fits, it seems unwise to use unresolved questions about style to dismiss Paul's authorship of the disputed letters.

RECONSTRUCTED HISTORY

Decisions about authorship bleed into our conception of the history of the early church. Rejecting Paul's authorship of some of the letters in his name has led to amended views of early church history. Skeptics of Paul's disputed letters reconstruct the history of early Christianity to conform to their new conclusions. Two popular features of this revised

---

42. See also Luke Timothy Johnson, *The First and Second Letters to Timothy*, AB 35A (New York: Doubleday, 2001), 71.

43. Especially in upper-class circles, secretaries were known to record letters dictated word-for-word, to take down discourse in shorthand and then rewrite it, or, more rarely, to make contributions to the content and style of the letter (Richards, *Paul and First-Century Letter Writing*, 65–77).

44. Ibid., 109–11.

45. Baum has suggested that both the wider vocabulary and cleaner sentence structure of the Pastoral Epistles exhibit stronger characteristics of written communication than the ten other more orally oriented Pauline letters (Armin D. Baum, "Semantic Variation within the *Corpus Paulinum*," *TynBul* 59 [2008]: 288–90). Ellis calls attention to significant amounts of preformed material in the Pastoral Epistles (E. Earle Ellis, "Pastoral Letters," *DPL* 664–65).

history are the idea of a school of Paul and a phenomenon known as early Catholicism.

The school of Paul theory alleges that after Paul's death, an informal group of adherents to Paul's theology tried to continue to spread Paul's influence. Some of these disciples of Paul even attempted to write letters in his name, hoping to address new theological challenges with fresh words from "Paul."[46]

Early Catholicism posits that shortly after Paul's time the early Christian movement began to evolve into a more organized network, foreshadowing its later development into a single, highly structured institution. Proponents of this view discern that most of the disputed letters betray indications of early Catholicism with their interest in church leadership, centralized truth, and organizational permanence.

There are problems with both of these theories. First, we have no historical support that any school of Paul ever existed. While early Christian writings (from the late first and early second century) commend Paul (*1 Clem.* 5.5–7; 47.1; Ign. *Eph.* 12.2; Ign. *Rom.* 4.3; Pol. *Phil.* 3.2; 9.1) and at times even attempt to echo his perspectives (Ign. *Trall.* 5.2; Ign. *Rom.* 9.2; Ign. *Phld.* 6.3), none show an interest in recapturing the golden days of Paul by recreating his voice for a new generation or furthering his impact through the ongoing development of his teachings. In fact, they unabashedly refer back to Paul as a revered authority from an earlier time, and they propagate his teachings by quoting or alluding to them rather than by putting new words in his mouth. Our examples of known attempts to imitate Paul (rather than appeal to him) do not surface until later in the second century, with the pseudepigraphal letters mentioned earlier (3 Corinthians and Epistle to the Laodiceans).

The early Catholicism hypothesis simultaneously perceives too much development from Paul's early letters to the disputed, later ones, and too much conceptual similarity between his disputed letters and known writings from the late first or second century. First, scholars contend that later imitations of Paul in the disputed letters turn Paul's dynamic teachings into inflexible traditions. But Paul talks about a "pattern of teaching" (Rom. 6:17), passing down traditions (1 Cor. 11:2), and imparting what he had been taught about the faith (1 Cor. 15:3), which previews the traditions and sound teachings that are to be embraced and disseminated in the disputed letters (2 Thess. 2:15; 3:6; 2 Tim. 1:13–14; 2:2). Second, scholars group the organizational structure of the Pastoral Epistles more with the Apostolic Fathers than with Paul's undisputed

---

46. See Hans Conzelmann, "Paulus und die Weisheit," *NTS* 12 (1965–1966): 231–44; Martinus C. de Boer, "Images of Paul in the Post-Apostolic Period," *CBQ* 42 (1980): 359–80; James D. G. Dunn, "Pauline Legacy and School," *DLNT* 887–93. Ehrman dismisses a formal version of a school of Paul theory that supposes the existence of some sort of philosophical school devoted to Paul's teachings (Ehrman, *Forgery and Counterforgery*, 172–74).

letters. But Ignatius of Antioch addressed overseers who gave leadership to the elders and deacons of the churches under their care (see for instance Ign. *Eph.*. 4.1; Ign. *Magn.* 6.1; Ign. *Trall.* 3.1; Ign. *Smyrn.* 8.1–2). In contrast, the overseers of 1 Timothy and Titus serve as a group in their ministries to local churches while operating under apostolic oversight. The overseers in 1 Timothy and Titus are known as the elders, not a group governing the elders.[47]

Theories of Pauline pseudepigraphy have resulted in altered views of early church history. But that reconstructed history has in turn shaped the interpretation of Paul's letters, injecting a layer of artificiality into the letters, because of the fiction that they are seen to prop up. Neither the school of Paul nor the early Catholicism hypothesis offers a convincing portrait of early church history, but these reconstructions have significantly altered many scholars' interpretations of the disputed letters.

CANONICAL IMPLICATIONS

Discounting Paul's authorship of as many as six of his letters has also deeply affected how believers view the canon of Scripture. An authoritative New Testament canon, recognized by common consensus across all major branches of the church, has provided vital nourishment and direction for God's people. Every time the Bible is read or explained in front of a congregation (starting with Paul's churches—1 Thess. 5:27; Col. 4:16), believers hear God speaking to them, by his Spirit. Students should engage in careful research to see Paul's letters in their proper historical context and even evaluate the plausibility of their projected settings, but readers would do well to take a deep breath and reconsider alternatives before dismissing the authenticity of certain letters. Is it worth sidelining such powerful and rewarding material in Scripture in deference to theories of authorship that are far from convincing?

Some theologians insist that even if later admirers wrote some of Paul's letters, nothing needs to change theologically about how the church values these letters as Scripture. They say that the authoritative place of Paul's letters is not dependent upon Paul having written them, especially if the pseudonymous authors did not intend to deceive readers. But I agree with Ehrman that non deceitful pseudepigraphy doesn't work as a proposal.[48] The disputed letters of Paul are either genuine or forged. If they are fraudulent, then the trustworthiness and authority of those

---

47. The terms overseer (ἐπίσκοπος) and elder (πρεσβύτερος) seem to be interchangeable in 1 Timothy and Titus, as seen in the smooth transition from elder (Titus 1:5) to overseer (Titus 1:7). See also Acts 20:17, 28.

48. Ehrman, *Forgery and Counterforgery*, 128–32.

letters begin to crumble.[49] When modern scholars cast a cloud over many of these books with hasty assertions of forgery, confidence in the spiritual value of those letters can't help but dwindle. The crowds have herded in the direction of skepticism in the past several hundred years, but that continued drift need not be inevitable.[50]

A few experts have wondered whether some of the skepticism about the disputed letters has gained momentum from scholars' distaste for the letters' controversial teachings on issues such as authority and submission in families and churches or the role of women in the home and church.[51] When Paul's vision for life is derived from the seven undisputed letters alone, it is a bit easier to reconcile Paul's teachings with the favored ideas of the modern world (ideas of freedom and equality, for instance). But we should be wary when teachers privilege only the letters and chapters from Paul that fit current sensibilities. The church's health depends on its embrace of all parts of God's inspired Scriptures.

CONCLUSION

As long as there are unresolved questions in our minds about whether Paul wrote the letters in his name, we might find ourselves holding the disputed letters at an arm's length. As serious students of Paul's letters, we want to know that what they proclaim and prescribe for our lives was written by a legitimately commissioned representative of Christ.

Evaluations of whether or not Paul wrote the letters attributed to him should start with theological compatibility and historical fit. Do the teachings match with the ideas from Paul's widely accepted letters, when proper allowance is made for distinct occasions for each letter? Could the events have realistically occurred during the historical setting in which Paul lived and ministered? We have seen that Ehrman relies heavily on arguments based on theology and the assumed historical development of the church. But through the survey of these topics in this chapter we have demonstrated that these protests are overblown. Once questions about theology and history have been resolved, that leaves just style. We could speculate what caused the differences in style among the various letters, but it seems rash to discount Pauline authorship on the basis of style alone. If the theology and history fits, the cleanest solution is to acknowledge Paul's authorship of all thirteen letters.

---

49. Pseudonymity is nowhere as directly deceptive as it is in the letter genre. The author's real identity and the author's and recipients' actual circumstances are so deeply embedded in a letter that it requires direct fabrication of identities and circumstances in order to maintain the charade that the named author actually wrote the letter.

50. A scholar as influential as N. T. Wright has called for renewed openness to the authenticity of 2 Thessalonians, Colossians, and Ephesians (Wright, *Paul and the Faithfulness of God*, 56–58).

51. Johnson, *First and Second Letters to Timothy*, 56–57; Wright, *Paul and the Faithfulness of God*, 58.

As long as we are leaving ourselves an "out" when we read Paul's letters (that a letter or passage didn't really come from Paul), we may avoid seeking more promising interpretative options or wrestling with the challenging teachings that we encounter. Reading with confidence that Paul wrote these letters will allow us to jump headfirst into Paul's teachings. We can read all of Paul's letters with curiosity, and with the determination to let God shape us through them.

■ ■ ■

CHAPTER SIX

HOW CAN I GET THE MOST OUT OF STUDYING PAUL'S LETTERS?

M ost people list travel as an interest or priority in life. It can be thrilling to explore new lands and experience all of the sights, sounds, tastes, and even smells of unfamiliar cultures. Each trip holds such great potential, but sometimes we miss opportunities to make the most of a journey. Ideally, each trip to another locale would stretch us and enrich our lives, but this does not always happen automatically. With a little advance preparation, alertness during our travels, and reflection on our adventures we can improve our chances of having a meaningful experience that makes a difference in our lives.

Studying Paul's letters presents great opportunities for life change, but that growth is not automatic either. Knowing what we want to get out of the journey and then following through on the plan can make all of the difference. In this chapter we will discuss goals for studying Paul's letters and examine strategies that will help us accomplish those goals. After finishing this chapter and the next one, readers should be equipped to compile letter summaries for each of Paul's letters.[1]

TWO MAIN GOALS

Overarching goals fall into two main categories: meaning and relevance. First, we want to discern the *meaning* of the letters in their original settings. What was going on in Paul's world, and in the lives of the original recipients of the letters? How did the letters address problems or encourage the believers who received the letters? Returning to our travel analogy, it might be tempting to think of a trip as simply *our* experience in a

---

1. I first enjoyed creating letter summaries in an informal setting as part of a missionary team in East Asia. We used one form of this process for our Bible study times together. An example of a completed letter summary can be found in the appendix of this book.

different culture. But the culture itself is worth understanding and exploring. In fact, one could argue that a traveler has an artificial experience if he or she is interested only in having personal "moments," using the scenery and people as mere window dressing for trip photos and memories. A more substantial and authentic journey consists of really getting to know a culture and its people. The same is true for studying Paul's letters. Digging deeply into Paul's letters with an eye toward grasping his message to the original audience actually creates more fertile ground for our own growth. That leads us to the next goal.

Second, we hope to appreciate the *relevance* and value of the letters for our lives and churches today. What seems fascinating about the letters? What unanswered questions spark our curiosity and make us want to continue to study the letters? What truths challenge the way we think about God and life with him? How should we respond to God in worship, trust, or obedience, based on what we have read? These questions are crucial, particularly when we study the letters in an academic context, where it can be tempting to overlook or shortchange questions of spiritual significance. If our only goal is mastery of content, we will have missed the wonder, beauty, and power of the message conveyed in the letters. Paul wrote the letters to open a window into the saving plans of God and the fullness of life in Christ. As we yield ourselves to the Spirit's work in our lives while reading the letters, we can join with believers across generations who have found themselves challenged and inspired by the truth Paul relays to us.

OVERALL STRATEGIES FOR MEANING AND RELEVANCE

What strategies help us accomplish these goals? I will introduce the broad categories first and then address each one in more detail. The quest for meaning consists of three specific interrelated areas: background, analysis, and synthesis. With background, we want to understand more about the author(s), recipients, and historical circumstances that prompted the author to write the letter in the first place. Analysis consists of a methodical tracing of the argument of the letter and detecting main themes and repeated ideas throughout the letter. We will devote the next chapter to how to successfully discern and articulate the argument of the letter in the form of an expanded outline. Synthesis involves identifying key verses that constitute major turning points of the argument or that encapsulate ideas in main movements of the argument, sensing what characterizes the tone of the letter, and deciding upon a title for the letter.

Once your observation skills have been tested while determining meaning, you will transition to finding the relevance of the letter. This stage requires thoughtful reflection. First, consider how this letter applies to your life, how it applies to your church, or how it applies to the broader Christian community of your country or around the world. Second, record questions that remain in your mind after you have studied the letter. What unresolved questions caught your attention? What would be fun to explore further? Though these two topics (application and lingering questions) will not require as much time as the sections on meaning and relevance, the process should not be rushed. You will want to set aside undistracted time to formulate quality applications and questions for further investigation.

BACKGROUND: AUTHOR, AUDIENCE, DATE AND PLACE OF WRITING, OCCASION, AND PURPOSE

Begin your journey by noting the listed author or authors of your letter. Go ahead and include the co-senders who appear alongside Paul in the opening verse of the letter. Though Paul's voice may be the dominant one, other coauthors are listed there (as opposed to the closing greetings in the letter) for a reason.[2] You could also note how Paul identifies himself—as an apostle, servant, or prisoner, for example. Get in the habit of citing the verses that you base any conclusions upon. The next step is more challenging. Determine whether Paul's authorship of the letter is debated in current scholarship. You will need to consult outside resources for this, whether the chapter on authorship in this book, introductory notes to a study Bible, or an introduction to a commentary.

I will use Ephesians as an example throughout the rest of this chapter (the final assembling of all of the material for the letter summary of Ephesians may be found in the appendix). Paul lists only himself as a sender of the letter. He calls himself an apostle (1:1) and a prisoner (3:1; 4:1). On the basis of both theology and style, some specialists dispute that Paul actually wrote the letter, so there is significant debate about the identity of the author.

Next, discover more about the recipients. How does Paul describe them? Does he address them as a single church or as multiple churches (look for clues in both the opening and closing greetings). Does Paul speak to the church as a whole, and/or does he single out certain leaders or individuals? Again, cite the verses that supply the information you use.

For Ephesians, the first verse pinpoints "God's holy people in Ephesus, the faithful in Christ Jesus" as the recipients. Straightforward enough. But it is actually more complicated (I promise that you won't encounter such a technical problem in the other letters!). Your Bible probably has a footnote about verse 1. Some early copies of Ephesians do not include a named city at all. It is quite possible that "in Ephesus" was originally absent in the letter and that scribes added a place name later. That would explain the fairly general feel of the contents of the letter. A little research suggests that Paul wrote to multiple churches in the region of the province of Asia,

---

2. See Richards, *Paul and First-Century Letter Writing*, 33–36.

so I note in the letter summary that the recipients are likely believers in Ephesus and other cities in the province of Asia.

For the probable date and place of writing, start with any signs within the letter and then refer to study Bibles, commentaries, a Bible atlas, or the chapter in this book on the chronology of Paul's letters. Indicate whether there is some uncertainty about how this letter fits into the timeline. Don't worry about giving a specific year, since even the experts have to estimate this. It is more helpful to correlate the letter to Paul's various missionary journeys or other periods of Paul's ministry, as well as with the cities where he was stationed at the time. You will sometimes find passing references to locations within the letter, so cite the verse that reveals a probable location, where applicable.[3]

Most scholars who hold to Paul's authorship of Ephesians believe that Paul wrote it during his first imprisonment in Rome. Paul mentions his imprisonment in 3:1, 4:1, and 6:20, though no hints of major strain from the imprisonment emerge in the letter. This would correspond to the relatively uneventful Roman imprisonment recorded at the end of Acts. There is some debate about where Paul was imprisoned (perhaps in Caesarea or Ephesus instead of Rome), but not enough to need to record the various options.

The next two steps are crucial to the whole letter summary process. To truly appreciate any given letter's contribution we must determine the *occasion* and *purpose* of the letter. These are related but distinct ideas. The *occasion* of a letter highlights the circumstances that motivated Paul to write the letter in the first place, while the *purpose* describes what Paul hopes to accomplish through writing the letter. For instance, if a college student writes a letter to mom or dad, the occasion of the letter might be that the student has run out of money, while the purpose is to ask mom or dad for a loan. The occasion and purpose go hand in hand, and it is easy to conflate the two. Paul's purpose *responds* to the occasion, so the purpose is very much influenced by the occasion. The occasion of a letter is often some problem that the church was facing. In your wording, the occasion should talk more about what happened before Paul wrote the letter, while the purpose should reflect what Paul hopes will change in the recipients' lives and churches moving forward.

The occasion of a letter is rarely stated directly, but it can be ascertained through what is known as a "mirror-reading" of the letter. A mirror-reading of a letter involves reading with the goal of determining the likely circumstances the author is addressing. Scholars often employ this process of mirror-reading narrowly to understand

---

3. Paul sometimes includes specific information about his travel history or plans in his letters (1 Cor. 16:8; 2 Cor. 2:13; 1 Thess. 3:1; 1 Tim. 1:3). Some of these details are more helpful than others for determining Paul's exact location at the time he wrote a letter.

the specific characteristics of a false teaching that Paul was countering in a letter. But mirror-reading can be applied more broadly to identify the occasion of Paul's letters. Through a mirror-reading of a letter, we can catch indirect "reflections" of the problems or circumstances Paul or his readers faced. We cannot see these problems and circumstances directly, since we do not have written records of those circumstances from the point of view of the letter's recipients. Instead, we have Paul's *response* to those circumstances. At times Paul refers to an occasion quite overtly, while in other cases he provides glimpses into the nature of those circumstances by referring to them in passing. In either case, be sure to provide verses from the letter itself as support for your impressions about the occasion for the letter.

The different occasions vary across Paul's letters. At times the occasion is concentrated tightly within the church's own internal struggles and needs. At other times there are tensions or complications in Paul's ongoing relationship with the recipients. Paul's own circumstances could also have some bearing on the occasion of the letter. Try to have fun doing the detective work of discovering the most likely occasion for the letter. That effort will pay off for discerning the purpose and argument of the letter.

The occasion of Ephesians is notoriously difficult to pin down (the occasions for the other letters you will read will not be as unclear). The letter comes across as the most general letter of all of Paul's writings. He never calls out a specific false teaching or sin problem in the letter. This is not surprising, especially if Paul wrote the letter to suit the needs of multiple churches, some of which were relatively unfamiliar to him. About the best we can do with our mirror reading of Ephesians is to note Paul's heavy doses of prayer and encouragement to the readers and the unusually long section on being spiritually equipped for spiritual battle (Eph. 6:10–18). Perhaps Paul felt that the churches of that region were at risk of spiritual discouragement or of losing their sense of confidence in the midst of a hostile environment.

The purpose of the letter should correspond to the occasion. For the purpose, try to observe the "why" behind the "what" Paul teaches in the letter. Why did Paul take the time to pen this letter? What did he hope to accomplish? What extended doctrinal or practical teachings does he promote? Locating the purpose of the letter gives you a head start on analyzing the argument of the letter, since the purpose should encompass major emphases in the letter. In some letters Paul even previews the letter's main topics in an introductory section. Again, any purposes you choose should fit well with the occasion you described.

Ephesians appears to have the following purposes: to further establish the believers in their individual and corporate identity in Christ (1:3–14; 2:1–22), to instruct the readers about how to grow as a unified and holy body of believers (4:1–5:21), and to help them depend on Christ's authority for spiritual battle (1:15–23; 6:10–18). These topics are Paul's response to the spiritual needs he heard about in that region.

ANALYSIS: ARGUMENT AND REPEATED IDEAS

We will skip discussing a letter's argument for now, since we will devote the entire next chapter to talking about tracking the argument of a letter and arranging insights in the form of an expanded outline. But another important task to tackle during the analysis phase is to make note of recurring words, phrases, and topics throughout the letter. ·

Authors tend to divulge what they care about by talking about certain topics over and over. When Paul mentions "joy" and "rejoice" multiple times in Philippians, we should probably stop and take notice. The Gospel of John includes the word "believe" nearly one hundred times! When I look for repeated words, phrases, and topics, I approach it like a treasure hunt, waiting to see what gems I will uncover. Keep a running list of words that surface repeatedly. Underline and circle them in your Bible. Even better, make a copy of the letter from your Bible and then mark up the copy with colored pencils or various symbols that will allow you to view the repeated ideas visually once you are finished.

Here are a few hints about the process. First, group cognate words and different forms of the same word together. So "saved" and "salvation" and "Savior" should be counted together, as should "justify" and "justified." Second, disregard words such as articles ("the" or "a(n)"), conjunctions, pronouns, and prepositions, unless they are part of some distinct phrase in the letter (such as "in Christ" in Ephesians). Words for the Persons of the Trinity are fair game, but you might go the extra mile by noting if one Person or title is especially prevalent in the letter. Third, look for brief phrases and prominent concepts in addition to words. Fourth, focus on each word while reading, so that you will be alert to repetition. Some recurring words appear in clusters, so those are easier to spot. It takes more talent (and luck) to notice words that are sprinkled throughout the letter but are never concentrated that densely in one section. I generally start marking a word when I notice it surfacing multiple times. When a word sounds familiar, I go back to see if I can spot it earlier in the letter. You can also use a search feature on a website such as Bible Gateway to confirm your suspicions that a word is common in a letter. Finally, how many words should you single out? For even short letters you should aim for a half-dozen or so, while longer letters could yield more than a dozen. If you name too many distinct words, however, you run the risk of diminishing the benefit of the process, since the most significant words may get lost in the crowd.

When you are ready to record your list of the most frequent words, phrases, and topics, order them roughly from most to least frequent. Try to distinguish between identical words and phrases on the one hand and nonidentical concepts on the other by putting exact wording in italics. The more detail you observe and document, the more you will appreciate and have a lasting record of the unique texture of each letter.

When I study Ephesians, many interesting repeated words and phrases jump off from the page. I have italicized the actual wording and left the more general concepts in regular font in the following list: *in Christ* and its equivalents (*in him* and *in whom*, etc.), the *heavenly realms*, *walk* (ESV) or *live* (NIV), *body* (of Christ), *mystery*, *grace*, *love*, God the *Father*, unity/oneness, the authority of Christ, and the Holy Spirit as a *seal/pledge*.

SYNTHESIS: KEY VERSES, TITLE, AND TONE

The process of synthesis requires readers to see the forest in addition to the trees. Words and sentences form paragraphs, and paragraphs constitute whole letters. These letters communicate interrelated thoughts that support one or more major ideas. Paul conveys these ideas with differing tones that influence the way the ideas are received. Accordingly, you will want to complete several tasks related to synthesis. First, determine what key verses are featured prominently in the letter, and then support your decisions. Second, form judgments about how the whole letter ties together, then assign the letter a title. Third, try to discern the tone of the letter and describe the tone in a few words. We will examine these three goals in turn.

Key verses communicate either major turning points in the argument or a thesis statement for the entire letter (or for major movements in the argument). Key verses are not simply verses that are meaningful to you or popular verses in today's churches. Leave those types of verses for the application section later in the letter summary. Key verses emerge from Paul's original meaning, according to his argument in the letter.

Look for verses that stand at the seams of the letter—places where Paul makes a significant shift from one topic to another. For instance, does Paul make a notable transition from doctrine to practice in the letter? Also, ascertain whether Paul has indicated his letter's thesis near the beginning or a summary near the end of the letter. For instance, a thesis statement may occur in Hebrews 1:1–3 ("in these last days he has spoken to us by his Son . . . [who] provided purification for sins [and] sat down at the right hand of the Majesty in heaven"), and a possible summary statement surfaces in 1 Peter 4:19 ("So then, those who suffer according to God's will should commit themselves to their faithful Creator and continue to do good"). Note that for the longer passage in Hebrews I condensed the wording, while I quoted the entire verse from 1 Peter. For your letter summaries, feel free to provide snippets of wording from longer passages and a whole sentence for briefer verses when you list your key verses.

When you choose a few key verses, briefly state your rationale for your decisions. In other words, indicate how the verse marks a transition, previews a major theme, or summarizes a main point in the letter. Try to avoid commenting only that the verse was powerful or simply restating what the verse says. Show how the verse functions effectively in the letter's content and structure.

When I choose key verses for Ephesians, I start with 1:9–10, which functions as a thesis statement for the letter. Next, 4:1 stands out as the verse that signals a major transition in the letter, from doctrine to practice. Paul makes this clear with his use of "therefore" and by referring back to the calling he described in chapters 1–3 as motivation for how the readers should pursue unity and maturity in Christ. Beyond these first two choices, there are no other clear contenders for key verses, but if I revisit the purposes I observed for the letter, I could choose a verse that highlights one of those main purposes. For example, 1:3 introduces the blessings that are central to the believer's identity. Also, 2:14–16 provides the theological basis for unity that Paul prescribes for his readers later in the letter. I ended up choosing the former as my third key verse. The number of key verses will depend on the letter. Quality is better than quantity, which means that you should make your support for your choice clear.

Settling on a title for the letter is a science and an art. The title should be something you derive from the careful process of working from the ground up on your outline (to be discussed in the next chapter). Each paragraph of the letter feeds into major sections, and when the reader considers the major sections together, the sections can be summed up in a title. The title won't likely do justice to all of the ideas in the major sections, but do what you can to encompass a few of the main ideas, and specify their relationship to one another. That is the "science" part of constructing a title. The "art" part involves tapping into your creativity with language. The best titles are engaging and memorable. They stay grounded in the actual content of the letter while illuminating that content through fresh and thoughtful wording.

Here are a few other pointers about titles. First, try to avoid titles that are too historically confined to Paul's setting. Universalize the title so that it resonates with Christians in all situations. That means using present tense where possible and omitting Paul in the title. Second, aim for a title that is both crisp and substantive. Long titles are easily forgotten. Finally, a strong title fits unmistakably with a single letter. The title, "Preparing for the Return of Christ" could be refined so that it doesn't describe 1 Thessalonians and 2 Thessalonians simultaneously.

One possible title for Ephesians is, "The United Church's Riches and Calling in Christ." The title speaks to issues for churches in all times and all places. The eight words contain some of the letter's major themes, and the title corresponds to the major sections of the outline I constructed (see next chapter).

Perceiving the tone of the letter comes next. Detecting a letter's tone correctly indicates that you have an accurate grasp of the letter's contents and force. Paul displays a wide range of tones in his letters. He can be combative in some letters and encouraging in others. Try to find the right adjectives or phrases to describe the tone of each letter. For Ephesians, I chose "lofty, not very personal, and positive."

APPLICATION

We short-circuit the Bible study process if we never reach the application stage. The Bible is meant to be applied, and Paul's letters are no exception. When the Bible is underapplied, spiritual stagnation often follows. Think of the Dead Sea, which cannot sustain life within it. There is no outlet for its waters, and all of the salts that flow into the sea just settle there instead of being washed elsewhere. God did not design our lives as collection pools for biblical knowledge. He wants his truth to cascade into all areas of our lives. God communicated in Scripture to facilitate life change, growth, and ministry to others.

Make a list of applications from the letter, and as you describe each application, aim to be faithful, creative, and specific. The best applications emerge only after you have a firm understanding of the letter's meaning to the original audience. Respect the meaning of the text by keeping the applications consistent with the text's meaning and implications. Be creative by prayerfully imagining how your life or relationship with God could change if the words of a verse or passage took root in your life. Be specific by pinpointing actual relationships to target, action steps to take, or specific reasons to worship God. Ask, "What relationship does God want me to address—with God, family, friends, enemies—because of this passage?" Consider identifying and articulating concrete applications about love, holiness, stewardship, joy, vigilance, and other topics that stand out to you from verses in the letter. Strong applications will also direct your heart toward God, in specific words of praise and thanksgiving.

Here is a sampling of some of my application statements from Ephesians:

- Praise God for the spiritual blessings that he has given me and will give me (1:3–14).
- Reconciliation with Christ brings diverse people together (2:14–18).
- There are nonnegotiable doctrines that Christians must rally around (4:4–6).
- Various spiritual gifts should lead to unity and growth (4:11–13).
- New life must show itself in tangible ways (4:20–32).
- I should identify the correct enemy and resist through prayer and confidence in Christ (6:10–13).

When you list applications, include verse references as well, so that the connection to the text will be made explicit. Whether you list applications for an assignment or for your own study, the purpose is to get into the habit of thinking about your response to God's Word. But that still leaves the actual business of applying what you have identified! Be intentional about follow-through with one or two of your applications. Come up with a plan that can be pursued, so that you do not stop at simply thinking good thoughts or feeling good feelings.

QUESTIONS FOR FURTHER INVESTIGATION

Give kids a scavenger hunt to complete at a museum (with specific items and exhibits to find), and you will observe different reactions. Some kids just want to complete the task as quickly and efficiently as possible. Their goal is to find all of the exhibit pieces and check all of the boxes. Other kids use the hunt as a catalyst for further discovery. When they find something on the list, sure, they enjoy finishing a step, but they also stop to appreciate the find (after all, their wise teacher included the work on the list for a reason). They may even stick around long enough to notice some of the fascinating exhibits nearby as well.

We often read our Bibles like the task-oriented kids, rushing through the process to move onto other things. Even careful Bible study can devolve into mastering the steps of analysis and synthesis in order to feel that we have achieved a goal. We need to remember to cultivate a spirit of curiosity and exploration while we read. One of the best ways to do this is to ask questions while we read. What captures your interest as you read? What puzzles you or intrigues you? What would you enjoy investigating further?

Having a sense of wonder comes more naturally to a child than to an adult, but we would do well to imitate the wonder of many children when we study Paul's letters. I once even heard a teacher tell young readers to start questions with "I wonder . . ." as a prompt. That is good advice. Though there is a place for skeptical questions ("Did Paul really write this letter?" or "Why does Paul seem to overlook the injustice of slavery?"), we want to ask healthy doses of wonder-filled questions. Does Paul describe ideas that seem beyond what you can currently grasp? Ask about those. Do you sense that several ideas in the passage are more closely related than you can currently perceive? Ask about that as well. You may even find differences in how English versions of the Bible translate a certain passage. Those differences can be good fodder for questions.

There are a number of questions to pursue in Ephesians. For instance, what does the language of "chosen" and "predestined" mean in the context of chapter 1? How does the church display God's wisdom to the rulers and authorities of the heavenly realms (3:10)? What is the relationship and/or difference between being sealed and filled with the Holy Spirit (1:13–14; 4:30; 5:18)? What does it mean that Christ descended to the "lower, earthly regions" (NIV) or "lower parts of the earth" (NASB)? What is the meaning of 5:14 ("Wake up, sleeper")? Is there a link to Romans 13:11–12?

Be sure that your questions lead you towards, and not away from, the meaning of the passage. It can be easy to get distracted by incidental questions that were not important to the original author and readers of the passage. Good questions help us move closer to the original meaning of the passage. But don't get overly concerned about asking the "right" questions. Try to tap into that sense of wonder we talked about earlier.

A SUGGESTED ORDER OF TASKS

I have tried to explain the various features of a letter summary in the conceptual categories of background, analysis, synthesis, and relevance. When you go through the process on your own, however, you may find it easier to proceed in a different order. I recommend reading through the letter a first time to form opinions about the author, audience, occasion, purpose, tone, and basic divisions in the argument of the letter. On your first pass you can also begin marking key verses and repeated words, phrases, and ideas. The second time through, examine the argument more closely. Craft appropriate summary statements for each division of the argument, group smaller paragraphs into larger sections, and create descriptions for those sections too (these procedures will be explained in detail in the next chapter). For your third reading, try a different translation and look for applications and lingering questions you have about the letter.

Once you have collected all of your thoughts about the letter, you might consider editing and organizing them for future use (an example for Ephesians is given in the appendix). These letter summaries are fun to consult later for personal study, but they are also useful to distribute to others on occasion. For instance, you could share your summary with a Bible study group during the first week you begin studying a letter together. Even if you are invited to speak to a group about just one passage from a letter, giving listeners a letter summary will help orient them to how your passage fits into the broader letter.

A NOTE ON TRANSLATIONS

I recommend consulting two different Bible translations when you study a letter. Sometimes the variance in wording between two translations kindles a recognition of something important for the letter's meaning or relevance. Disparities in how sentences are translated can also signal that the verse contains some ambiguity in the grammar. For example, does Paul intend to talk about "the obedience that comes from faith" (NIV) or "obedience to the faith" (NKJV) in Romans 1:5?[4] Conflicting opinions can also arise because of textual uncertainty (when ancient manuscripts support different

---

4. Most translations preserve the ambiguity in the Greek: "the obedience of faith" (NASB, ESV, HCSB, NET, NRSV).

readings). You can usually spot these when versions include a footnote for an alternate translation for a verse. For instance, there is debate about whether 1 Thessalonians 2:7 should say "we were gentle among you" (ESV, NASB, NKJV, NRSV, HCSB) or "we were like young children among you" (NIV, NET). These versions, except for the NKJV, include footnotes mentioning the other option for the verse. It is always nice to become aware of what scholars disagree about for a verse.

Which translations should you use? For your initial study, choose a version that sticks closely to the wording and structure of the original Greek. The NASB and ESV translations are examples of versions that follow this philosophy. For your second round, you might try a translation that aims for more of a "thought-for-thought" approach. The NIV, HCSB, NET, and NRSV are all good choices here. Though paraphrases such as the Message have their uses, avoid them for this type of study, because the original meaning and structure of the text can become obscured in the paraphrasing process.

CONCLUSION

I hope that you are beginning to see the potential benefits of studying Paul's letters in this detailed manner. You will become well acquainted with the letters and see their unique contributions. You will also begin to note recurring themes across the letters. Having time set aside for application will allow you to discern what the Spirit wants you to implement. By formulating questions you will appreciate how much more there is to explore with the letters' meanings. In the next chapter we will give additional attention to tracing the argument of a letter and see how this has the potential to unlock even more truth and insight into each letter.

In the end, these tasks all propel you into a journey of first-hand immersion into the letters of Paul. They bring you into a captivating world of people, places, and ideas that you can experience for yourself. Committing to the careful work of self-discovered learning promises to put you into a better position to hear and respond to God's truth for your life.

■ ■ ■

CHAPTER SEVEN

HOW CAN I DISCERN PAUL'S TRAIN OF THOUGHT IN HIS LETTERS?

Misunderstandings happen all the time in communication. When my wife and I text our kids and go back and forth with brief comments that are sometimes out of order, one or the other party sometimes sends a "???" message to indicate that he or she is lost. The conversation partner can no longer follow where the conversation is going. Does that ever happen to you? It takes effort and sensitivity to communicate well with other people. Paul's letters are an especially challenging form of communication, since we aren't familiar with the readers' world or circumstances, and we only hear one side of the conversation. Furthermore, at times Paul communicates with layers of intricacies, and even subtleties, to impart just the right instruction and tone. These are significant challenges. But with patience and attentiveness, we can learn to follow Paul's train of thought more accurately and thereby avoid misunderstandings.

We call the train of thought in certain types of discourse an *argument*. This academic term is potentially misleading, because arguments need not be argumentative. Arguments attempt to persuade readers or hearers, through reasoning and interpersonal appeals. Well-constructed arguments carefully and coherently present evidence, examples, and justifications for certain beliefs or proposals. A successful argument results when readers emerge with a clear idea of the author's agenda and find it compelling. But that requires work from the readers! We have to be ready to take an author's ideas seriously and seek to understand even when the meaning is not immediately obvious.

In this chapter we will step through the process of tracing Paul's argument in his letters and putting that argument into outline form. This takes a methodical approach and attention to detail, but the payoff is rewarding. There is a thrill in the "a-ha" moments you'll have when you see Paul's ideas in a new light. Philippians 2:12 ("work out your salvation with fear and trembling") was puzzling to me until I saw its place in the greater argument of the letter. I had previously read the passage as a call to individual, introspective reflection on whether one's personal salvation was secure. But in the broader argument the verses extol putting feet to our faith in a corporate way, as a community of faith. The verses are sandwiched between passages that emphasize others-centeredness (Phil. 2:1–11) and shining Christ's light to the world through harmonious relationships (Phil. 2:14–16). This suggests that in verses 12 and 13 Paul wants believers to jointly work out (= live out) their faith through humble and cooperative relationships with one another, so that the world may see Christ reflected in their interactions.

The longer I have studied Paul's letters, the more inclined I am to persistently unpack the argument of a section that contains puzzling verses. That has become my knee-jerk reaction to ambiguous verses, because I have found that the process really works! Paul's letters display coherent and elegant arguments. They are writings that yield unexpected treasures for those who seek them. Let's take a look at how to develop this habit.[1]

STEP ONE: DIVIDE THE TEXT INTO PARAGRAPHS

The building blocks of arguments are paragraphs. Each paragraph communicates a main thought, and successive paragraphs build upon each other and communicate an overall argument.[2] That means that the first step in ascertaining the argument is to divide the letter into paragraphs. Look for seams between paragraphs that form the boundaries between one topic and another. Rarely will you see abrupt shifts in topics. Instead, Paul will make smooth transitions from one idea to another, related idea.

For the longer letters (Romans, 1 Corinthians, 2 Corinthians) you may need to group several paragraphs together and thus start with larger divisions. You want to avoid having so many items in your outline that you lose the forest for the trees. By combining related paragraphs, you can streamline your outline and retain a sense of overall direction in the letter. If you aim for two or three groupings per chapter, you will still have thirty-two to forty-eight individual sections for Romans and 1 Corinthians, and twenty-six to thirty-nine sections for 2 Corinthians. For the shorter letters, you can err on the side of finer divisions in the material. For every letter, you want at least two levels in the outline, and for the longer letters, three levels can be appropriate in certain places. You'll notice that on my

---

1. For a detailed look at developing an outline from the Greek New Testament, see Jay E. Smith, "Sentence Diagramming, Clausal Layouts, and Exegetical Outlining," in *Interpreting the New Testament Text: Introduction to the Art and Science of Exegesis*, eds. Darrell L. Bock and Buist M. Fanning (Wheaton, IL: Crossway, 2006), 100–131. Many of Smith's ideas transfer well to outlining the argument from English versions of the text.

2. See Gordon D. Fee and Douglas Stuart, *How to Read the Bible for All Its Worth*, 3rd ed. (Grand Rapids: Zondervan, 2003), 64–65.

completed Ephesians outline (in the appendix) I vary between two and three levels of content.

STEP TWO: DEVISE STRONG TITLES FOR EACH PARAGRAPH

Paragraphs are united by a common point or theme. Our second step, after dividing the letter into distinct paragraphs, is to identify the theme of each paragraph and assign it a title. Look for what is distinct about the content of a given paragraph. What main points does Paul highlight in the paragraph? Be sensitive to the *why* of each paragraph in addition to the *what*.[3] In other words, look for hints about why Paul says what he does, in keeping with the awareness that Paul's letters are occasional documents. Paul writes with multiple purposes in mind, according to the needs of the readers. He includes each paragraph to help accomplish his purposes for writing. Being alert to the "why" gives you a greater chance of picking up on the direction or flow of the argument as well as the inner connections within Paul's letters.

Attempt to include both a subject and complement in each title. This means that you want to explain something about a topic in the letter, rather than simply stating the topic. Subject-complement statements provide more complete summaries of a paragraph. The subject states the paragraph's general topic, while the complement notes what the author is affirming about the subject.[4] For instance, "Grace and works" is insufficient for James 2:14–26. "Grace and works" designates the topic or subject but doesn't express what James says about the subject. Without further elaboration, the passage could mean anything from "Grace and works are incompatible" to "Grace and works are interchangeable." We just don't know, since the complement is absent. Much better is "True faith must be accompanied by works." That subject-complement statement is barely longer than the original attempt, but it packs a lot more useful information into it. Including both a subject and a complement helps ensure that you have a precise understanding of the paragraph. Vague generalities often indicate fuzzy thinking. Looking for both subject and complement also helps you treat the paragraph as part of an argument. Paul's letters aren't simply strings of topics. They are well-developed arguments that communicate substantive ideas informed by Paul's knowledge of God and his concern for his readers.

When you compose your titles for each paragraph, use third-person language (he, she, it, they, etc.) rather than first-person (or second-person) language (so, not "we should bear one another's burdens"). This helps force you to keep your focus on the original meaning Paul conveyed to his readers. The one caveat here is to avoid using "Paul" in all of your

---

3. Ibid., 65.
4. See Smith, "Exegetical Outlining," 105–17.

titles ("Paul tells the Galatians to bear one another's burdens"). You can typically omit referring to Paul and his readers by name ("Believers fulfill the law of Christ by bearing one another's burdens" is sufficient without naming Paul or the Galatians), since they are always looming in the background and need not be mentioned each time. When Paul does describe his own circumstances or actions (his calling, imprisonment, travel plans, and prayers or concerns for his readers), then you can include him in the paragraph title. The same goes for the readers, when their specific problems are front and center ("Paul is dismayed that the Galatians are being duped by a false gospel"). Try to guess why I included "Paul" in certain titles of the Ephesians example later in this chapter.

As far as verb tense goes (past, perfect, present, or future tense), try to reflect the time frame from the perspective of Paul and his original readers. When Paul talks about past events (such as Christ's death and resurrection) use past or perfect tense (perfect tense conveys more of an idea of ongoing effects of a past event). Examples are "God humbled Paul by allowing a debilitating hardship in his life" (past tense), or "God has given believers new life in Christ" (perfect tense). When Paul addresses current or future realities from the original readers' perspective, use present or future tense, as with "Christ has authority over all things in creation and reconciliation" (present) or "Christ will raise believers from the dead when he returns" (future).

Avoid titles from Bibles. For one thing, that short-circuits the learning process. But paragraph titles from Bibles typically list only subjects, rather than both subjects and complements. This editorial feature provides a convenient reference for readers who are looking for specific passages, but it does not shed light on the unfolding argument. Try not to follow the paragraph (or section) divisions from Bibles either. Those have been added by editors but don't necessarily reflect the best way to partition the discourse. In fact, sometimes there are several defensible groupings for a collection of verses. For instance, does Ephesians 5:21 ("Submit to one another out of reverence for Christ") belong to the prior material (in which different expressions of a Spirit-filled life are encouraged) or subsequent material (which depicts what submission and love look like in a marriage)? There are good arguments, grammatically and conceptually, for both options. You can read the section carefully and see what makes most sense of the discourse.

Strong paragraph titles share several common features. First, they grasp the substance of a paragraph and yet are worded succinctly and memorably. Using too many words runs the risk of obscuring the progression of the argument from paragraph to paragraph. Second, titles that reflect the uniqueness of a paragraph are superior to generic titles that could point to a number of different passages. Third, it is especially effective when successive paragraphs have titles that reflect the logical relationship between the sections (through repeated wording in particular). Fourth, look for opportunities to relate titles of individual paragraphs to ideas in larger section titles. Don't force that process, but stay alert for when such connections will increase the visibility of the argument of the letter. In your outline you want to make the argument of the letter as explicit as possible and reflect Paul's purpose for the direction of his discourse.

When you are finished with the first two steps, you should have a list of titles for all of the paragraphs of the letter. At this point, you have one level of an outline completed. You are now ready to add a second level.

STEP THREE: GROUP PARAGRAPHS INTO LARGER SECTIONS

Paul transitions in subtle ways from paragraph to paragraph but also in more pronounced ways at various points in his letters. You now want to identify those more drastic seams in the letter and create groupings of paragraphs into sections. From here on we will distinguish between (smaller) paragraphs and (larger) sections.

Take a stroll through your paragraph titles, while referring regularly to the letter itself.[5] Do you see some natural groupings, where several titles in a row exhibit some relationship to one another? Bracket those titles into a group. Repeat that procedure with the rest of your paragraphs. Not every paragraph will fit well with surrounding paragraphs. In such cases, just keep that original paragraph on its own.

For small letters, you might make only two or three section groupings (you should make a minimum of two). For larger letters you could have as many as a dozen sections. You will need to conduct another round of groupings for those larger letters, as we will describe later.

STEP FOUR: ASSIGN TITLES TO THE SECTIONS

Once you delineate those sections, create a title for those new sections. The title for a section should correspond to its component parts.[6] That means that the title should tie together ideas from as many of the subordinate paragraphs as possible, without creating a cumbersome sentence that loses its focus. It's a fine balance that is more an art than a science! Remember to give subjects and complements to each of your section titles, so that they communicate complete thoughts and not just general topics.

By providing titles for the sections, you are creating a second level on your outline. These titles will be arranged before all of the subordinate paragraph titles (created in the second step) are listed. The section titles regulate and shape the paragraph titles underneath them. They

5.   Ibid., 122.
6.   Ibid., 117–22.

don't replace any of the titles but span the range of all of the verses organized under them.

MAKE AN ADDITIONAL ROUND OF GROUPINGS AND TITLES, IF NEEDED

For larger letters, you may be able to make even larger groupings (for instance, you could create three major groupings in Romans—chapters 1–8, chapters 9–11, and chapters 12–16). For any additional major groupings (we could call these "mega-sections"), follow the same procedure as above for producing appropriate titles for each grouping. These third round of titles constitute the top level of your outline (I, II, III, IV, etc.).

You could also subdivide an existing paragraph, if you find that a further breakdown of the passage would expose more of Paul's argument. For new smaller divisions (we could call these "mini-paragraphs"), create new titles without eliminating the original paragraph title that governs the smaller passages. This third level would become the bottom level of the outline (labeled as 1, 2, 3, 4, etc.).

You may also want to tweak the wording of your original titles as you articulate new titles for mega-sections. This could help avoid redundancy (if a mega-section title basically repeats a section title) or make connections between titles more obvious. Make sure any changes keep the title anchored to the content of the section it describes.

EXAMPLE: EPHESIANS

For my first pass of Ephesians, I made paragraph divisions (combining some related paragraphs together) and composed the following titles:

Paul the apostle greets faithful believers with grace and peace (1:1–2)

The Father has an eternal plan to bless believers, in Jesus Christ (1:3–6)

Believers are forgiven through Christ's blood, in preparation for Christ's reign over all things (1:7–10)

The Spirit's presence ensures that believers will receive all blessings (1:11–14)

Paul prays that believers would grasp their riches in Christ, who rules over all (1:15–23)

Formerly "dead" believers have been saved and made alive in Christ (2:1–10)

Formerly excluded Gentiles have been included in God's people by Christ's sacrifice (2:11–13)

Formerly divided believers (Jews and Gentiles) have been made one in Christ (2:14–18)

Jewish and Gentile believers who are united in Christ are God's new temple (2:19–22)

Imprisoned Paul recalls his divine mandate to reach the Gentiles (3:1–13)

Paul prays that believers would grasp the abundant love of Christ (3:14–21)

Believers should humbly unify around their common confession of faith (4:1–6)

Christ has equipped diverse believers to grow together towards maturity (4:7–16)

Believers should put off their old, corrupted selves and put on their new identity in Christ (4:17–24)

Believers should live as new people in their speech, conduct, and attitude (4:25–32)

Believers should live as imitators of God, with sacrificial love and holiness (5:1–5)

Believers should aspire to shine Christ's light in a dark world (5:6–14)

The Spirit should guide believers in discernment and corporate worship (5:15–20)

The Spirit should shape relationships between wives and husbands (5:21–33)

The Spirit should shape relationships between children and parents (6:1–4)

The Spirit should shape relationships between masters and servants (6:5–9)

Believers should be equipped in Christ for spiritual battle (6:10–20)

Paul shares final greetings of peace and grace (6:21–24)

For step three, I looked for natural groupings among the paragraphs. Some paragraphs seemed to stand well on their own (since there were significant transitions in thought before and after them), so I left those alone. I grouped others together:

Paul the apostle greets faithful believers with grace and peace (1:1–2)

The Father has an eternal plan to bless believers, in Jesus Christ (1:3–6)

Believers are forgiven through Christ's blood, in preparation for Christ's reign over all things (1:7–10)

The Spirit's presence ensures that believers will receive all blessings (1:11–14)

Paul prays that believers would grasp their riches in Christ, who rules over all (1:15–23)

Formerly "dead" believers have been saved and made alive in Christ (2:1–10)

Formerly excluded Gentiles have been included in God's people by Christ's sacrifice (2:11–13)

Formerly divided believers (Jews and Gentiles) have been made one in Christ (2:14–18)

Jewish and Gentile believers who are united in Christ are God's new temple (2:19–22)

Imprisoned Paul recalls his divine mandate to reach the Gentiles (3:1–13)

Paul prays that believers would grasp the abundant love of Christ (3:14–21)

Believers should humbly unify around their common confession of faith (4:1–6)

Christ has equipped diverse believers to grow together toward maturity (4:7–16)

Believers should put off their old, corrupted selves and put on their new identity in Christ (4:17–24)

Believers should live as new people in their speech, conduct, and attitude (4:25–32)

Believers should live as imitators of God, with sacrificial love and holiness (5:1–5)

Believers should aspire to shine Christ's light in a dark world (5:6–14)

The Spirit should guide believers in discernment and corporate worship (5:15–20)

The Spirit should shape relationships between wives and husbands (5:21–33)

The Spirit should shape relationships between children and parents (6:1–4)

The Spirit should shape relationships between servants and masters (6:5–9)

Believers should be equipped in Christ for spiritual battle (6:10–20)

Paul shares final greetings of peace and grace (6:21–24)

I created new section titles for the larger groupings. These new titles joined the titles that were retained from paragraphs that did not get grouped with others to become a new level of the outline. The new section titles are in bold, and the paragraphs they encompass are arranged under them:

Paul the apostle greets faithful believers with grace and peace (1:1–2)

God has a plan to bless believers through the Son and by the Spirit (1:3–14)

> The Father has an eternal plan to bless believers, in Jesus Christ (1:3–6)
> Believers are forgiven through Christ's blood, in preparation for Christ's reign over all things (1:7–10)
> The Spirit's presence ensures that believers will receive all blessings (1:11–14)

Paul prays that believers would grasp their riches in Christ, who rules over all (1:15–23)

Formerly "dead" believers have been saved and made alive in Christ (2:1–10)

God has made formerly divided Jews and Gentiles into a new, unified, holy people in Christ (2:11–22)

> Formerly excluded Gentiles have been included in God's people by Christ's sacrifice (2:11–13)
> Formerly divided believers (Jews and Gentiles) have been made one in Christ (2:14–18)
> Jewish and Gentile believers who are united in Christ are God's new temple (2:19–22)

Imprisoned Paul recalls his divine mandate to reach the Gentiles (3:1–13)

Paul prays that believers would grasp the abundant love of Christ (3:14–21)

Diverse believers united in Christ should grow together towards maturity (4:1–16)

> Believers should humbly unify around their common confession of faith (4:1–6)
> Christ has equipped diverse believers to grow together towards maturity (4:7–16)

Believers should put off the old and put on the new in practical ways (4:17–32)

> Believers should put off their old, corrupted selves and put on their new identities in Christ (4:17–24)
> Believers should live as new people in their speech, conduct, and attitude (4:25–32)

Loving and holy believers shine as Christ's light in a dark world (5:1–14)

> Believers should live as imitators of God, with sacrificial love and holiness (5:1–5)
> Believers should aspire to shine Christ's light in a dark world (5:6–14)

Believers should pursue Spirit-filled lives and relationships (5:15–6:9)

> The Spirit should guide believers in discernment and corporate worship (5:15–20)
> The Spirit should shape relationships between wives and husbands (5:21–33)
> The Spirit should shape relationships between children and parents (6:1–4)
> The Spirit should shape relationships between servants and masters (6:5–9)

> Believers should be equipped in Christ for spiritual battle (6:10–20)

> Paul shares final greetings of peace and grace (6:21–24)

Finally, I looked for logical groupings of the above sections and created titles for those larger groupings of mega-sections. These will become the major section titles for the whole letter, and the other levels will be indented below them:

> God has richly blessed Jews and Gentiles by making them alive and united in Christ (1:1–2:22)

> Paul fulfills his calling to instruct and pray for Christ's united church (3:1–21)

> The united church should grow together in love and shine as Christ's holy people in a dark world (4:1–6:24)

That creates three levels for the outline. I use Roman numerals for the three main sections (mega-sections), A, B, C, etc. for the next level (sections), and 1, 2, 3, etc. for the smallest divisions (paragraphs). See the appendix for the final arrangement and formatting of the outline.

CONSTRUCTING YOUR OUTLINE

Keeping in mind some conventional practices for designing outlines will help you achieve a better finished product.[7] Here are some guidelines:

- Be sure to specify the verse range for each section and paragraph, next to your titles.
- Verse ranges for the larger sections should encompass all of the verses included in the corresponding paragraphs, and there should be no gaps of verses among the paragraphs.
- Indent your outline properly, so that it is clear which sections or paragraphs are parallel to one another and which are subordinate. Similarly, make sure that your outline numbers and letters

---

7. Ibid., 100–104.

are correctly aligned with parallel sections or paragraphs of the same level.

- A section should have at least two paragraphs underneath it. If a section has just one paragraph under it, that paragraph is redundant (it is just a restatement of the section above it). Eliminate the paragraph and let the section stand alone.
- If a title runs over one line, try to have the second line match up with the starting point of the first line.

It takes time to develop proficiency in outlining the argument of a letter, but the payoff is well worth it. Paul's letters come alive when we see how they fit together as coherent wholes. And, since outlining requires us to locate the component parts as segments of larger movements in the argument, it ensures that we don't overlook anything important or miss the relevance of a given passage. Moisés Silva observes that "our ability to understand a letter (or any other document) is tied to how accurately we perceive its structure."[8] Outlining the structure of Paul's argument is central to the whole task of interpretation.

---

8. Walter C. Kaiser, Jr. and Moisés Silva, *Introduction to Biblical Hermeneutics: The Search for Meaning*, rev. and exp. ed. (Grand Rapids: Zondervan, 2007), 182.

■ ■ ■

CHAPTER EIGHT

ARE THERE SUCH THINGS AS "CORRECT" INTERPRETATIONS OF PAUL'S LETTERS?

n 2004 my wife and I started watching an intriguing show on television called *Lost*. We were drawn in by the plot, the characters, and above all the quest to know answers to the mysteries on the island where survivors of an airplane crash were stranded. During the first couple of seasons I scoured each episode for clues about the history of the island and the secrets it held. Every scene seemed to be ripe with indicators about the ultimate meaning of the story.

As it turned out, there was less meaning in the show than many of us had assumed. While it is still debatable how much the directors themselves knew where the story was going, it became clear that every detail and every plot twist was not part of a brilliant master plan that would one day make sense of everything. While the show was still entertaining on some levels, I no longer watched the episodes with the same focus and curiosity that I had before. Viewers were still letting the show's episodes impact them in different ways, but there was evidently no shared meaning, driven by the show's writers and directors, that governed each scene and interaction.

A multiple-season show designed primarily to entertain will have a difficult time investing each scene with a greater purpose. When it comes to Paul's letters, though, we should expect the quest for meaning to pay dividends. Paul's letters were written to address specific occasions, so he writes every letter with a purpose. Each section of the letter supports his larger purpose (or purposes) for his readers, as part of the unfolding argument of the letter. Ultimately, each passage of each letter also ties into God's perfect, eternally ordained story for this world. What happens, then, when we begin to treat Paul's letters more as episodes of *Lost* than as the historically rooted, purposeful letters of Scripture that they are? When we adopt views about meaning and interpretation that lose sight of the actual, intended meaning of a letter, we run the risk of undermining some of the motivation to really study Paul's letters.

CLARIFYING THE TASK OF INTERPRETATION

As readers of Paul's letters we want to understand individual passages as well as the ideas in the letters as a whole. To do so we must interpret Paul's letters. But before we embark on the process of interpretation we must consider what our objective is. Are we looking for a single, correct interpretation of any given passage, or are there multiple valid interpretations for passages in Paul's letters? Can we wade through various proposed interpretations and deem some as superior to others? What process of interpretation yields the best results? Begin by formulating your own initial answer to these questions. Think about the questions for a moment and identify some reasons you responded the way you did. These are important questions to delve into, since the way we answer them will shape how we read and study Paul's letters.

We will break down this topic into smaller parts. First, how should interpretation be distinguished from application? Second, what does authorial intent entail, and how is it central to the task of interpretation? Third, how does speech-act theory help us appreciate and discern the intended effect of Paul's words? Fourth, how does the specific wording and content of a verse and the surrounding context reveal the intended meaning of a verse or passage? Fifth, how should we factor in our own interpretive fallibility without losing our drive to find the correct meanings of passages? Finally, what is at stake with our assumptions about meaning and the interpretive strategies we adopt?

INTERPRETATION AND APPLICATION

First, let's explore the difference between interpretation and application. Some students end up conflating these two topics, which adds to the confusion over whether there are correct meanings for passages in Paul's letters. We could start by noting that interpretation seeks what Paul's letters *meant* to the original audience, while application identifies what the letters *mean* for later readers. But we can see right away that interpretation and application encroach on each other's space with these definitions, since they both concern themselves with meaning. The difference between *meant* and *mean* is subtle enough to create ambiguity.

Bringing the ideas of "meaning," "implication," and "significance" into the conversation allows us to talk more precisely about what we are doing when we interpret and apply Paul's letters.[1] We will use the word

---

1. For the difference between meaning and significance, see Kevin J. Vanhoozer, *Is There a Meaning in This Text? The Bible, the Reader, and the Morality of Literary Knowledge* (Grand Rapids:

"meaning" to denote the ideas that Paul wished to communicate through his writings, as observed in the words, sentences, and paragraphs Paul used to articulate his ideas. With this breakdown, "meaning" is reserved for what Paul meant when he addressed the original readers. The term "implication" refers to any principle that is compatible with Paul's overtly stated meanings. Paul did not necessarily write with these implications in mind but would see them as logical extensions of what he wrote. Implications are not confined to the historical circumstances of the original author and readers but still take their cues from the original meaning. "Significance" is an even broader term. It recognizes the intersection of Paul's original meaning or resulting implications with the present reader's circumstances. Readers find written material to be significant when it has some relevance to their lives. Viewing these three concepts together, the historically particular meaning of a text opens up into broader implications and significance for readers' lives.[2]

How can the concepts of meaning, implication, and significance sharpen our definitions of interpretation and application? We can reserve the term "interpretation" for the process that has the original meaning of discourse as its target. That tighter definition of interpretation corresponds with what is known as exegesis within the field of biblical studies.[3] Interpretation or exegesis requires evaluating possible meanings and determining what meaning was most likely intended by the author. Application, on the other hand, builds off of the implications and especially the significance of a text to a reader.[4] Interpretation narrows in on the single, most likely meaning of a passage in its original context, whereas application opens up to the many possibilities of how the passage can shape our lives. For example, when Paul says in Ephesians 3:13, "I ask you, therefore, not to be discouraged because of my sufferings for you, which are your glory," the *meaning* is that Paul's original readers should be encouraged that God works through Paul's imprisonment (3:1) and other sufferings for the greater spiritual good of his readers. Once we confirm that this interpretation fits the wording and context we can call this a correct interpretation of the verse.[5] An *implication* of this verse is that righteous suffering represents a victory rather than a defeat in God's plans. A point of *significance* from this verse is the comfort that Christ's persecuted church even today doesn't suffer in vain. There are several valid applications readers could implement from the implication

---

Zondervan, 1998), 259–63. Adding implications into the mix is Robert H. Stein, "The Benefits of an Author-Oriented Approach to Hermeneutics," *JETS* 44 (2001): 457–61.

2. Fee and Stuart put language of "historical particularity" in the foreground of their guidelines for Bible study (Fee and Stuart, *How to Read the Bible for All Its Worth*, 21).

3. Fee and Stuart define exegesis as "the careful, systematic study of the Scripture to discover the original, intended meaning" (ibid., 23).

4. Stein, "Author-Oriented Approach to Hermeneutics," 461.

5. Though this rough summary captures the gist of the verse, we would still want to examine the meaning and possible eschatological connotations of "glory" more closely.

and significance of this passage. We could prayerfully evaluate our willingness to suffer for Christ, confront areas of our lives in which we have settled for comfort over obedience, or pray for renewed strength and perspective for the persecuted church around the world.

A clear-cut division between interpretation and application runs the risk of oversimplifying discussions that have a long history of philosophical nuance.[6] The academic discipline of hermeneutics promotes careful reflection on a range of issues related to how we interpret and apply texts.[7] But since this is a book to equip us for diving into Paul's letters and reading them well, we will tolerate certain simplifications. In the end, the more we distinguish between interpretation and application on a practical level, the more we can devote our energies to doing each task well.[8]

AUTHORIAL INTENT

When we confine our definition of interpretation to perceiving the meaning of passages in their original historical contexts, the concept of authorial intent takes center stage. We must allow Paul's personal involvement in writing his letters to factor into how we understand them. Paul's letters consist of intentional communication from author (Paul) to readers (the churches and individuals he addressed).[9] The content of the letters is sensible only when we see how it is embedded within actual moments and events in history that affected Paul and his readers.

Texts do not float about detached from the authors that wrote them, especially whenever the primary purpose of a text is to relay comprehensible information and ideas to an audience.[10] Paul's letters were designed for this basic purpose, not as works of art to be admired independently from his missionary and pastoral aims. Paul's goals and strategies thus regulate the way his letters should be interpreted. The concept of authorial intent respects the time, cost, and effort Paul invested into

---

6. Even E. D. Hirsch Jr., a champion of seeking the original meaning of a text, worries about the consequences of separating interpretation and application too completely (E. D. Hirsch Jr., "Meaning and Significance Reinterpreted," *Critical Inquiry* 11 [1984]: 210–12). While his concerns are noted, they can be addressed by simultaneously differentiating between interpretation and application and affirming the close relationship between the two.
7. For a comprehensive treatment of philosophical questions regarding hermeneutics, see Vanhoozer, *Is There a Meaning in This Text?*
8. We will devote the entire next chapter of this book to applying passages from Paul's letters.
9. Wolterstorff calls this intentional communication "authorial discourse" and defends the legitimacy of making this a focus of interpretation (Wolterstorff, *Divine Discourse*, 132–70).
10. Advocates of New Criticism and Structuralism have argued that works of literature do attain a life of their own after they are written. The historical context and author's purpose for writing get eclipsed by literary structure and literary features in the text (see the overview in Vanhoozer, *Is There a Meaning in This Text?*, 26–27, 82). Regardless of the merits or weaknesses of such approaches, Paul's letters are not composed as literary pieces but as channels for communicating with his readers (see Stein, "Author-Oriented Approach to Hermeneutics," 455).

communicating valuable insights to his readers.[11] We all hope to be understood when we communicate instructions or ideas that matter to us. Paul was no different, and the Spirit who speaks through Paul desires to reveal God's heart and plans as well.

At the same time, we don't have access to Paul's mind and motivations. We can't consult him in person to discover what his true intent was. Our entryway into Paul's aims comes through the letters themselves. That means that we eschew attempts at playing amateur psychologists with Paul and keep the focus on the discourse we find in Paul's letters. Reading according to authorial intent means reading with plausible assumptions about the historical situation reflected in Paul's writings. It consists of forming hypotheses about the occasion of each letter and interpreting the words, grammar, and content with sensitivity to what we know about the socio-historical backdrop of early Christianity in the Roman world. All of this demands our careful attention to the text of Paul's letters, especially the developing argument of each letter.

What about the role of readers in constructing meaning from their experiences interacting with the text? Is there a danger of entombing Paul's writings in the first century by insisting that true meaning is dictated solely by the author's address to the original readers? Does God speak freshly through Paul's letters to readers today, and could the identification of that fresh word be a valid interpretation of Paul's letters? Champions of reader-response criticism expand the concept of interpretation to allow room for meanings readers come away with when they read texts. We can acknowledge the validity of meanings that sincere readers perceive for their own lives (guided by the Spirit's leading) but still treat such meanings as a separate topic, grouped under application instead of interpretation. Though the philosophical assumptions behind reader-response theory deserve careful treatment, we will set aside the reader's personal engagement with Paul's letters for the time being and reexamine how readers draw implications and significance from Paul's letters in the later chapter on application.

Affirming the priority of authorial intent in interpretation properly credits the writer with composing the work in the first place, but the fact that Paul was empowered and directed by the Spirit when he wrote further complicates matters. Could we argue that God's involvement in the writing process injected deeper truths that extended beyond Paul's intended meaning in rare instances?[12] The problem with a fuller message expanding beyond Paul's awareness is, what would be the process of discerning that message? If a proposed meaning is not observable in Paul's actual discourse, how would believers gain access to those truths?

---

11.   Besides the materials needed to write the letters, Paul and his team may have employed professional scribes to assist him in his letter writing (Richards, *Paul and First-Century Letter Writing*, 91).

12.   This idea, known as *sensus plenior*, is more familiar from discussions of prophetic texts in Scripture.

If we respond that individual believers could discover Spirit-guided messages specifically for them, wouldn't that have crossed into the realm of application anyway?

The divine oversight of apostolic teaching doesn't eliminate the fully human quality of Paul's correspondence with his readers. Even if God's communications through Paul were to contain some fuller meaning, that divinely ordained meaning would never replace Paul's original meaning but would only enhance and supplement it. Otherwise, the idea of authentic communication (relaying a purposeful message with the expectation of being understood) would break down. Paul certainly wrote to communicate truths to his original readers. We see this in Paul's appeals to his readers to comprehend his words (Gal. 3:7–9; 2 Tim. 2:7), in his clarifications of his intent (Rom. 1:13–15; 2 Cor. 13:10; Col. 2:1–2), in his desire that his readers be informed (Rom. 11:25; 1 Cor. 12:1; 1 Thess. 4:13), and in his steps to ensure that he is not misunderstood (1 Cor. 5:9–11; Phil. 3:12).[13] Paul also relies on a variety of styles of persuasive arguments in his letters (Rom. 4:9–12; 7:1–3; 1 Cor. 12:12–26; Gal. 3:2–5), suggesting that his discourse is meant to be understood, weighed, and accepted.

Being sensitive to authorial intent means entering the world of the original readers. As readers from a much later era we must try to adopt the perspective of the original readers as much possible when we interpret the original meaning of Paul's letters. This is challenging in some ways but feasible in others. On the one hand, many of Paul's original readers had the advantage of an existing relationship with Paul, which gave them a surer context for interpreting what he was saying. Modern readers have to carefully but persistently put ourselves in that original setting and seek to discern the messages Paul conveyed to the recipients. We do that by reconstructing the occasion of the letter, determining Paul's purpose, and tracking how Paul carries out that purpose through the argument of the letter. On the other hand, the earliest recipients were just normal people, not highly educated, trained theologians who were instructed in the latest theories of communication and knowledge. From Paul's letters we see indications that he believed that his readers could process what he was saying, and this accords with the way that communication typically works.[14] We too can proceed with the expectation that Paul communicated to be understood, as long as we take a careful, sensible, and informed approach to interpreting Paul's letters.

13.　Though statements such as "I do not want you to be uninformed" (1 Cor. 12:1; 2 Cor. 1:8; 1 Thess. 4:13) reflect conventional formulas in letters, their widespread use in letters attests to a fundamental desire for understanding in communication.

14.　We can assume that literal or direct communication, according to basic rules of a language, is the default setting of most communication. In certain genres, we make adjustments to our understanding, in keeping with the conventions or rules of that genre. See Wolterstorff, *Divine Discourse*, 191–99.

SPEECH-ACT THEORY

Since the idea of authorial intent retains the essential link between authors and their writings, we must read authors with an eye towards the goals they hope to achieve. Authorial intent, by definition, requires us to associate words on a page with the aims of the author. The field of speech-act theory helps alert us to authors' goals when they use language. Speech-act theory is a branch of linguistics that encourages readers to interpret texts by looking at not only *what* authors said, but also *why* they said it.[15] When linguists study communication, they examine both the meaning of communication and its effects. Human communication has not only content but also force.[16] Sometimes words caution us or cause us to slow down ("watch out!" or "be careful!"), prepare us for unsettling news ("you might want to sit down"), invite us to partake in an activity or experience ("let the games begin" or "bon appetit"), or spur us on to more intense effort ("defense!" yelled at a sporting event).

Paul's discourse also has a purpose. Paul shares words not just as ideas, but as ideas that have the potential to change his readers' lives. On several occasions Paul specifies the desired effect or response he hopes to see in the readers. He clarifies, "I am writing this not to shame you but to warn you as my dear children" in 1 Corinthians 4:14. Two chapters later, on another topic, Paul acknowledges that "I say this to shame you" (1 Cor. 6:5). Another time Paul tells Timothy the explicit purpose of his words: "I am writing you these instructions so that, if I am delayed, you will know how people ought to conduct themselves in God's household" (1 Tim. 3:14–15).[17] Reading these passages according to Paul's authorial intent is quite straightforward because of these overt indicators of purpose.

Even when Paul does not disclose his goals so obviously, we can learn to infer Paul's purpose from the wording and content he includes in his letters, as well as from a knowledge of his missionary goals. For instance, Paul talks about readers as "saints" (Phil. 1:1; Col. 1:2) who have been "chosen" (Col. 3:12; 1 Thess. 1:4) and "called" (1 Cor. 1:2; 2 Tim. 1:9) by God. Those words represent *what* Paul is saying about the recipients. But *why* is he saying those words? He wants to help form and shape his readers' identity in Christ. When the readers hear these words, Paul wants them to be strengthened in their sense of who they are as God's children.

---

15. Beyond this, speech-act theory considers the resulting effects when readers receive the communication, but we will set aside matters of readers' responses until we return to application in the next chapter.

16. This content is known as the *locution*, and the force is the *illocution*. The resulting effects on the hearer or reader is labeled the *perlocution*.

17. Paul also articulates his purpose for writing in 2 Corinthians 2:4; 5:11–12; 7:12.

They belong to God (as set-apart saints) not by accident but because of his initiative ("chosen" and "called"). Superior interpretations of these passages recognize the formative function of such language in the lives of Paul's original readers. Asking *why* Paul wrote the things he did can help reveal the purpose of the material he included.

CONTENT AND CONTEXT

A passage's correct interpretation is simply Paul's intended meaning (including both the content and the force of the words) when he wrote the letter. This meaning is best ascertained from the content of the passage within its immediate literary context.[18] Paul's discourse consists of combinations of words that express thoughts according to the ways the words are arranged together. This arrangement aligns with the grammatical and syntactical norms of a language, which consist of language patterns that function in the service of conveying meaning.[19] To grasp the meaning of a verse or passage, readers must spend time becoming acquainted with the details of the content, looking at word definitions and the grammatical and syntactical features of a sentence. Students must become deeply familiar with the verse or passage through repeated reading and giving focused attention to each clause or phrase. Since few of us are studying Paul's letters in the original Greek, we should consult multiple translations (giving preference to rather literal translations) to gain as accurate a view of the content as possible.

Beyond the actual words and content of the passage itself, nothing provides better guidance for interpretation than the context in which the content appears. Context also assists us in the vital task of tracing the argument of the letter. Letters are written as wholes, to be read from start to finish. When you put together a puzzle, every piece fits and contributes to the larger picture. In Paul's letters, the individual passages contribute to the larger message. That, in turn, helps us see how each section of the letter fits into the broader argument.

The nature of language is that words, sentences, and even paragraphs have meaning only within a broader context. Words alone don't have a fixed meaning. For instance, the word "flesh" (σάρξ) has a range of meanings in Paul's letters. The actual meaning in any given place depends on the words and ideas surrounding that word. In 1 Corinthians 3:1–3 flesh has a negative connotation that is in contrast to spiritual maturity. But in 1 Corinthians 15:39, flesh describes physical bodies. The same word

---

18.   See Fee and Stuart, *How to Read the Bible for All Its Worth*, 27–28.

19.   It is helpful to think about grammar as the study of how the various forms of words communicate meaning, while syntax looks at the purposeful organization of words within sentences (J. William Johnston, "Grammatical Analysis: Making Connections," in Bock and Fanning, *Interpreting the New Testament Text*, 57).

has different meanings in different contexts. The same goes for sentences. When some people read Philippians 4:13 ("I can do all things through him who strengthens me," ESV) in isolation, they conclude that God will help them achieve their dreams. But in context, it is clear that Paul is saying that even when his dreams come crashing down (through setbacks or lack of basic resources) God gives him the strength to endure. Even the meaning of entire paragraphs depends on the contributions of neighboring paragraphs. In 1 Corinthians 9:1–12a Paul's doesn't defend the rights of apostles in order to secure a more comfortable life for himself. On the contrary, Paul highlights those apostolic rights before showing how he has discarded those rights for the sake of a more effective ministry (1 Cor. 9:12b–23). His personal example supports what he has challenged his readers to do in the preceding section (1 Cor. 8:1–13)—to be willing to sacrifice their own rights out of concern for others' spiritual well-being.

Let's examine a well-known verse to observe the power of content and context in action. In Romans 8:28 Paul proclaims, "And we know that in all things God works for the good of those who love him, who have been called according to his purpose." First, we'll analyze the content of the verse. A check of different translations reveals the consistent presence of "and," a conjunction that ties this verse to the one prior to it. This further emphasizes the importance of reading this verse in context, which we will do shortly. Paul's insertion of "we know" indicates that he is communicating a truth that is already familiar to his readers.[20] One discrepancy in the translations is whether God is the explicit subject of "works for the good." The absence of God as a stated subject (in ESV, NKJV, NET, NRSV, HCSB) suggests that the other translations (NIV, NASB, NLT) are inserting God as the understood subject. This involves a judgment call on the part of the translators (it could be "God works all things together" or "all things work together").[21] The idea of "working together" implies a greater plan that makes sense of the discrete events that occur in a person's life. Paul's choice of present tense for "works together" gives this assurance a timeless quality (not something confined to the past or hoped for in the future alone). Paul's use of "all" captures the unlimited scope of events, whether good or bad, that get worked together for a larger purpose. The working together results in "the good," and this good is experienced by a specific group that is described in two complementary ways. First, they are "those who love him (God)," and second, they are "those who have been called according to his purpose." The first description recognizes the recipients

---

20. The insights of speech-act theory can be applied here to surmise that "we know" subtly strengthens the force of the whole statement by framing it as knowledge the readers already know but just need to re-implement in their thinking.

21. The Greek original does not include God as a stated subject. Paul's idea that "all things work together for the good" likely assumes God as the sovereign agent behind this outcome. This would fit both the surrounding context and Paul's overall theology in his letters.

as actively involved in their spiritual lives. They love God in the midst of his greater oversight of their lives. The second qualifier uses the significant word "called," which surfaces again in Romans 8:30 and shifts the focus to God's initiative. Their calling is "according to his (God's) purpose," which provides clearer definition of what God's calling of these believers looks like. He calls them in view of the purpose he has for them.

On its own, the verse assures us of God's benevolent intentions towards believers, but what that looks like remains ambiguous apart from the greater context. Does this mean that God spares believers from difficult experiences in life? Or that something good will always come out of tough times? How do you understand this verse?

Look at the larger context of Romans 8:28. Paul initiates a discussion about Christian suffering and glory in Romans 8:17–18. Paul does not shy away from the painful reality of suffering, though he notes how suffering drives the children of God towards hope and longing for God's ultimate deliverance (Rom. 8:18–25). Believers, who are living in the "not yet" era, in which they are still exposed to the corruption of a fallen creation, groan for that day of God's arrival. Along the way God's Spirit assists believers in their prayers for strength and hope (Rom. 8:26–27). Note that the Spirit prays specifically "in accordance with the will of God" when believers "do not know what we ought to pray for." The Spirit taps into God's wiser, better plans when believers can't see those plans in the midst of the fog of life.

Within this context, we encounter the promise that God is always working for his greater purposes and for believers' ultimate benefit (Rom. 8:28). Contextually, these purposes and believers' ultimate benefit (8:28) must align with God's perfect will (8:27). Believers rest in the assurance that God is carrying out his perfect plans for their world and their lives, even when they feel lost in the fog. The verses that follow proceed to unfold the specifics of that plan. God is conforming his chosen and redeemed people into the image of his Son, who shares his life and status as Son with his many brothers and sisters (Rom. 8:29). This process reaches its climax when believers experience the full glory of Christ when he returns (8:30).

The context of Romans 8:28 illuminates the meaning of the verse. When God promises to work for believers' good, he does *not* promise to rearrange temporary circumstances so that believers can be delivered from hardship or disappointment. Rather, he affirms his commitment to continuing the good work of spiritual transformation that he has already started in believers' lives and is committed to completing (see also Phil. 1:6). God's good work is so much greater and more permanent than the "good work" his children often long for from him. But the Spirit that God has given to dwell in believers' lives helps shape our prayers and expectations in the direction of God's greater good work for our lives.

INTERPRETIVE FALLIBILITY AND TRUTH-SEEKING

The best biblical interpreters know their limits. Though they diligently pursue interpretations that do justice to Paul's arguments and aims, they realize that their interpretations are prone to bias and the constraints of their limited experiences and perspectives. They retain a healthy suspicion about the influence of the pre-understandings they bring to Paul's letters. Humble interpreters also know that the wonders of God are beyond their complete comprehension. They seek God with sincerity and a hunger for truth, but they admit that they can never exhaust their knowledge of God in this lifetime. Paul himself acknowledged the following: "For now we see only a reflection as in a mirror; then we shall see face to face. Now I know in part; then I shall know fully, even as I am fully known" (1 Cor. 13:12).

As fallible interpreters we must always hold our interpretations loosely, checking them against what other believers think and what Christians have understood throughout history. God never designed us to be independent interpreters who try to grow spiritually in isolation from other believers. Ephesians 4:11–16 describes the beautiful picture of believers growing together, as part of a larger body, with teachers and pastors playing important roles. That growth can be supported by our individual Bible study, but individual Bible study does not replace participation in local churches, where we study the Bible together and hear the Bible read, taught, and preached.[22]

This humble attitude in interpretation shouldn't diminish our eagerness to seek truth. Sincere interpreters genuinely value God's truth over any convenient manipulations of truth for self-serving ends. Proverbs 23:23 gives the following exhortation to believers: "Buy truth and do not sell it, get wisdom and instruction and understanding" (NASB). The best interpreters eagerly seek God's truth and invest the time and focus needed to do so. We can read Paul's letters with optimism about our ability to understand them and glean wisdom from them. Our humility and zeal can work together when we study Paul's letters. We humbly view our interpretations as provisional and open to further adjustment. But that very commitment to ongoing refinement keeps us hungry to study Paul's letters and seek greater understanding. We never know when we will have another "aha" moment that will provide greater clarity about Paul's message.

WHY OUR ASSUMPTIONS ABOUT MEANING AND INTERPRETIVE PRACTICES MATTER

A few years ago I was on a jury in a criminal case that involved some serious charges. We heard testimony from various people involved in the

---

22. See also Timothy Ward, *Words of Life: Scripture as the Living and Active Word of God* (Downers Grove, IL: IVP Academic, 2009), 171–74.

case, including a victim, the defendant, police investigators, and technical experts. The prosecutor and the defense attorney offered divergent theories about what happened in the case. The jury was introduced to concepts such as accomplice liability, the difference between force and the threat of force, and differing degrees of counts against the accused. The judge informed us that it was our job to understand the relevant sections of law and apply those to the evidence we heard. We were not supposed to speculate on events beyond what was presented or bring in our own cultural assumptions to decide on guilt or innocence. That was easier said than done! It took a conscious effort to let the evidence speak for itself and keep a narrow focus on interpreting and applying the law. But we realized what was at stake—justice for the victim and a fair trial for the defendant.

The stakes are high for how we understand and carry out our task of interpreting Paul's letters. Consider for a moment the personal consequences of abandoning the pursuit of the correct meaning of a passage. Motivation gets undercut when we are not convinced that there is a meaning worth pursuing. Habits of regular Bible study that engage both mind and heart feed on the belief that objective truth can be found in Paul's letters. Self-deception becomes a greater risk without a commitment to a stable meaning. We are too prone to distorting passages to better suit our skewed visions of faith or to stay more in step with the fashionable values of the day. Awareness of the intentionality of communication acts as an anchor to keep us grounded in what God has revealed about himself, through Paul.

Nurturing a common faith within the church also depends on believing that we can retrieve the original meaning of Paul's letters. Growth in Christ is a shared endeavor, and that growth springs from knowledge and understanding of how God has revealed himself in the Scriptures. The English pastor Charles Simeon once said about his preaching, "My endeavor is to bring out of Scripture what is there, not to thrust in what I think might be there."[23] We need that same commitment in our churches today. Healthy churches seek the Scriptures together and stand ready to live according to what they discover.[24] In order to have constructive, growth-inducing conversations about the meaning of Paul's letters, we need a shared target—the original meaning Paul intended for a passage. Multiple, scattered, subjective interpretations will not lead the church on the path toward understanding and maturity. That is more of a recipe for splintering and factions. As we will see in the next chapter, even good

---

23.   Simeon's quote is preserved in Handley Carr Glyn Moule, *Charles Simeon* (London: Methuen & Co., 1892), 97.

24.   Wise churches also respect the consensus beliefs developed throughout the centuries of the church. Paul's own affirmations of central Christian beliefs (1 Cor. 15:3–5; Eph. 4:4–6; 2 Tim. 2:8) continue to be expressed in the rule of faith, the ecumenical creeds, and later church confessions and doctrinal statements. Believers and churches read the Bible with the wisdom of nearly two thousand years of church history ringing in their ears.

applications, which can be more varied in expression, should emerge from credible, supported interpretations of passages.

CONCLUSION

Interpretation and application are both valuable endeavors, but interpretation is the first task. Interpretation seeks original meaning, while application works from the implications and significance of the text. Accordingly, interpretation privileges the intended meaning and desired effects of the author's discourse. Paul's communicative purpose establishes the criteria for the best interpretation of any given passage. Paul reveals his purpose through the words he chooses and the overall context of what he writes in a letter, so reading passages carefully in context is our most valuable strategy for arriving at the best interpretation of Paul's material.

The task of humble but fruitful interpretation requires prayerful focus, use of consistent and tested methods, and ongoing motivation to understand Paul's letters. Quality interpretation of Paul's letters is characterized by careful observation, curiosity, and attention to literary form and context. When we encounter a passage whose correct interpretation seems elusive, we may need to double down on our efforts to discern the best interpretation, in conversation with believers from the past and present.

■ ■ ■

CHAPTER NINE

HOW CAN I WISELY APPLY PAUL'S TEACHINGS?

S ometimes people characterize themselves or others as "'book smart' but not 'street smart.'" This terminology recognizes a difference between knowing the right answers for a test and being equipped to make wise decisions out in the real world. What should you do if you get a flat tire on the road? Knowing the physics of simple machines and mechanical advantage won't help if you can't figure out how the parts of your tire jack fit together!

Bible readers also get off track when they accumulate biblical knowledge without putting into practice what they are reading. Christianity is meant to be lived, not just understood. Biblical truth is fuel for a growing relationship with God. Knowing how to apply two-thousand-year-old texts in beneficial and appropriate ways is not automatic. It takes wisdom to move from the original meaning of Paul's letters to faithful responses that capture the potential of Paul's teachings for transformed living in current contexts. But as with all worthwhile endeavors, there are ways to develop proficiency in practicing good application.

RESPONDING TO PAUL'S LETTERS AS DIVINE DISCOURSE

With typical literature we don't automatically prepare to apply what we read. Yes, thoughtful literature may cause us to reflect on our lives and apply lessons from what we have encountered, but we don't often view application as central to the process of reading. Why do we give such attention to application with Paul's letters? These letters written nearly two thousand years ago are significant to our lives today, because they convey not only human discourse but also divine discourse. God appointed Paul and other sanctioned spokespersons to teach divine truth that has abiding authority for the church. God's chosen servants spoke as ambassadors on God's behalf (Mark 3:13–15; John 14:26; 16:13–15; 1 Cor. 4:1; 15:3–11; 2

Cor. 5:18–20; Gal. 1:1, 11–12; 1 Thess. 2:13; 2 Peter 3:16).[1] These apostolic pioneers for the church taught truths whose value was not confined to the original readers alone. The reach of their teachings extended to all nations and even to the generations beyond them (see Matt. 28:18–20; John 17:20; Acts 1:8; Eph. 2:20; 2 Tim. 2:2; Titus 3:8; 2 Peter 3:2; Jude 17).[2]

Believers today view Paul's letters in the same way that Paul viewed the Old Testament. According to Paul, in the Old Testament God speaks truths that are still authoritative and significant for new covenant believers, once allowances are made for the effects of Christ's redemptive ministry (Rom. 3:23–24; 15:4; 1 Cor. 10:11; 2 Tim. 3:15–17; see also 1 Peter 1:10–12). The apostle Paul and other authors of New Testament documents likewise fulfill their divinely ordained responsibility to announce spiritual truths that have enduring relevance for all believers.[3] We embrace what Paul says as beneficial and normative for our lives today since Paul writes as one of God's authorized representatives, imparting God's truth to God's people. That means that beyond Paul's goals for his original readers, we need to consider God's goals for us through Paul's teachings. This puts the task of application front and center for readers of Paul's letters.

God speaks through Paul's words in order to bring about a response or change in our lives. In Isaiah 55:10–11 God says, "As the rain and the snow come down from heaven, and do not return to it without watering the earth and making it bud and flourish, so that it yields seed for the sower and bread for the eater, so is my word that goes out from my mouth: It will not return to me empty, but will accomplish what I desire and achieve the purpose for which I sent it." God's words through Paul are designed to strengthen and nurture the relationship God desires with us. God uses Paul's letters, which God breathed out by his Spirit, to teach, rebuke, correct, and train us (2 Tim. 3:16). The Holy Spirit that dwells in us helps make God's message effective in our lives. This reminds us to view Bible verses not as mere static words on a page but as part of God's communicative and relational overtures to his people.[4] We read, interpret, apply, and respond to Paul's letters because we cherish the relationship that grows through that process.

FROM INTERPRETATION TO APPLICATION

Interpretation and application go hand in hand. Interpretation without application is woefully incomplete, while application unmoored from interpretation is too arbitrary. Both interpretation and application require

---

1. See the extended discussion of this topic in the chapter, "Why Should I Listen to Paul?"
2. On this point, see also Ward, *Words of Life*, 43.
3. The association between the commissioning of Old Testament prophets and New Testament apostles is explored in Wolterstorff, *Divine Discourse*, 50–51, 288–95.
4. Ward provides helpful insights into the ways that God communicates through the human authors of Scripture (Ward, *Words of Life*, 78–89).

discipline, skill, and practice. Yes, there is something instinctive about reading to understand (interpretation) and modifying beliefs, values, attitudes, or practices based on what we have read (application). But we often encounter difficult cases in both interpretation and application that are not so straightforward. Being informed about the best principles and practices for interpreting and applying prepares us to make the most of our time studying the Bible. We looked primarily at interpretation in the last chapter, so now we will ponder application.

When we move from interpretation to application we step out of the readers' world into our world. The particular setting and circumstances of the original readers give way to the specific settings and circumstances of the world we live in. We might think of this as the difference between working within the text (interpretation) and venturing out beyond the text (application). The original meaning in the readers' world continues to guide our thinking, but with application we probe the implications and significance of that original meaning to our current settings and challenges. Paul's original, intended meaning creates ripple effects of implications that reach the shores of our lives, touching significant needs, concerns, and dreams. We interpret the original meaning with the expectation of also applying what we read, knowing that the same Spirit who empowered Paul in his ministry and teachings seeks to implant Paul's teachings into the soils of our lives (1 Cor. 2:11–16; 2 Cor. 3:12–4:6; Gal. 5:16–26; Eph. 1:17–19; Col. 1:9–13; 2 Tim. 2:7; see also Mark 4:1–20 and parallels).

One way that interpretation sets the stage for application is in the intended purpose of any given section of discourse. As we learned from the previous chapter on interpretation, we seek the original meaning of Paul's letters by examining both what Paul said (the content) and why he said it (the purpose). Both of these components should shape our application as well. The content of Paul's teaching supplies the subject matter for our application, but the purpose or intended force of the utterance guides the direction of our response. Simply put, different types of speech call forth different responses. Paul expects readers to respond to commands with obedience and rebukes with repentance. When Paul praises God, he invites readers to join in with wonder and adulation, and Paul's thanksgivings turn readers' attention to what they also ought to give thanks for.

For us, this means that application shouldn't be reduced to a series of character-improvement steps. Sensitive application encompasses a whole range of prayerful responses to Paul's teachings. Paul's letters impact believers cognitively, affectively, and volitionally. In other words, his teachings influence how we think, what we feel, and what we do. Paul's discourse elicits responses that affect the whole person, so we should seek to follow these prompts with application that involves all aspects of our being.

APPLYING ACROSS TIME AND CULTURE

When we apply Paul's letters we must keep in mind our location as both spiritual insiders and cultural outsiders.[5] Our insider credentials create promising footholds for application, while the reality that we are stepping into unfamiliar cultural terrain means that we should approach the climb with great care.

Don't forget how much we share in common with the original recipients of Paul's letters. We live in the same era of salvation history as they did, which creates much common ground.[6] We look back to the same pivotal moments in God's saving plans and value a shared history that makes sense of where we are today. All believers located in this new covenant era are joined in a permanent, internally transforming relationship with God through Jesus Christ. We all live between the resurrection and return of Christ. God has given all believers his indwelling and empowering Spirit to guide us in this interim period. We are all part of God's universal church, reflecting God's truth, love, holiness, and reign to a world that is separated from him. We are all called to be one as a diverse but unified body whose members have been redeemed by God and reconciled to him. Because of these commonalities, we can confidently engage the content of Paul's letters with an expectation that they will still be relevant and powerful for our lives today.

Even with this baseline of shared life in Christ, we are still outsiders to the historical and cultural context of Paul and his first readers. There are thus instances in which we have to make significant adjustments in order to apply Paul's teachings in appropriate ways. One general rule about the turn from interpretation to application is that the more the original discourse was shaped by the occasion of the letter, the more we will need to be intentional about adapting our applications to our distinct contexts. Conversely, when the letter's original occasion did not exert a pronounced influence on what Paul taught in a passage, we will be able to apply Paul's words more directly into our contemporary settings. When Paul's discourse can be fitted for our circumstances without major

---

5. People who aren't children of God through Christ will read Paul's letters as both spiritual and cultural outsiders, increasing the likelihood that they will find Paul's message about Christ to be "foolishness" (1 Cor. 1:18; 2:7–8). Paul wrote his letters to and for believers in Christ.

6. This makes applying New Testament letters more clear-cut than applying Old Testament material or even the Gospels. The people of God in the Old Testament related to God within old covenant parameters, so many of the commands and promises made sense specifically within that broader system. In the Gospels, Jesus's followers lived in a transition period between Christ's incarnation on the one hand and his death and resurrection on the other. Their circumstances were thus governed by a different sort of "already and not yet" than ours, which is book-ended by Christ's resurrection (and ascension) and his return. Material in the Old Testament and the Gospels is still God's truth for us, but we have to factor in spiritual settings that are more foreign to us than the spiritual backdrop in Paul's letters.

reconfiguration, identifying valid applications is quite straightforward. Of course, the actual *doing* of the application still looms as a formidable personal challenge! But at least in many instances we can be confident about how to begin responding to God's words through Paul. That still leaves the challenging passages that require more thought and skill in crafting legitimate applications.

Undergirded by the faith we share with Paul's initial readers, we carefully delve into letters that first make sense within an original historical setting. Along the way, we keep our eyes open to how Paul's messages need to be put into action in much different settings today. This process requires detecting which concepts ingrained in Paul's letters are not limited to single contexts but pertain more broadly to believers everywhere.

TRUTH CONTEXTUALIZED THEN AND NOW

Readers of Paul's letters carry teachings from a distant world into their own settings. Reading with alertness to both the original historical context as well as our current cultural contexts ensures that we don't misapply what we read. Nevertheless, this transition from interpretation to application includes an intermediate step. We don't teleport immediately from one particular world (theirs) to another particular world (ours). The journey is more like an airplane flight, in which we spend some time in the air, acclimating to the "time change," and thinking about the universal relevance of Paul's teaching. Sometimes we need little time in the air, when the circumstances in Paul's original setting match quite well with our current environment. With other passages we need more time during the flight, when certain cultural features relevant to Paul's world seem quite foreign to our settings. In both cases, we ponder the universal, enduring ideas within Paul's teachings that have value for our lives. Then, we apply these truths in concrete ways to our lives. This process spotlights what is known as the contextualization of truth.[7]

Paul himself demonstrates the contextualization of truth in his letters. Paul draws upon ideas and spiritual principles and contextualizes them for his readers' circumstances. He takes universally significant truths and embeds them into specific settings. Our task is to do the same thing, weaving his teachings into our contexts. That means we work ground-up from Paul's letters, looking at specific teachings tailored for Paul's original readers in order to find the overarching truths inherent in those teachings. Then we move back down to our world, returning with truths that can be integrated into our distinct settings.[8]

---

7. For a more comprehensive analysis of this topic, see Grant R. Osborne, *The Hermeneutical Spiral: A Comprehensive Introduction to Biblical Interpretation* (Downers Grove, IL: InterVarsity, 1991), 326–38.
8. Ibid., 335.

This process involves carefully inspecting the particularities of Paul's guidance to his first readers in search of broader undercurrents or implications in his teachings. To do so, we ask the question, "What underlying theological values or principles does Paul appear to draw upon in his specific instructions?" For instance, in his counsel to married and single Christians in 1 Corinthians 7, Paul affirms values such as undivided devotion to God, keeping commitments, mutuality in marriage, and purity. Later, in his discussion of spiritual gifts, prophecy, and tongues (1 Cor. 12–14) Paul extols orderly worship, the priority of love, the goal of edification, and appreciation for diverse gifts. In Romans 14:1–15:5 the values of harmony among believers, refraining from judging others, keeping a clear conscience before God, freedom in Christ, and concern for the spiritual health of others permeate Paul's practical advice to the weak and strong.

In each of these passages, Paul reflects universally pertinent principles (for believers living within the new covenant era) and applies them to the questions and challenges the original readers faced. The coherent ideas that form the substructure of Paul's belief system materialize in his advice to readers in their specific circumstances. By looking at Paul's actual teachings in their particularity we can infer the basic contours of that underlying set of guiding principles. This also means that the more acquainted we are with Paul's overall theology, the more readily we will recognize the theological principles operating within his specific teachings.

Once we discern the fundamental theological ideas inherent in a passage, we proceed to apply that wisdom to current contexts. Ideally, we want to find points of contact between the original circumstances and current circumstances, so that the enduring truth we found can be suitably applied to the new context.[9] While historical and cultural gaps will be present with any application, we can still identify situations in which similar spiritual or relational dynamics are in play. For example, we can find similar currents at work between promoting oneness in Christ between Jews and Gentiles (Rom. 10:12; Gal. 3:28; Col. 3:11) and cultivating unity in Christ among believers of different backgrounds, countries, and cultures today. Paul's instructions for the Philippians to warmly welcome Epaphroditus (Phil. 2:25–30), who had to return prematurely from serving Paul in prison because of a serious illness, corresponds to honoring those who have served well in some ministry or volunteer role but are stepping aside ahead of schedule because of events beyond their control. Contextualization seeks to preserve the spirit of Paul's teachings in countless similar situations that have arisen since he first wrote.

---

9. Osborne, *Hermeneutical Spiral*, 334; Fee and Stuart, *How to Read the Bible for All Its Worth*, 75–80.

CHARACTERISTICS OF LEGITIMATE APPLICATIONS

The Spirit helps different believers and churches apply Paul's teachings in numerous ways, according to how the implications of a passage intersect with the needs of the moment. There is no single "correct" application for a passage in Paul's letters. But we can still distinguish between wise and misguided applications by asking some evaluative questions. These questions serve as quality checks, filtering out applications that aren't faithful to the specific passage or Paul's broader theology, or that impose extraneous ancient cultural standards that believers today aren't required to adopt.

First, have we derived the application from the original meaning of the passage? Paul's intended meaning should direct the course of the resulting application. Second, does the application prioritize one of the major points of the passage, rather than an incidental detail that Paul never intended to hold up as a template? Learn to discern Paul's preferred responses from the content, purpose, and tone of the passage. Third, does the application keep in mind the totality of Paul's teachings and even the broader witness of the Scriptures? Bible readers should avoid applying an individual passage in a way that is oblivious to teaching from elsewhere in Scripture. For example, applying either 1 Corinthians 7:25–35 (which praises the spiritual advantages of singleness) or Ephesians 5:22–33 (which captures the spiritual beauty of marriage) in isolation, without considering the teaching from the other passage, might lead us to devalue either marriage or singleness among believers. But the existence of both passages confirms that Paul championed both options. Fourth, does the application leave behind unnecessary ancient cultural baggage that Paul dealt with but did not advocate in his teaching? For instance, the head coverings mentioned in 1 Corinthians 11:2–16 were not Paul's idea but were cultural givens in that setting. We can draw upon Paul's wisdom for navigating the head-covering controversy without implementing the actual practice of using head coverings.[10]

FOSTERING MEANINGFUL APPLICATION

We should insist on legitimate applications, but legitimate applications may still be ineffective applications. Our habits of Bible study don't often lead to fruitful application. Specifically, we tend to practice shallow, unreflective, and unimaginative reading. Good application stems from ruminating over the spiritual insights in Paul's letters as well as remaining alert and open to creative expressions of those truths in our lives.

Quality Bible study allows ample time for reflection and internalization in the transition from interpretation to application. Reflective

---

10.   See Fee and Stuart, *How to Read the Bible for All Its Worth*, 83.

reading enhances responsive reading. Spiritual truth needs to percolate in our thoughts in order to make a lasting difference. The specific words, phrases, and clauses of a passage need to circulate in our minds. There are a number of Scripture engagement methods that force us to slow down and focus long enough to facilitate reading for spiritual growth.[11] The process of prayerful reflection and savoring truth invites the Spirit to use God's truth to comfort, convict, motivate, and strengthen us as needed.

Another important part of the application process is imagination. Readers should try to imagine how God's truths in Paul's letters could make a difference in the various dimensions of their lives. Truth should be applied in areas of worship, relationships, stewardship, and obedience. When we read Paul's letters we should open ourselves to the sanctifying work of the Spirit in these different spheres. We should be prepared to be awakened, unsettled, and shaken from the status quo. Develop a vivid picture of how God's message to you needs to take shape in your life. Imagine how God could change a specific area of your life using the truth you encountered in Paul's letters.

Searching for specific, even measurable action points can help ensure that our stated applications are not just empty ideals. We want to articulate how we will follow through on the application steps we have identified. Specific plans of action can also become fodder for prayer, as we look to God for strength and wisdom to integrate these responses into our lives.

APPLICATION—EXAMPLES

Here are three examples of how the process works. The first is an example in which the teaching was general enough so that the original and current contextualization looks quite similar. The second example is one in which the original teaching was targeted towards a highly specific occasion, but where the transfer of truth to other settings is still quite clear. The third is one in which the reader has to make significant adjustments to incorporate the broader truths into current realities.

Let's start with 1 Thessalonians 5:4–11, which is part of Paul's thorough instructions on living in expectation of Christ's return. Though the Thessalonian believers may have experienced some confusion over eschatological teachings (1 Thess. 4:13), Paul approaches the subject generally by reiterating many of Jesus's own teachings about his return. In the passage Paul develops a sharp contrast between children of light and children of darkness. Children of darkness are oblivious to Christ's imminent arrival and live for their own pleasures. Children of light, however, are alert and vigilant, knowing that their Lord might return at any time. Paul exhorts

---

11. | Bible Gateway hosts an extensive collection of helpful articles on Scripture Engagement prepared by the Taylor University Center for Scripture Engagement: https://www.biblegateway.com/resources/scripture-engagement.

his readers to live in keeping with their identity as children of light. They should actively arm themselves with faith, love, and hope for the spiritual challenges they face. They should rely especially on the salvation and eternal life that Christ secured for them when he died for them, and they should encourage each other with the hope of his return.

All of these truths from 1 Thessalonians 5:4–11 relate directly to the believer's life today. We can apply points from 1 Thessalonians 5:4–11 as directly as the original readers were expected to. Be strengthened in our identity as children of light. Live as children of light by embodying the virtues of faith, love, and hope. Express praise and thanks for Christ's sacrificial death for us and his certain triumphant return. In this case, the applications are quite straightforward. They now just need to be expressed in specific and creative ways in the face of the challenges and opportunities of our current environment. Many other passages in Paul's letters carry over to our world in similarly clear-cut ways.

Our second example provides us with communication about a very specific episode in the readers' lives. In 2 Corinthians 2:5–11 Paul revisits a painful situation that had likely arisen when one of the Corinthian believers had openly resisted Paul's input found within the letter of 1 Corinthians. When Paul had confronted this defiance it had caused strain in his relationship with the Corinthians, but they had eventually responded to his insistence that the troublemaker repent.[12] In this passage, Paul calls for restoration of the offender and a reaffirmation of love for him. Paul assures church members that he has added his own forgiveness to theirs, so that there is no lingering animosity between Paul and the Corinthians. Any relational affronts have been resolved in Christ's sight, which protects them from Satan's divisive schemes.

Unlike with our first example, the occasion for this passage features prominently in our interpretation. A specific incident looms in the background of the passage, and while Paul does not elaborate on the details of the confrontation, both he and the readers were well aware of them. But note several universal truths that still emerge from the passage. First, sin leads to grief that is destructive, but appropriate confrontation about the sin can bring constructive grief, leading to repentance (2 Cor. 2:5–6). Second, the outcome of repentance should be the restoration of the repentant individual to good standing within the church, accompanied by unambiguous affirmations of love for the individual (2 Cor. 2:7–8). Third, forgiveness is central to preserving the unity and spiritual health of a church (2 Cor. 2:10–11). We might apply these general truths by deciding to speak frank but gentle truth to a fellow believer who has fallen into sin and destructive patterns of living. Or, we could help a returning prodigal get warmly welcomed and reassimilated into healthy Christian fellowship. Finally, we could work toward forgiveness and

12.   See Bruce, *Apostle of the Heart Set Free*, 274–75.

reconciliation in a specific strained relationship. When we measure these applications against the criteria for legitimate applications (discussed in an earlier section), we can confirm that they are faithful to the parts and whole of 2 Corinthians 2:5–11 and that they accord with Paul's teachings elsewhere. Furthermore the applications successfully retain central truths of the passage without recklessly replicating parts of the passage that don't transfer smoothly to our lives (for instance, we aren't apostles and thus should be wary of testing others' obedience to us, as Paul did according to verse 9).

Finally, we'll look at a classic example of a passage that assumes a very specific cultural backdrop that is quite unfamiliar to our world.[13] In 1 Corinthians 8 Paul begins an extensive discussion about whether believers should eat meat that has been sacrificed previously to idols.[14] Interpreting this passage well requires careful definitions of "weak" and "strong" and "conscience," sensitivity to how Paul subtly affirms but also modifies the views of his readers, and some awareness of the ways meat moved from temples to marketplaces and residents' homes. Once we have done our due diligence with interpretation, we can locate some theological principles from the passages. First, believers should prioritize loving other believers over having spiritually enlightened views on disputed matters. Second, in their choices about disputed matters believers should avoid harming the consciences of other believers by inducing them to go against their convictions. Third, Christ died for all believers, including weak believers, and he identifies himself with the well-being of weak believers.

The challenge of applying the passage consists in recognizing comparable contemporary situations into which to deploy these principles. In parts of east and southeast Asia I have encountered cultural contexts that resembled the circumstances that Paul described in 1 Corinthians 8. Such circumstances are relatively rare in North America, on the other hand. How can these principles still be applied in a legitimate manner? What are some scenarios in which similar issues surface? The weak believers in Corinth were concerned that meat offered to idols was spiritually contaminated, even if they were served the meat in a spiritually neutral setting. Similar misgivings could arise with the practice of Halloween, which is often celebrated in neutral ways but has some darker spiritual connotations for some people who know the history of the holiday. Could believers appeal to Paul's teachings from the passage for their own decisions about participating or not participating in Halloween? The "strong" could find reasons from the passage to enjoy their freedom, knowing that the spiritual forces sometimes associated

---

13.   See the similar treatment of this passage in Fee and Stuart, *How to Read the Bible for All Its Worth*, 77–79.

14.   The topic resurfaces in 1 Corinthians 10.

with Halloween have no real power in their lives.[15] At the same time, those same families could still be sensitive to the consciences of those around them when deciding whether to participate in neighborhood Halloween activities or in some alternative such as a church festival. As Paul reminds us, love is more important than enlightenment.

The comparisons to the situation of 1 Corinthians 8 are less obvious but still in the ballpark concerning the question of drinking alcohol in moderation.[16] Some "strong" Christians enjoy limited quantities of alcohol in good conscience, supported by their knowledge that the Bible doesn't prohibit moderate alcohol consumption. Some "weak" Christians worry about their own susceptibility to addiction or feel that alcohol's connection with drunkenness and other social vices in many cultures creates a guilt by association, so they abstain from all drinking. The connections to the original disagreements about eating meat dedicated to idols are less pronounced than was the case with Halloween, since drinking alcohol doesn't have the same overt associations with spiritual forces. But we could still carefully apply some of Paul's guidance about eating meat sacrificed to idols to our questions about drinking. The principles of others-centeredness and respecting convictions and conscience can be applied beneficially as we make decisions about when and where to drink (if at all). As with eating meat dedicated to idols, "strong" believers could make distinctions between the different settings in which alcohol is served. Paul appears to promote different approaches depending on whether the meat was served at the temple (1 Cor. 8:10), sold in the markets (1 Cor. 10:25), or shared at an acquaintance's home (1 Cor. 10:27). A Christian today might choose to abstain from drinking in certain off-campus parties or bars while having a drink when they are served wine at a friend's house, for instance, based on principles from 1 Corinthians 8 and 10.[17] Since the question of drinking doesn't correspond as neatly to the issue of meat sacrificed to idols, Christians might hold their conclusions from these passages more loosely and avoid dogmatism in their discussions with others.

CONCLUSION

Applying Paul's letters is at once both a simple, natural part of reading the Bible and a complex endeavor that requires skill, discernment, and imagination. Christians do well to appreciate the great privilege of meeting

---

15. This application would hold for the more family-oriented expressions of Halloween. In Paul's continuing discussions of meat offered to idols (1 Cor. 10) he does condemn more direct entanglements in idolatry (1 Cor. 10:14, 20–21), which should make us wary of any Halloween practice that blatantly glorifies evil.

16. Excessive drinking and drunkenness is more clearly prohibited in Paul's letters (Rom. 13:13; Gal. 5:21; Eph. 5:18).

17. Other factors to consider, not as connected to the passage itself, include the legal drinking age in various countries as well as the cultural norms of those countries with regard to drinking.

with God when we read Paul's letters, since God's Spirit moves to apply truths to our lives through the process of Bible reading. Sincere truth-seekers can expect to see God knit the powerful ideas of the Bible into their lives. Still, wise steps of application that take into account the original content, purpose, and context of a passage, discern broader theological truths within the passage, and creatively import those truths into modern contexts increase the potential for fruitful application. This important part of Bible study is both an art and a science that offers room for growth through practice and experience.

■ ■ ■

CHAPTER TEN

WHAT ARE SOME SPECIFIC INTERPRETIVE CHALLENGES IN PAUL'S LETTERS?

I magine a man who is about to attend his first family reunion with his fiancée's relatives. He is eager to become more acquainted with his fiancée's world, and he knows some general things about her family and its history, but he is still hesitant about plunging into a situation with so many unknowns. Once his fiancée steps in to help by providing details about each of her relatives and their charming peculiarities and interrelationships, he feels much more confident about meeting everyone.

I hope that this chapter will help you become more acquainted with Paul's letters by alerting you to some of the specific challenges you will encounter when you study them. Paul's letters as a whole are quite accessible to the motivated reader, but certain passages can be intimidating or possess unexpected complexity. This chapter will introduce you to some interesting literary features and debated passages in the various letters of Paul. We will also examine a procedure for weighing strengths and weaknesses of competing interpretive proposals for the meaning of debated passages in Paul. Instead of offering verdicts on preferred interpretive options for contested passages, this chapter will orient you to the issues and prepare you to make informed decisions on the most likely meanings of the passages.

ROMANS

Romans, along with Galatians, displays Paul's use of a rhetorical style known as the diatribe. Diatribe style is marked by crisp sentences, logical argumentation, and lively engagement with objections anticipated from imaginary conversation partners.[1] In particular, Paul repeatedly

---

1. For a more exhaustive study see Stanley Kent Stowers, *The Diatribe and Paul's Letter to the Romans*, SBLDS 57 (Chico, CA: Scholars Press, 1981).

uses the Greek μὴ γένοιτο ("by no means!") to reject misguided conclusions people might draw from simplistic interaction with his ideas (Rom. 3:4, 6, 31; 6:2, 15; 7:7, 13; 9:14; 11:1, 11). Note how Paul goes back and forth from question to answer in Romans 3:1–8. Verses 1, 3, 5, and 7 pose questions based on false inferences drawn from Paul's teachings. In verses 2, 4, 6, and 8 Paul definitively dismisses the queries, twice commencing his denunciation with "by no means!" (μὴ γένοιτο, in 3:4, 6). Once you become comfortable with the diatribe style you will be able to appreciate how Paul uses it to drive home points he doesn't want the readers to miss about God's faithfulness, God's law, human sin, and believers' response to the gospel. Readers both then and now get these topics muddled in both understanding and application.

Three sections of Romans often puzzle readers. Romans 2:6–16, 7:7–25, and 9:1–11:36 feature intricate theological discussions that should be interpreted within the broader discourse of the letter. Even with the overall context as a guide, scholars still disagree on the exact meaning of these sections.

In Romans 2:6–16 Paul examines the reality of individuals standing before God at the final judgment and the possibility of being justified before God. Both Jews and Gentiles will face judgment and have their deeds evaluated. Paul affirms some things in this passage that seem to conflict with his views elsewhere. For instance, in verse 7 Paul says, "To those who by persistence in doing good seek glory, honor and immortality, he (God) will give eternal life." Similarly, verse 13 states, "For it is not those who hear the law who are righteous in God's sight, but it is those who obey the law who will be declared righteous." Paul goes on to suggest that the Gentiles' consciences can function as a law and testify to Gentiles' righteousness on occasion (2:14–15). How do these claims align with Paul's teaching about being justified by grace, through faith and not works (Rom. 1:16–17; 3:21–24; 4:4–5; 5:1–2)? We must consider the case that Paul is building throughout the letter and discern how Romans 2:6–16 fits into the broader argument. Two attractive possibilities are that he is anticipating the good works the Spirit produces within Jews and Gentiles who have trusted Christ (Rom. 2:29; 8:3–4), or that he is raising the theoretical possibility of reaching God's standard for righteousness before driving home the reality that sinful Jews and Gentiles all fail to reach that standard (Rom. 3:19–23).[2] As you read the passage with the overall letter in mind, what do you see as Paul's purpose for the section? This difficult passage provides a good opportunity to explore larger questions about how good works should factor into a believer's life.

---

2. Moo sees these as the best options out of a number of possible interpretations (Douglas J. Moo, *The Epistle to the Romans*, NICNT [Grand Rapids: Eerdmans, 1996], 139–43). See also N. T. Wright, "Justification by (Covenantal) Faith to the (Covenantal) Doers: Romans 2 within the Argument of the Letter," *The Covenant Quarterly* 72 (2014): 95–108.

Romans 7:7–25 probably stands out in your mind as a fascinating passage that explores the depths of sin and the continual struggle to overcome it. The meaning of the passage is heavily debated. Does it recount Paul's past or ongoing experience, or does Paul use "I" rhetorically, without describing his own specific battles against sin? By extension, does the passage reflect the experience of a devout Jew that tries to follow the Mosaic law, of a believer in Christ striving for obedience, or of self-empowered humanity more generally?[3] When you investigate the meaning of this passage, try to read it in the broader context of Romans 6–8 and determine what primary question Paul hopes to answer with the vivid discourse in the section. This passage raises important questions. Are Christians doomed to perpetual defeat in their struggles against sin? Should believers feel optimistic or pessimistic about the possibility of overcoming sin? What difference does the indwelling Spirit make for believers?

Similarly, Romans 9–11 should be interpreted according to questions or concerns that lurk behind the chapters.[4] Only then will the treatment of divine election, the concept of a remnant within the people of God, the imagery of the olive tree, and the frequent Old Testament quotations and allusions make better sense. Paul does signal his agenda at several points in the three chapters, so be alert to those clues when you read. Note that after Paul ponders the deep theological issues in these three chapters he concludes with words of amazement and wonder at God's magnificent character and plans. Perhaps we too can emerge from these chapters with a greater appreciation of God's sovereignty, wisdom, and mercy.

FIRST CORINTHIANS

The intriguing "Corinthian slogans" create some interpretive complexities in 1 Corinthians.[5] The slogans approximate the "sound bites" of our day. Sound bites are streamlined and often one-sided summaries of complex topics, often meant to insinuate that the simplified position is all that needs to be said on the matter. Similarly, Corinthian slogans were brief sayings about the Christian life that had a grain of truth to them but were woefully incomplete. Typically, they were used to rationalize an attitude or action about the Christian life, particularly regarding the exercise of Christian freedom. Examples include, "I have the right to do anything" (1 Cor. 6:12; 10:23), which was used to rationalize an extreme application of Christian freedom, and, "An idol is nothing at all in the world" (1 Cor. 8:4), which disregarded any unease someone might feel about partaking

---

3. See Moo, *Romans*, 442–51; Richard N. Longenecker, *The Epistle to the Romans*, NIGTC (Grand Rapids: Eerdmans, 2016), 650–74.
4. See for instance Michael F. Bird, *Romans*, SGBC (Grand Rapids: Zondervan, 2016), 307–11.
5. For a helpful introduction to the topic, see Jay E. Smith, "Slogans in 1 Corinthians," *BSac* 167 (2010): 68–88.

in meat offered to idols. Paul highlights these slogans before showing their inadequacies, bringing up other important considerations the Corinthians had failed to account for. English Bible translations often indicate the likely presence of a slogan by putting the saying in quotation marks.[6]

Some Corinthian slogans are widely acknowledged, while others are contested. For instance, scholars agree that "Food for the stomach and the stomach for food" (1 Cor. 6:13) is one of the aberrant beliefs some of the Corinthians held, but they are split over whether the words that follow ("and God will destroy them both") belong to the slogan as well.[7] Among Bible versions that specify where slogans begin and end, the NIV and NET include the second part in the slogan, while the NRSV, HCSB, and NLT do not. Because the slogans are not marked out explicitly in the original Greek, translators have to make judgment calls about where they begin and end, and whether they are there at all. Other slogans whose existence is debated are, "Every sin a person commits is outside of the body" (1 Cor. 6:18, NET; see also HCSB) and "It is well for a man not to touch a woman" (1 Cor. 7:1, NRSV; see also NET, HCSB).[8]

When we read these passages we should see them as windows into the ongoing two-way communication between Paul and his readers. With the slogans Paul gives voice to positions the Corinthians held before he comments on these positions. To properly interpret the passage containing the slogan, we first need to assess whether the slogan in question does actually represent the Corinthians' sentiments rather than Paul's. That dictates whether we filter the slogan through Paul's rejoinder to it or embrace wholeheartedly the affirmation "as is." Then, once we are confident we have located a Corinthian slogan, we need to interpret, from Paul's response to the slogan, how much Paul challenged or qualified the Corinthians' assumptions.

Paul demonstrates keen insight and theological expertise in the way he confronts the Corinthian slogans that were leading his readers astray. We can learn from his example. We need to perceive and challenge the underlying theological assumptions of errant practices in our churches today. When we see polluted water downstream (disordered practices

---

6. The original Greek does not use quotation marks, and neither does the ESV, NASB, or NKJV. Other versions (NIV, HCSB, NET, NRSV, NLT) insert them to make it more obvious when Paul disassociates himself from the views that are stated.

7. The slogan "Food for the stomach and the stomach for food," taken on its own, may have reflected the flawed view that believers shouldn't resist bodily (or sexual) appetites, since they were considered perfectly "natural." If, on the other hand, the slogan included "and God will destroy them both," the slogan as a whole may have given voice to the mistaken belief that bodily indulgence didn't matter in the end, since only the spiritual realm lasts.

8. Though no major English translation identifies the restriction on women speaking up in the congregational meetings in 1 Corinthians 14:34–35 as a Corinthian slogan, a few scholars have put forward that possibility (see for instance Neil M. Flanagan and Edwina H. Snyder, "Did Paul Put Down Women in First Corinthians 14:34–36?" *Foundations* 24 [1981]: 218–19). The content of 1 Corinthians 14:34–35, consisting of two fairly long sentences, seems to be a poor candidate for a Corinthian slogan.

among believers), we can be sure that the source of the pollution is somewhere upstream (confused theological thinking, often in the form of simplified sound bites). This is true for our own lives as well. Our sins and poor decisions sometimes stem from unchallenged and unbalanced theological beliefs. The Corinthian slogan passages are important passages that require our close attention, thoughtful interpretation, and ready response.

SECOND CORINTHIANS

The challenges in 2 Corinthians involve the overall composition of the letter. Some scholars dispute the *integrity* of the letter, which means that they suspect that the letter in its current form is a compilation of two or more of Paul's writings that were initially separate from one another. Along the same lines, scholars posit that 2 Corinthians contains *interpolations*, or segments of material that were inserted after the original letter was written.[9] These alleged interpolations may have been written by Paul or by someone else.

If you read 2 Corinthians in one sitting, you may notice that the tone seems to shift from the end of chapter 9 to the beginning of chapter 10. Experts have surmised that 2 Corinthians 10–13 was originally part of an earlier "severe" letter (the letter allegedly mentioned in 2 Corinthians 2:2–4, 9; 7:8–9, 12) that later became attached to 2 Corinthians 1–9. Readers will need to balance the evidence of a change in tone against the presence of some common themes in the first and second parts of the letter.[10] The claim that chapters 10–13 were imported from an earlier letter must also account for the reason why two originally independent letters were made to look like a single letter, since the compiler would have had to omit the conclusion to chapters 1–9 and the introduction to chapters 10–13. Furthermore, why was the letter assembled in reverse order (since the theory alleges that chapters 10–13 were written first)?

There are other plausible scenarios for how the two sections of the letter fit together. First, Paul may have turned his attention to a smaller, troublesome group within the Corinthian congregation in the final chapters, after applauding the majority of the church in the earlier chapters. Paul had been struggling to promote a vision of Christianity that championed God's strength through human frailties and suffering, while some of the Corinthians endorsed a more triumphalist version of Christian living. Some in the church had finally come around to Paul's way of viewing things, but a small group of holdouts still rejected Paul's perspective. Second, Paul may

---

9. For an overview of some of the proposed interpolations see Scott J. Hafemann, "Corinthians, Letters to the," *DPL* 176–77.
10. These themes include the ideas of strength through weakness (which Paul praises in chapters 1–9 and defends in chapters 10–13), Paul being "commended" in his actions (2 Cor. 3:1; 4:2; 5:12; 6:4 with 10:12, 18; 12:11), and legitimate and illegitimate "boasting" (multiple times in both sections of the letter).

have written 2 Corinthians over a period of time. Perhaps he wrote chapters 10–13 after receiving additional information about certain believers' resistance to Paul's apostolic authority and his vision for a "jars of clay" ministry (see 2 Cor. 4:7–12).[11]

Beyond 2 Corinthians 10–13 the strongest candidate for an interpolation is 2 Corinthians 6:14–7:1. The material on holiness and idolatry sounds like Paul's teaching (resembling what he said in 1 Corinthians 10:14–22), but it doesn't fit that comfortably into the surrounding discourse of 2 Corinthians 6–7, raising the possibility that the segment was previously part of a different letter. In the material immediately before and after the section Paul pushes for more openness and affection in his relationship with the Corinthians, repeatedly focusing on his and their "hearts" (2 Cor. 6:11, 12; 7:2, 3). In 2 Corinthians 6:14–7:1, however, there are no overt traces of this interest in mutual relational commitment. On the other hand, Paul's admonition, "Make room for us in your hearts" (7:2) sounds quite repetitive of "Open wide your hearts also" (6:13), casting doubt on the theory that the one verse was written right after the other. If Paul had momentarily pursued a different line of thought (2 Cor. 6:14–7:1), the repetition would help reorient Paul's readers to the original discussion.[12] Why, then, the digression of 2 Corinthians 6:14–7:1? It is possible that Paul felt that other allegiances were drawing his readers away from their bonds with him, so he wanted to address those misguided alliances before returning to his relationship with his readers. In short, the verdict is that it is possible but not necessary that 2 Corinthians 6:14–7:1 is an interpolation.

It helps to be aware of the strengths and weaknesses of the various proposals for and against the integrity of 2 Corinthians. The conclusions you reach will affect the level of coherence you expect from Paul's discourse in the letter. Readers who accept the integrity of the letter will assume more of a smooth progression in the discourse, while those who suspect that material has been combined or inserted after the fact will allow for more abrupt changes in thought at the points where the interpolations begin and end.

GALATIANS

With Galatians we jump headfirst into some of the most lively debates about Paul's letters in recent memory. In a later chapter you will learn more about the so-called New Perspective on Paul, which challenges traditional ways of reading Paul's letters.[13] New Perspective proposals have generated fresh questions about Paul's primary thesis in Galatians. Does Paul narrow in on

---

11. Strengths and weaknesses of various options are noted in Carson and Moo, *Introduction to the New Testament*, 429–36.
12. See C. K. Barrett, *A Commentary on the Second Epistle to the Corinthians*, HNTC (New York: Harper & Row, 1973), 194; Carson and Moo, *Introduction to the New Testament*, 439.
13. See the chapter, "What Are the Experts Saying about Paul These Days?"

first-century concerns about the assimilation of the Gentiles into the new covenant people of God, or does he tap into even deeper contrasts between human effort and the mercies of God? To determine Paul's overall direction in Galatians, readers must decide what to do with Paul's discourse about works, faith, justification, and righteousness, as well as ascertain the significance of the various contrasts Paul develops in the letter.

First, try to define some key terms and phrases in Galatians. Two crucial phrases are "works of the law" and the "faith of Christ."[14] Scholars debate the precise referent and scope of the works of the law (Gal. 2:16; 3:2, 5, 10). Is the phrase restricted to works prescribed by the Jewish law, as given to Moses and spelled out in the Pentateuch? Or does the phrase legitimately include all good works, whether performed by Jews or Gentiles? For "faith of Christ" and its equivalents (Gal. 2:16, 20; 3:22), the options are either the believer's trust in Christ or Christ's own exercise of faith or faithfulness in his service to God. Take special note as well of the various occurrences of the closely associated words "justify" (Gal. 2:16–17; 3:8, 11, 24; 5:4) and "righteousness" (Gal. 2:21; 3:6, 11, 21; 5:5). What exactly do the words mean in each occurrence, and what conclusions can we draw about what Paul hopes to emphasize with that language?[15] Though Bible dictionaries, commentaries, and grammatical resources can help with all of these questions, looking closely at the literary context yields dividends like nothing else does.

Second, Galatians is filled with contrasts that are relevant to the question of whether Paul is focused primarily on ecclesiological questions of reconciliation within the body of Christ or soteriological concerns about individuals' right standing before God. Paul contrasts faith and works in several instances, and these contrasts are central to the question. Specifically, "works of the law" stand in opposition to "faith of Christ" twice (both in Galatians 2:16) and against "hearing with faith" (ESV) on two other occasions (3:2, 5).[16] Other associated pairings include the distinction between promise and law (Gal. 3:14–29; 4:23–28), and the contrasts between freedom and slavery (Gal. 4:8–5:1), the cross of Christ and circumcision (5:2–6; 6:12–15), and the Spirit and the flesh (Gal. 3:2–3; 4:29; 5:13–25; 6:7–8). Once again, readers should develop an opinion about whether to understand these contrasts narrowly, within the pressing problem of Jew and Gentile relations in the early church, or whether Paul saw the right standing of Jews and Gentiles before God as a subset of the universal need

---

14. As will be noted in a later chapter, "faith of Christ" is the literal translation of πίστις Χριστοῦ. English Bible versions typically translate the phrase as "faith in Christ." But some interpreters argue that the "faith of Christ" (or the "faithfulness of Christ") is a legitimate alternate translation of the grammatical construction.

15. To become familiar with the range of options for the interpretation of any given instance of "God's righteousness," see Larry R. Helyer, *The Witness of Jesus, Paul and John: An Exploration in Biblical Theology* (Downers Grove, IL: InterVarsity, 2008), 257–61.

16. For me, this adds to the likelihood that the "faith of Christ" is equivalent to "hearing with faith" in the letter.

to experience God's grace through faith and not works.[17] The chapter on current scholarship later in this book will furnish you with some additional background to these discussions.

The New Perspective on Paul has prompted people to take a second look at Paul's argument throughout Galatians. In no other letter does he speak with such urgency. Paul scanned the horizon and noticed a large mass of ice in the waters ahead. The Galatians were on a course straight toward that iceberg. In his God-given wisdom Paul realized that as daunting as the tip of the iceberg seemed, the ultimate danger that could take down the ship lurked beneath the water level. See if you can notice both the tip of the iceberg (the immediate problem Paul spotted) and the rest of the iceberg below the water (the problem that Paul believed struck at the heart of his gospel message). Only when we correctly perceive the fundamental problem will we appreciate Paul's stunning vision of life in Christ.

EPHESIANS AND COLOSSIANS

Ephesians 5:22–6:9 and its streamlined cousin in Colossians 3:18–4:1 feature material on household relationships. The instructions are organized similarly to discussions in Jewish teachings and Greek philosophy. Scholars have labeled these instructions about household management "household codes" (in German, *Haustafeln*). Aristotle breaks down the organization of households into three pairs of relationships—masters and slaves, husbands and wives, and fathers and children (Aristotle, *Politics* 1.3, 12–13). For Aristotle, effectively run households organized in hierarchical frameworks made society stronger. Jewish historian Josephus shares his counsel on how husbands should assume their positions of authority over their wives, who should submit to their husbands (Josephus, *Ag. Ap.* 2.25). The Jewish philosopher Philo likewise offers advice for husbands and wives and adds his brief opinions on the importance of parents directing and ruling over their children (Philo, *Hypothetica* 7.3, as found in Eusebius, *Praep. ev.* 8.7.3). Paul wades into similar waters in Ephesians 5:22–6:9 and Colossians 3:18–4:1, providing instructions about these same three relationships and holding to a similar ordering of each relationship. Still, Paul departs from the other thinkers in the tone and content of his prescriptions. Most important, he ties his instructions to the greater purpose of honoring Christ and reflecting his love and reign. This Christ-centered focus affects how all parties should implement Paul's directives.

Once interpreters have compared and contrasted Paul's household teachings with these passages and others, they must decide how much weight to place on the differences and how much on the shared material.

---

17. Differing perspectives on these topics can be found in N. T. Wright, *Justification: God's Plan and Paul's Vision* (Downers Grove, IL: InterVarsity, 2009), 111–40; Douglas J. Moo, *Galatians*, BECNT (Grand Rapids: Baker, 2013), 21–31.

Should believers implement primarily the unique contributions of Paul's instructions or the common material (found in both Paul's letters and sources outside the New Testament) as well? Does Paul intend to supplement and subtly critique the inadequate cultural prescriptions for household relationships with a more robust and compelling Christ-centered vision?[18] Or does he have apologetic aims in mind, to help believers reflect harmonious relationships valued by the broader world as part of the church's effective outreach to unbelievers?[19] More fundamentally, how much should knowledge of household codes from the ancient world influence our exegesis in the first place? These are intriguing interpretive and philosophical questions to address.

The language of election, predestination, and the eternal purposes of God in Ephesians 1:3–14 presents another interpretive challenge. God "chose" believers (1:4 and 1:11, using two different terms) and "predestined" them (1:5 and 1:11) according to the plans he set in motion from before the creation of the world (1:4; see also 1:11). In this passage Paul doesn't ponder the abstract philosophical paradox between predestination and free will. Instead, he incorporates this strong language of God's sovereignty to advance his argument. The focus of that argument, however, is open to debate. We still need to decide whether Paul describes primarily the mystery of individual predestination or the corporate integration of believing Jews and Gentiles into the chosen one (Christ).

In Colossians Paul critiques the views of false teachers who seem to be harassing some of the Colossian believers (Col. 2:8, 16). To fully appreciate Paul's instructions in the letter it helps to inspect the perspectives Paul opposed. We must use a "mirror-reading" method to form an opinion on the specific nature of the false teachers' doctrines.[20] From Paul's refutation of specific beliefs and practices we can gain a picture of the ideas his opponents were disseminating. To what extent did Jewish beliefs shape their teachings? There are several possible references to Jewish practices and mindsets in the letter (2:11, 16, 21), though Paul's assessment of these as worldly (2:20) and "based on merely human commands and teachings" (2:22; see also 2:8) suggests that he viewed them as distortions of or additions to the God-given law he praises elsewhere (Rom. 3:2; 7:12; 9:4; Gal. 3:19; see also Mark 7:7–9). Is there evidence in the false teachings of syncretism, a mixing of Jewish beliefs with practices that derive from other belief systems? The introduction to the section (2:8) and the full descriptions of the various practices (2:18, 23) don't seem to describe an

---

18. Timothy G. Gombis, "A Radically New Humanity: The Function of the *Haustafel* in Ephesians," *JETS* 48 (2005): 317–30.

19. Craig S. Keener, *Paul, Women & Wives: Marriage and Women's Ministry in the Letters of Paul* (Peabody: Hendrickson, 1992), 145–47.

20. See the introduction to mirror-reading in the chapter, "How Can I Get the Most out of Studying Paul's Letters?"

unadulterated Judaism.[21] Spending time exploring a possible profile of the aberrant teachings in Colossae allows us to appreciate more deeply Paul's carefully crafted rebuttal and advocacy of something better in Christ (see Col. 3:8b, 17b, 19, for starters).

PHILIPPIANS

Philippians 2:5–11 stands out as the most memorable and theologically complex passage in the letter. Scholars debate whether Paul wrote this hymnic passage or whether he borrowed and edited material that early Christians used in worship settings. Either way, Paul integrates this tribute to Christ's humility and exaltation smoothly into the letter. The passage reinforces Paul's immediately preceding exhortations to humbly serve other believers (Phil. 2:1–4). More broadly, Christ's lowly descent followed by his glorious vindication establishes a paradigm for believers' current suffering and eventual exaltation, which are themes advanced throughout Philippians.

The passage's description of Jesus's humility in particular has created confusion over the years. Scholars have debated the meaning of a handful of terms and phrases from the first half of the passage (2:6–8), which reveals the contours of Christ's divinity and humanity.[22] First, what does Paul mean when he says that Jesus was "in very *nature* God" (using the Greek word μορφή, which is sometimes translated as "form")? Second, what should we make of the subtle but significant differences in the translations of Jesus's stance toward equality with God (Phil. 2:6)?:

- He "did not consider equality with God something to be used to his own advantage" (NIV; see also NRSV, HCSB).
- He "did not count equality with God a thing to be grasped" (ESV; see also NASB, NET).
- He "did not think of equality with God as something to cling to" (NLT).
- He "did not consider it robbery to be equal with God" (NKJV).

Third, how should we interpret Christ emptying himself (NASB, HCSB, NRSV, NET) or making himself nothing (NIV, ESV) in Philippians 2:7? Scholars distance themselves from past attempts to interpret Christ's emptying as a removal of certain divine attributes during Christ's incarnation. They look instead to clues from the participial phrases that follow—"taking the

21. For varying perspectives, see N. T. Wright, *Colossians and Philemon*, TNTC (Leicester: Inter-Varsity; Grand Rapids: Eerdmans, 1986), 23–28; Clinton E. Arnold, *The Colossian Syncretism: The Interface between Christianity and Folk Belief at Colossae* (Grand Rapids: Baker, 1996), 228–44; David W. Pao, *Colossians and Philemon*, ZECNT (Grand Rapids: Eerdmans, 2012), 25–31.
22. See the careful discussions of the issues in Gordon D. Fee, *Paul's Letter to the Philippians*, NICNT (Grand Rapids: Eerdmans, 1995), 198–211; Moisés Silva, *Philippians*, 2nd ed., BECNT (Grand Rapids: Baker, 2005), 99–106.

very nature of a servant" and "being made in human likeness." The key to interpreting this passage is to read the individual lines as parts of the whole passage, avoiding reading more into any individual word or phrase than necessary.[23] Look for confirmation of your interpretation from other passages in Paul's letters and from how wise theologians in the past have explained the section. Let this inspiring vision of Christ's humility and glory add fuel to your worship and leave you with a pattern to follow in your life.

FIRST AND SECOND THESSALONIANS

These two letters have similar backgrounds and some overlapping material. Be sure to explore the way Paul connects hard work, love, and holiness to the return of Christ in these letters. Paul renounces any appeal to Christ's imminent return as an excuse for a passive mindset among Christians. Paul's stern words against lazy believers (1 Thess. 5:14; 2 Thess. 3:6–13) should be read in this light.

Paul's pronouncement about the wrath of God visiting Jewish persecutors of believers in Judea has puzzled many commentators (1 Thess. 2:16).[24] When Paul says, "The wrath of God has come upon them at last," does Paul speak as a prophet, predicting a judgment that is future but certain (or already in motion because of the inauguration of the kingdom of God on earth)? Or does he discern God's punishment in an actual crisis in history that had recently struck the Jews of Judea? And should the words at the end of the sentence (εἰς τέλος) be translated as "at last" (NIV, ESV, NRSV, HCSB), indicating finality, or "completely" (NET; see also NASB, NKJV), expressing the full extent of the wrath? Yet another option is that Paul means "until the end," which, like "at last," is a temporal notion, but conveys an opposite understanding—that the Jews' reception of wrath in their current history was not permanent (they would be spared God's ultimate wrath, along the lines of the dramatic reversal envisioned in Romans 11:25–26).[25] Overall, this passage fits into Paul's broader treatment in 1 and 2 Thessalonians of the theme of believers' assurance during suffering and persecution. God does not turn a blind eye to his people in the midst of their suffering. This provides a great comfort to all of God's afflicted children.

Paul draws upon apocalyptic imagery in 2 Thessalonians 2. He uses the enigmatic language of "the rebellion" and "man of lawlessness" and "a powerful delusion" to describe the advance of evil in the last days. Particularly confounding is Paul's language about a "restraining" (ESV, NRSV, NKJV,

---

23. Silva, *Philippians*, 103.

24. For three different perspectives on this passage, see Charles A. Wanamaker, *The Epistles to the Thessalonians: A Commentary on the Greek Text* (Grand Rapids: Eerdmans; Exeter: Paternoster, 1990), 116–18; Gary S. Shogren, *1 & 2 Thessalonians*, ZECNT (Grand Rapids: Zondervan, 2012), 115–17; Jeffrey A. D. Weima, *1–2 Thessalonians*, BECNT (Grand Rapids: Eerdmans, 2014), 175–78.

25. Wanamaker, *Epistles to the Thessalonians*, 117–18; Weima, *1–2 Thessalonians*, 178.

NASB, HCSB) entity whose function it is to "hold back" (NIV, NET) lawlessness (2 Thess. 2:6–7) until the time designated by the Lord. Paul refers to the restrainer in both the neuter and masculine gender, suggesting some interplay between a concept/force and a person in the activity of restraining. Readers can sift through several popular options for the identity of the restrainer and develop a preliminary conclusion on the likely referent for the wording.[26]

When you read 1 and 2 Thessalonians, take the opportunity to ponder these realities of an eternal kingdom of salvation and judgment. There is more to life than what immediately meets the eye. Believers can drill down into a more substantive existence when they realize that through Christ they are already participating in that eternal kingdom. Our lives are invested with the greatest significance imaginable. We should live each day with that higher calling in mind.

PASTORAL EPISTLES

In 1 and 2 Timothy and Titus Paul uses the Greek expression πιστὸς ὁ λόγος on five occasions (1 Tim. 1:15; 3:1; 4:9; 2 Tim. 2:11; Titus 3:8).[27] This distinct wording never appears in any of Paul's other letters. Commentators and Bible translators have typically opted for the translation of "this is a trustworthy saying," or something similar. They then attempt to link the expression to a saying that either immediately precedes or follows the construction. An arguably superior proposal is that the expression functions more generally as a reference to the inspiring gospel-oriented teaching that Paul hopes to impress upon Timothy and Titus.[28] A translation of "the word is faithful," or even the doxologically tinged "faithful is the word!" may more powerfully convey Paul's interest and sentiment in those passages. The reader will need to determine whether the first view can be supported with tangible "sayings" in the near context and look at whether Paul's characterization of doctrine and "the word" throughout the three letters aligns with the second theory about πιστὸς ὁ λόγος being a general affirmation of the power and beauty of God's truth.

First Timothy and Titus provide a more detailed look into the leadership structure of the early church. Try to set aside your picture of a modern-day church and use your powers of observation to discern how the churches at Ephesus (1 Timothy) and Crete (Titus) were organized. Look at the similarities and differences between qualifications for the roles of deacon and overseer, along with the potential relationship between overseers and elders (whether these are two terms for the same leaders in the churches). What systems of accountability are set in place for the elders of the churches?

---

26. For help in navigating through the options, see Weima, *1–2 Thessalonians*, 567–77.
27. The construction consists of a noun (λόγος) modified by an adjective (πιστός) in predicate relationship to the noun.
28. See L. Timothy Swinson, "Πιστὸς ὁ λόγος: An Alternative Analysis," *STR* 7 (2016): 57–76.

In addition, are the widows in 1 Timothy 5 operating as part of a formal ministry within the church at Ephesus? What are their responsibilities? Finally, try to determine the nature of Timothy's and Titus's ministries to the churches at Ephesus and Crete. From these observations, what do you see as the most valuable takeaways for churches today?

PHILEMON

Philemon is the shortest of Paul's letters but is in some ways the trickiest to interpret. That is because of the uncertain occasion and backstory of the letter, not to mention Paul's ultimate agenda in writing the letter. We have to draw some tentative conclusions about the circumstances behind the letter by using a mirror-reading strategy. Why is Onesimus with Paul, and what brought him to Paul? Was it a providential crossing of paths or an intentional meeting? Was Onesimus serving Paul with Philemon's blessing, or had he run away from Philemon? Did Paul know of specific offenses that Onesimus had committed against Philemon, or is Paul just speaking hypothetically (Philem. 18)? What legal constraints did Onesimus face as Philemon's slave, and did Paul likewise have some legal obligations in his interactions with Onesimus and Philemon? How had Paul become acquainted with Philemon (1:19b)? These are among the questions that scholars raise about the letter.[29]

Once we determine the history leading up to the letter, we are still left with the ambiguity over Paul's ultimate agenda in his letter to Philemon. Paul applies indirect rhetorical pressure at various points in the letter (Philem. 8, 19b, 21), but to what end? Relational reconciliation between Philemon and Onesimus? A spiritual reconfiguration of their relationship? Temporary release of Onesimus to Paul for continued assistance in his imprisonment? Permanent freedom from slavery that would allow Onesimus to serve alongside Paul as a missionary? This is a letter that sparks stimulating discussion for groups of readers that have studied it carefully!

WEIGHING THE VIEWS OF EXPERTS USING THE PROCESS OF VALIDATION

The exegetical challenges in this chapter represent just a sampling of the passages and issues for which there are differing views. Though readers can form well-reasoned opinions about the meaning of many passages in Paul's letters, students would benefit from consulting commentaries to resolve some of the more difficult passages. For any debated passage students can dig deeper into the competing positions and chart a methodical course to reach a sound conclusion about the meaning of the passage. Readers can weigh strengths and weaknesses of arguments for and against

---

29. See the overview of issues in Pao, *Colossians and Philemon*, 343–47.

specific interpretations using a process known as validation.[30] The goals of validation are to thoroughly understand the strengths and weaknesses of each interpretive option and then to arrive at a conclusion about the most plausible explanation for a passage.

We can use the method of validation on any debated verse or passage in Paul's letters. How do we recognize these disputed sections of discourse in the first place? One way is to look for where English versions of the Bible translate a verse or passage in significantly different ways. A second way is to consult a commentary that alerts readers to the presence of various possibilities for a verse or passage.

After you have identified the gist of the disagreement and where it surfaces in the passage, articulate how the resolution would affect the interpretation of the passage. This is a good opportunity to pause and decide whether the passage is worth validating in the first place. The debated issue should be meaningful and consequential enough to pique your interest and keep you motivated throughout the process.

Next, students should identify the distinct interpretations proposed for the debated issue, using differences in English translations and the opinions of commentators as a guide. You may need to group some scholars together even if their views contain some subtle differences, as long as they agree on the central issues. Scholars don't tend to fall lockstep into tidy categories. Use your best judgment to sort commentators into groups that hold to the same general positions. Give priority to commentaries written in the past several decades, since they are more up to date on the arguments for and against the different viewpoints. Give priority as well to commentaries that methodically wade through strengths and weaknesses of major positions. Finally, try to find actual advocates for at least two widely held interpretations, since you want to hear the best arguments for a given perspective.

The next steps constitute the heart of the validation process. Consulting the work of commentators and other experts, locate several arguments advanced for each proposed interpretation. To ensure a thorough analysis and your own well-grounded conclusions, assess the strengths and weaknesses of the commentators' arguments first. Make sure that you comprehend the view and arguments you are evaluating. This may require reading and re-reading paragraphs from the sources until you are confident that you understand the author's train of thought. Examine any parallel passages the writer uses to support a position, and confirm that those passages actually correspond to the author's point. Next, form an opinion about the overall logic of the various authors' arguments. Do the authors offer convincing reasons for adopting their interpretations? Are

---

30. I am grateful to my colleague William A. Heth for sharing his ideas about the validation process he has used for decades with his advanced Greek students at Taylor University. See also David K. Lowery, "Validation: Exegetical Problem Solving," in Bock and Fanning, *Interpreting the New Testament Text*, 155–66.

they aware of the complexities of the issue? Do they consider and respond to potential weaknesses in their own views and apparent strengths in opposing perspectives? As you carry out this process, imagine yourself as a judge who impartially and thoroughly weighs all of the evidence before reaching a conclusion. And keep in mind that support for an interpretation must move beyond a simple appeal to experts. Seek to understand the arguments put forward and use your best judgment and knowledge of Paul's teachings to assess the strength and validity of the arguments.

Once you are confident that you have sufficiently evaluated the support for different positions, decide upon your preferred interpretation, providing the main reasons for your choice. Indicate and briefly explain your level of certainty about your conclusion. There is no shame in feeling somewhat doubtful about the best choice, but it helps to make a decision one way or the other. You are always free to change your mind later! Finally, show how your chosen interpretation fits within the broader discourse. This takes you back to the original question of significance. We pursue validation because we have reached a fork in the interpretive road. Once we decide upon a path, we can continue our journey toward understanding Paul's overall discourse.

CONCLUSION

There is so much to explore in Paul's letters. The topics introduced in this chapter highlight just a few of the intriguing passages and features you will encounter in Paul's letters. These debated ideas or unfamiliar phenomena aren't just fodder for intellectual debate and speculation. They touch upon the deepest questions about God, humanity, salvation, and God's eternal plans. Thankfully, much of what Paul writes is transparent to the sincere and careful reader. And even uncertainty about the puzzling passages won't derail our walks with God. Still, nothing should stop us from humbly seeking answers to the passages that confound us. The writings of seasoned interpreters and the method of validation we surveyed will help us make progress. More than anything, let your curiosity and thirst for truth propel you forward in inquisitive and responsive reading.

■ ■ ■

CHAPTER ELEVEN

FROM WHERE DOES PAUL GET HIS MATERIAL?

Once we recognize Paul as a flesh-and-blood servant of God who wrote to real churches in the context of his missionary work, we can explore the question of Paul's sources. Paul's words are inspired by God and authoritative for churches of all time, but Paul doesn't simply receive and record words by dictation from God, without any of his own personality and concerns shining through. Paul instead seeks to represent God's perspective on a host of matters, functioning as an apostle called by God. Paul acts as a steward of God's truth and an ambassador on God's behalf (1 Cor. 4:1–2; 2 Cor. 5:20; Eph. 6:19–20). Even as God's Spirit directs Paul while he writes, Paul simultaneously draws upon his own knowledge and insight into God's truth and how it should be applied. That brings the question of Paul's "sources" into play.

Why does determining Paul's sources really matter? Isn't it enough to know what Paul said without determining the sources of his ideas? But we have been reminded that *why* Paul writes what he does is relevant to *what* he writes. Sensitivity to sources actually contributes to our ability to properly interpret Paul's letters. We are more likely to discern Paul's meaning if we use the right keys for understanding. And what better keys than the actual sources Paul depended on, whether he drew upon them intentionally or more subconsciously? These sources shed light on the ideas that worked their way into Paul's thinking and convictions.

Paul's content for his gospel and teaching probably comes from a mix of sources. The primary influences seem to be a combination of Christ's revelation to him on the road to Damascus and Paul's extensive preexisting knowledge of the Old Testament. Paul fits those two pieces together to show how Jesus was the anticipated Messiah who fulfilled the promises of the Old Testament through his incarnate ministry. Secondarily, while Paul rarely quotes Jesus's teachings, his own teachings resemble Jesus's outlook in a number of significant areas. Paul adopts all of Jesus's actions, teachings, and saving works as the starting point for his ministry, but he selectively applies whatever fits the specific needs of his churches. Paul also likely relied on sanctified common sense to address very specific problems for which there was little or no precedent for resolving. He may have even integrated some preformed material from early Christian hymns or creeds. Finally, God revealed additional insights to Paul supernaturally, though it is uncertain whether these insights contributed significantly to his teachings.

DAMASCUS ROAD EPIPHANY

We know from both Acts and Paul's letters that the resurrected Christ appeared directly to Paul while he was en route to Damascus from Jerusalem. Acts 9:1–19, 22:6–16, and 26:12–18 give complementary accounts of how this event unfolded. From those chapters we get glimpses into what Paul had "seen and heard" from Jesus, which was to form the basis of what he proclaimed to others (Acts 22:14–15). He saw the resurrected Jesus, the same Jesus he had persecuted when Paul oppressed Jesus's followers (Acts 9:4–5; 22:7–8; 26:14–15). Since Paul immediately began to announce that Jesus was God's Son, the Messiah, he must have heard or inferred this from this initial meeting with Jesus (Acts 9:20–21).[1] Jesus's close identification with his followers ("Why do you persecute me?") may have struck Paul as well, being planted as a seed that would later grow into Paul's vibrant doctrine of union with Christ.[2] Jesus told Paul that he would proclaim a message of enlightenment, deliverance, forgiveness, and cleansing (Acts 26:17–18). Paul was ready to announce these truths; after all, he had just experienced those very things when Jesus intervened in his life. Jesus told Paul to carry this message to the Gentiles in particular.

These detailed versions from Acts are corroborated by Paul's briefer comments in his letters about the experience (1 Cor. 9:1; 15:8; Gal. 1:11–16).[3] Paul had seen the resurrected Jesus, whom he identified as God's Son (Gal. 1:16). This fundamental realization, that the crucified Jesus had been raised from the dead and was vindicated as God's Son, formed the core of Paul's message of good news, the gospel (Rom. 1:1–4; 2 Tim. 2:8).[4] Paul also mentions his commissioning by Christ to bring this message to the Gentiles (Gal. 1:16; see also Rom. 11:13; 15:15–16; Eph. 3:8; 1 Tim. 2:7).

---

1. "The Son of God" is a Messianic title, as observed in 2 Samuel 7:14 (in the context of the Davidic covenant) and Psalm 2:7, 12 (in the context of God's vindication of his anointed one—see verse 2).

2. See similar speculation by Bruce, *Apostle of the Heart Set Free*, 87.

3. Some people see echoes of Paul's Damascus Road experience in 2 Corinthians 4:6 and Philippians 3:12 as well.

4. See also Seyoon Kim, *The Origin of Paul's Gospel* (Grand Rapids: Eerdmans, 1981), 100–111; Udo Schnelle, *Apostle Paul: His Life and Theology*, trans. M. Eugene Boring (Grand Rapids: Baker, 2003), 98; Helyer, *Jesus, Paul and John*, 215.

This would be the same message of grace and power that God had put on display in Paul's life, through Paul's transforming encounter with Christ (1 Tim. 1:12–16).

Even though, as we will see below, more revelations followed, Paul treated this initial appearance of Christ and unveiling of truth as unique among his visions. They were on par with the experiences of the other disciples who had seen Jesus in the days following his resurrection (1 Cor. 15:3–11). Paul tirelessly proclaimed and vigorously defended the gospel he received that day. He condemned those who tried to pervert it (Gal. 1:6–9).[5] This divine manifestation of Christ left Paul with the central components of the message of good news he proclaimed throughout his ministry.[6]

OLD TESTAMENT SCRIPTURES

Paul did not witness these central truths about Christ in a vacuum. Paul received revelation when he met Christ and integrated it into the true and inspired story of how God was already at work in the world, particularly through his chosen people, the Jews. Paul thus interpreted his new awareness that Jesus was the resurrected Messiah through the lens of what God had already disclosed in the Old Testament. In several places Paul overtly highlights his belief that the Old Testament previews Christ's ministry. Paul's gospel was "promised beforehand through [God's] prophets in the Holy Scriptures" (Rom. 1:2). Christ's death for our sins was "according to the Scriptures" and his resurrection was "according to the Scriptures" (1 Cor. 15:3–4). The "Holy Scriptures" that Timothy had learned from his childhood were designed to point to salvation through faith in Christ Jesus (2 Tim. 3:15).[7] The Old Testament foretells Christ's saving ministry, but Paul insisted that it has even broader relevance to all of Christian living. The Old Testament Scriptures give encouragement, hope, and instruction to believers in their daily living (Rom. 15:4; 1 Cor. 10:11; 2 Tim. 3:16–17). Paul spoke of the Old Testament Scriptures as an unrivaled source book for Christian doctrine and practice.[8]

---

5. Markus Bockmuehl, *Revelation and Mystery in Ancient Judaism and Pauline Christianity* (Grand Rapids: Eerdmans, 1990), 137.

6. The initial events may have had ongoing ripple effects in Paul's thinking, so that Paul gradually realized the full theological significance of what he witnessed that day on the road to Damascus (Bruce, *Apostle of the Heart Set Free*, 80).

7. "Holy Scriptures" is translated from a different Greek phrase than the wording in Romans 1 or 1 Corinthians 15, but the referent in all three passages is most likely the same.

8. In each of these mentions of "the Scriptures" Paul has the Old Testament in mind. Few, if any, Christian writings (that would one day comprise the New Testament canon) had begun to circulate at the time that Paul wrote most of his letters. Most other works had not yet been written, and they definitely had not been gathered together in a collection. "The Scriptures" as a moniker still referred to the collected writings of the Old Testament.

Beyond these summary statements of the relevance of the Old Testament to Paul's teachings, Paul also indicates his indebtedness to the Old Testament through his many quotations and allusions to specific Old Testament passages throughout his letters. We will look more closely at how Paul interacted with the Old Testament in the next chapter. For now, we notice how prominent the Old Testament was as a source for Paul's teachings.

JESUS'S TEACHINGS

Paul never followed Jesus during Jesus's earthly ministry, so he had no direct knowledge of Jesus's teachings. Paul rarely cites Jesus's teachings in his letters either. So why do we think that Jesus was one of Paul's sources? There are several reasons we do so.

First, there are good reasons why Paul doesn't directly reemphasize Jesus's teachings. We have to remember Paul's vantage point and purpose for writing his letters. Though the Gospels had not been written down and distributed during most of Paul's ministry, the teachings from Jesus circulated orally. The later emergence of written Gospels testifies to the fact that Jesus's teachings were valued, preserved, and passed down in the early church. Early Christian ministers would have made a practice of covering that ground orally with new audiences.[9] In Paul's letters to *existing* churches Paul did not need to rehash the teachings and ministry of Jesus but could rather assume those teachings as a starting point.[10] Paul wrote letters in response to specific needs and issues in the church, so he concentrated his efforts in that direction. Furthermore, Paul wrote from a post-resurrection perspective. Jesus cannot be fully understood without his exalted reign now clearly in view (Rom. 1:3–4; Phil. 2:6–11; 1 Tim. 3:16). Kate Middleton will now forever be thought of as a princess. Men who have become popes are viewed through the prism of the papacy once they are elected for that office. Likewise, Jesus's resurrected glory puts everything leading up to that reality in a new light. Even Jesus's humble march to the cross and his death on it radiates with fuller meaning in the wake of Jesus's resurrection. Jesus's pre-exalted status and teachings are never forgotten, but Paul looks primarily to the crucified and exalted Jesus to guide, govern, and sustain the churches Paul addresses.[11]

Second, even though Paul became part of Jesus's team after Jesus's ascension, that does not mean that Paul was ignorant of Jesus's teachings.

---

9. Early Christian writers may have even purposefully kept the traditions about Jesus disentangled from their own works, for the sake of preserving the purity and independence of those traditions (Bauckham, *Jesus and the Eyewitnesses*, 278–79).

10. See Dunn, *Theology of Paul*, 186–87. It should be noted that New Testament works by other authors also branch off from the primary trunk of the Gospels and their comprehensive portrayal of Jesus's life and ministry (Seyoon Kim, "Jesus, Sayings of," *DPL* 488–89).

11. See David Wenham, *Paul: Follower of Jesus or Founder of Christianity?* (Grand Rapids: Eerdmans, 1995), 402–8; Schnelle, *Apostle Paul*, 106–8.

Paul must have had at least some preexisting knowledge of Christian teachings (since he had persecuted those believers), and he probably had conversations with early Christians such as Ananias (Acts 9:17–19), Barnabas (Acts 9:27), and Peter (Gal. 1:18) about the more detailed teachings of Jesus.[12] In fact, we know that Paul relied on established traditions of the early church because he says so explicitly on several occasions. Paul appeals to received traditions about Jesus's teachings on marriage (1 Cor. 7:10–11; see Matt. 5:32; 19:3–11) and Jesus's institution of the Lord's Supper (1 Cor. 11:23–25; see Mark 14:22–25 and parallels).[13] Paul also quotes (1 Tim. 5:18b) and refers to (1 Cor. 9:14) one of Jesus's known sayings: "the worker deserves his wages" (Luke 10:7; see also Matt. 10:10). On one occasion Paul even quotes a teaching from Jesus that does not appear in the four Gospels (Acts 20:35).[14]

Third, there are a number of areas in which Paul's ideas closely resemble Jesus's teachings. These are in addition to the instances, mentioned above, in which Paul directly refers to previous tradition about Jesus or a saying from Jesus. Let's examine some of these comparable teachings, noting both the conceptual parallels and the similar wording and imagery used.

We begin with Paul's obvious, though sometimes overlooked, continuation of one of Jesus's repeated central teachings. In the Gospels, Jesus predicts multiple times that he would suffer, die, and be raised again as the pinnacle of his earthly ministry (Mark 8:31; 9:31; 10:33–34; 14:27–28 and parallels; John 2:19–22). Large sections of all four Gospels are devoted to describing these climactic events. Jesus also insinuates that his ministry and death will have saving benefits for his people (Matt. 26:26–28; Mark 10:45; Luke 24:46–47; John 3:14–15; 12:23–24; see also Matt. 1:21 and John 1:29). The Passion accounts have multiple allusions to the enigmatic servant who suffers for the sins of others (Isa. 52:13–53:12), which helps portray Jesus's suffering as having saving significance.[15] Paul does justice to Jesus's emphasis by making Jesus's saving death and resurrection "of

---

12. See similar conclusions in Dunn, *Theology of Paul*, 187–88; Helyer, *Jesus, Paul and John*, 214.

13. For a discussion of the presence of Jesus's teachings in 1 Corinthians 7:10–11 and 11:23–25, see Kim, "Jesus, Sayings of," 475.

14. When we think about sources and literary dependence, determining direct dependence is tricky. Two writings may draw on a third, common source or on a saying that was widely known in shared circles. Dependence could also travel through intervening sources or be in the reverse direction (in this case, a written gospel could reflect wording from Paul, rather than Paul relying on orally relayed Jesus traditions). See Wenham, *Follower of Jesus?*, 14, 29–30.

15. The allusions span from Jesus talking about "pouring out" his blood for them (Isa. 53:12), his prayer in the garden (referring to the Lord's will—see Isa. 53:10), his silence while being interrogated and mocked (53:7–9), praying for his oppressors (53:12), being "pierced" and "crushed" (53:5), being "cut off from the land of the living" (53:8), to being vindicated and exalted (52:13; 53:12). Jesus also directly quotes from Isaiah 53 in Luke 22:37. All of this reveals that the true meaning of Jesus's death should be interpreted along the lines of Isaiah 53, where the righteous servant suffers for the transgressions of others (53:5, 12) and dies as a sin offering (53:10).

first importance" in his teaching (1 Cor. 15:3–4).[16] Paul gives the death
and resurrection of Jesus, along with the blessings that accompanied those
events, the prominence that Jesus gave them.[17]

Related to the death and resurrection of Christ, Paul upholds Jesus's
sweeping vision of God's grace and forgiveness being lavished on sinners.[18]
Jesus broke through barriers of societal norms to befriend sinners (Mark
2:15–17), and he offended the Pharisees by forgiving sins (Mark 2:5–7 and
parallels; see also Matt. 26:28). Many of Jesus's teachings describe God's
extravagant love and the forgiveness he extends to the undeserving (Matt.
5:3–10; 18:10–14; 20:1–16; Luke 6:35–36; 7:36–50; 15:1–32; 18:9–14;
19:1–10; John 3:16–17). Paul also champions the abundant grace of God
that brings salvation to all sinners (Rom. 3:21–26; 6:23; Gal. 2:15–21; Eph.
2:4–10; 1 Tim. 1:13–16; Titus 3:4–7). This shared grace among believers
removes societal barriers in Paul's churches, so that Jews and previously
"unclean" Gentiles can join together for meals and other meaningful
fellowship (Gal. 2:10–14; Eph. 2:14–18).

Paul's eschatology, or beliefs about final events in God's saving plans,
shows strong kinship to Jesus's teachings. Paul considered the kingdom of
God a major preaching topic and ministry goal (Acts 19:8; 28:23, 31; Col.
4:11) reflecting the priority Jesus placed on the kingdom of God (Mark
1:15 and elsewhere). This was a kingdom that promised both current (Col.
1:12–14; Matt. 12:28; Luke 4:14–21) and future (1 Cor. 15:24–28; 1 Tim.
4:1, 18; see Matt. 8:11; 25:34; Luke 13:28–29; 22:29–30) manifestations of
God's reign.[19] Paul's strong association between God's kingdom and corresponding ethical obligations for believers (Rom. 14:17; 1 Cor. 6:9–10; Eph.
5:5; 1 Thess. 2:12) retains the strong ethical dimension to the kingdom in
Jesus's teachings, as seen particularly in calls to repentance, humility, and
righteousness (Matt. 6:33; 18:1–4; Mark 1:15).[20] For both Jesus and Paul,
kingdom participation requires a complete, inner transformation brought
about by a gracious work of God's Spirit (1 Cor. 15:50–53; Col. 1:12–14;
John 3:3–8; see also Matt. 19:23–26; Gal. 1:3–5; 1 Thess. 5:9–10). Jesus and
Paul also reflect a joint understanding of the necessary suffering that must
precede kingdom glory (Acts 14:21–22; 1 Thess. 3:3; 2 Tim. 2:12a; Mark
10:42–45; John 12:23–26). Note from some of these examples that Paul's
kingdom vision is not limited to verses where the word "kingdom" appears.
Paul touts Christ's ultimate reign of peace and restoration as the wonderful
conclusion to God's plans for this world (Rom. 8:18–25; 16:20; Eph. 1:9–10;

---

16. Paul's numerous other references to Christ's death and resurrection include places where both
are mentioned together: Romans 4:25; 6:5; 8:34; 2 Corinthians 5:14–15; 1 Thessalonians 4:14.

17. Helyer notes the centrality of the cross in Jesus and Paul (Helyer, *Jesus, Paul and John*, 384–89).

18. See Wenham, *Follower of Jesus?*, 43–45, 59–63; Anthony C. Thiselton, *The Living Paul: An Introduction to the Apostle's Life and Thought* (Downers Grove, IL: IVP Academic, 2009), 4–6;

19. See Helyer, *Jesus, Paul and John*, 382–83.

20. Note further the connection between future inheritance and current godliness in those final
three passages, including the use of "inherit" (1 Cor. 6:10) and "inheritance" (Eph. 5:5).

Phil. 3:20–21; Col. 3:3–4; Titus 2:13). Jesus and Paul still promote distinct shadings in their descriptions of the kingdom, but Paul's overall kingdom proclamation was nonetheless congruent with Jesus's commentary.

Even on a more granular level, Paul adopts language and imagery that closely mirrors Jesus's wording about the future arrival of God's final kingdom, especially from Jesus's so-called Olivet Discourse (found in Matt. 24–25; Mark 13; Luke 21).[21] Paul speaks of the Lord descending with a trumpet sound (1 Cor. 15:52; 1 Thess. 4:16; see Matt. 24:31), with angels accompanying him (2 Thess. 1:7; see Matt. 24:31; 25:31; Mark 13:27), gathering his people to himself (2 Thess. 2:1; see Matt. 24:31; Mark 13:27), and meeting with believers "in the clouds" (1 Thess. 4:17; see Matt. 24:30; Mark 13:26; 14:62; Luke 21:27). Jesus and Paul employ "thief in the night" imagery to promote readiness for the return of Christ in the midst of dark and troubling times, and they broach the related topics of alertness and avoiding being spiritually asleep (1 Thess. 5:1–4; Matt. 24:42–44; Mark 13:32–37; Luke 21:34–36). Both Jesus and Paul describe a period of lawlessness, deceptive Satanic activity, and blasphemy leading up to the return of Christ as well (2 Thess. 2:3–12; see Matt. 24:4–25; Mark 13:5–23). Jesus and Paul both certainly reflect Old Testament imagery in their descriptions (from the book of Daniel and the account in Exodus of God's descent onto Mt. Sinai, for instance), but the combination of similar images in the Olivet Discourse and 1 Thessalonians 4–5 or 2 Thessalonians 2 suggests Paul's great familiarity with the contents of the Olivet Discourse in addition to the Old Testament.[22]

Paul's ethical teachings track with the heart of Jesus's teachings, since Jesus and Paul both summarize God's commands for how to treat others by appealing to the love command from Leviticus 19:18b. Jesus does this explicitly in response to the question about which of God's commands were most important (Matt. 22:36–40; Mark 12:28–31; see also Luke 10:25–28). Paul claims that God's moral and interpersonal requirements from the law are fulfilled when believers love their neighbors as themselves, as Leviticus 19:18b instructs (Rom. 13:8–10; Gal. 5:14). Both Jesus and Paul want to ensure that with regard to God's commands people don't miss the forest for the trees. They direct people back to the central interpersonal requirement of the law as an organizing framework for the rest of the law. Love is thus the supreme virtue (John 13:34–35; 1 Cor. 13:1–13; Gal. 5:6; Col. 3:14; 1 Thess. 4:9; 1 Tim. 1:5). Paul applies the centrality of love to specific situations in Romans 12:9–21, echoing Jesus's teachings on loving enemies. Paul admonishes, "Bless those who persecute you" (Rom.

---

21. Blomberg observes that Paul's source material from the Gospels seems concentrated in the Sermon on the Mount and the Olivet Discourse (Craig L. Blomberg, "Quotations, Allusions, and Echoes of Jesus in Paul," in *Studies in the Pauline Epistles: Essays in Honor of Douglas J. Moo*, eds. Matthew S. Harmon and Jay E. Smith [Grand Rapids: Zondervan, 2014], 142).

22. See Kim, "Jesus, Sayings of," 475–77; Wenham, *Follower of Jesus?*, 305–19.

12:14), mirroring Jesus's mandate to "love your enemies and pray for those who persecute you" (Matt. 5:44). Paul also cautions, "Do not repay anyone evil for evil" and "overcome evil with good" (Rom. 12:17, 21; see also 1 Thess. 5:15), preserving the spirit of Jesus's teaching to treat enemies in unexpectedly good ways (Matt. 5:38–48).[23]

Paul's description of the process of church discipline also coincides with Jesus's teaching from Matthew 18:15–20. Paul promotes the same careful procedure of confronting believers for unrepentant sin (1 Cor. 5:1–2; Matt. 18:16), beginning with a gentle encounter (Gal. 6:1; Matt. 18:15), securing witnesses for any accusations (1 Tim. 5:19; Matt. 18:16), being willing to remove a professing believer from fellowship for a time (1 Cor. 5:5, 9–11; 2 Thess. 3:14; Matt. 18:17b), making this drastic move a shared decision by the church (2 Cor. 2:6; 1 Tim. 5:20; Matt. 18:17a), and understanding the heavenly authority that such steps entail (1 Cor. 5:3–4; 2 Cor. 2:10; Matt. 18:18–20). Paul, like Jesus, commends this approach for believers in particular, not as a way to interact with people outside the church (1 Cor 5:11–13; Matt. 18:15).

Paul follows in Jesus's footsteps in a number of other areas.[24] He views God as a loving Father and even addresses him with the affectionate Aramaic term, *Abba* (Rom. 8:15; Gal. 4:6; see Mark 14:36). He champions the way of the cross—a life of sacrifice, suffering, and service to the Lord (Rom. 15:1–3; Phil. 3:7–14), embodying Jesus's vision of losing one's life to find it (Matt. 10:39; 13:44–46; 16:25). He talks about laying up treasures in heaven through financial generosity in this life (1 Tim. 6:18–19; see Matt. 6:19–21). Paul's reconsidered notions of what is clean and unclean can be traced back to Jesus (Rom. 14:14, 20; see Mark 7:15–19). Paul observes that God chooses the unexpected to belong to him (1 Cor. 1:26–29), reflecting Jesus's enjoyment of God revealing his truth to the little children rather than to the wise (Matt. 11:25–26; Luke 10:21). Paul's description of the surprising recipients of God's call matches the unremarkable reputation of Jesus's chosen disciples (see Acts 4:13).

It is easy to drive a wedge between Jesus and Paul, and many Christians today are sympathetic to the idea that Paul somehow departs from the pure outlook and teachings of Jesus. While Paul doesn't simply advance the same narrative that other disciples who had been with Jesus were already propagating, he still makes Jesus the "foundation" (1 Cor. 3:10–11) and "chief cornerstone" (Eph. 2:20) of his teaching. Paul prioritizes and unfolds the truths that Jesus himself put in the foreground—Jesus's death for sins and his resurrection from the dead. These were events that Jesus predicted multiple times but left undeveloped because of his disciples' lack

---

23. See mention of these passages, along with other possible parallels, in Dunn, *Theology of Paul*, 650–51.
24. Some of these are discussed in Kim, "Jesus, Sayings of," 477–80; Dunn, *Theology of Paul*, 189–95; Blomberg, "Quotations, Allusions, and Echoes," 133–42.

of understanding at the time (Mark 9:32; Luke 18:34). Jesus never intended for his teachings to be the final word. Jesus had commissioned his original disciples to continue his ministry by proclaiming to the world what they had witnessed about his death and resurrection (Luke 24:46–48). Jesus had appointed Paul to carry out that same task, especially to the Gentiles. Along the way, Paul reinforced the ideas of love, self-sacrifice, God's grace, and God's kingdom that were near and dear to Jesus's heart during his ministry.

SANCTIFIED COMMON SENSE

One passage from Paul's letters that often catches a reader's eye is 1 Corinthians 7. Aside from the practical (and sometimes difficult to understand) instructions on singleness, marriage, and divorce, Paul also speaks in intriguing ways about the sources of his advice. At one point he credits "the Lord" for the information he shares (1 Cor. 7:10), while at other times he volunteers that he speaks without relaying the Lord's specific command (1 Cor. 7:12, 25, 40). What is going on here?

Paul is not differentiating between which directives are mandatory and which are optional, as some readers assume when they first read this language. Instead, Paul is making careful statements about his sources that confirm what we have already seen about his reliance on Jesus's teachings. He wants to specify when he appeals to Jesus's prior teaching on marriage and divorce (as found in Matthew 5:32 or 19:3–9, for example) and make clear when he does not.[25] When Jesus has not spoken about some of the specific challenges facing the Corinthians, Paul offers his own wisdom on those topics. Paul is still an apostle when he communicates these teachings, and from that position as apostle, Paul provides his own "judgment" (7:25, 40) on these matters.[26] Even without a specific word from the Lord confirming his judgments, Paul still calls himself "trustworthy" (7:25) and sees himself as backed by the Spirit (7:40) in his assessments.

This passage opens a window to what Paul does in his other letters too. Since Paul's letters are occasional, or designed to answer specific questions and provide guidance for specific challenges, Paul often has to venture out from the direct teachings of the Old Testament and Jesus. A good example is in the letter to Philemon. Paul applies truth about equality in Christ and the power of the gospel of reconciliation to a specific, complex relationship between a master and slave. While Paul doesn't qualify his words in Philemon as he did in 1 Corinthians 7, he exhibits the same approach in both places—an approach that applies established Christian truth and is guided by sanctified common sense.[27]

---

25. See a discussion of the correlations between Paul's perspective (1 Cor. 7) and Jesus's (Matt. 19 and Mark 10) in Wenham, *Follower of Jesus?*, 242–50.

26. Note the similar language of Paul submitting his own judgment in 2 Corinthians 8:10.

27. See other case studies in Dunn, *Theology of Paul*, 674–712.

PREFORMED CHRISTIAN MATERIAL

At times Paul may have appealed to portions of early Christian hymns, creeds, or other traditional material that churches learned or recited in worship settings. Some scholars detect occasional poetic passages that surface in Paul's letters, and they apply additional tests to determine the likelihood that Paul includes material from elsewhere.[28] Some passages that are commonly identified as preformed excerpts include Romans 1:3–4, 1 Corinthians 8:6, Philippians 2:6–11, Colossians 1:15–20, 1 Timothy 3:16, and 2 Timothy 2:11–13. Many of these examples are worshipful reflections on the person and work of Christ.

It is difficult to prove whether these are preexisting liturgical expressions or manifestations of Paul's own poetic creativity. At times there are surprising conceptual and verbal connections between the fragments and the surrounding material in Paul's letters.[29] Whether Paul borrowed or wrote the material, the content marches in step with Paul's theology from elsewhere in his letters. If Paul did enlist these preformed traditions he did not depend upon them so much as sources for his understanding but rather included them because they communicated in a memorable way truths he already agreed with.

ONGOING REVELATION

Christ's initial revelation to Paul on the road to Damascus marked the definitive turning point in Paul's theological perspective. But Christ promised that Paul would see more of him beyond that first incident, and that Paul should be ready to testify about those experiences as well (Acts 26:16).[30] Paul also sometimes speaks about his teaching as a mystery that has now been revealed to him (and at times to other ministers), which may occasionally refer to direct insight the Lord gave him, beyond the first encounter. How much did these ongoing revelations influence the substance of Paul's teaching?[31]

---

28. See for instance Richards, *Paul and First-Century Letter Writing*, 97–99; Ralph P. Martin, "Hymns, Hymn Fragments, Songs, Spiritual Songs," *DPL* 420–21.

29. Consider for instance the striking appearance of cognate or compound forms of three words from Philippians 2:6–8 (μορφή, σχῆμα, and ταπεινόω) in Philippians 3:21 (σύμμορφος, μετασχη-ματίζω, and ταπείνωσις). This has the effect of connecting Christ's exaltation from Philippians 2:9–11 (as a reversal of his humiliation in 2:6–8) to the believer's glorification in 3:21.

30. God divulges information specific to Paul's travels and trials several times (Acts 18:9–10; 22:17–21; 23:11; 2 Cor. 12:9), but these revelations are different from the disclosures of theological truth that are under discussion here.

31. One popular theory that lacks a strong foundation is that Paul spent a period of time in mystical communion with the Lord in Arabia (Gal. 1:17), and that he received much of his theology during that season of isolation. But Galatians 1:17 never describes it that way, and other verses suggest that Paul immediately jumped into missionary outreach during that time (Acts 9:20–30; 2 Cor. 11:32–33). See Bruce, *Apostle of the Heart Set Free*, 81–82.

In one extended passage, Paul talks circumspectly about "visions and revelations from the Lord," which his detractors valued as the mark of a true apostle (2 Cor. 12:1). The passage this verse introduces occurs in a larger section where Paul attempts to beat his opponents at their own game of boasting by highlighting his surprising credentials as an apostle—his weaknesses, and God's strength through his weaknesses. But in 2 Corinthians 12:1–6 Paul does recount God visiting him in some supernatural ways. Paul speaks cryptically about "a man in Christ who fourteen years ago was caught up to the third heaven . . . and heard inexpressible things" (2 Cor. 12:2–4). Yes, he is talking about himself here, but he is speaking about himself in the third person to make a point about the misguided boasting his opponents have succumbed to.[32] It's his way of saying, "I could make a big deal about this, but I won't."

So, what do we know about this unusual experience Paul had? First, it does not match chronologically with his Damascus Road vision. From Galatians 2:1 and some other clues to Paul's timeline, we know that the "fourteen years ago" Paul mentions in 2 Corinthians 12:2 would have been years after that trip to Damascus. The second thing we know is that the mode and content of revelation differed significantly from what Paul experienced on the road to Damascus. Christ had descended and appeared to Paul on his journey to Damascus, but in this case Paul was somehow caught up into "the third heaven" or "paradise," which are both ways of describing the dwelling of God in a spiritual realm beyond our world.[33] Paul then describes the knowledge he acquired as "inexpressible" and involving things that "no one is permitted to tell" (2 Cor. 12:4). Paul suggests that he has not transmitted to others the things that he learned that day. The extraordinary content Paul received that day apparently did not become one of the sources of his teaching.

Paul still does mention that God promised to unveil additional truths to him (Acts 26:16). Could these correspond to the "mystery" language that Paul incorporates in some of his letters? Inspired by precedents in Daniel 2, New Testament writers typically use "mystery" to refer to truth that was previously hidden but has now been disclosed in the era of Christ. Sometimes, however, Paul's reception of revealed mysteries can be accounted for by his initial exposure to the resurrected Christ on the road to Damascus. As we have seen, Christ imparted major pieces of the puzzle to Paul that day, including his resurrection, his status as Messiah and Son of God, and Paul's appointment to be a minister to the Gentiles. A mix of those primary elements surface in a handful of Paul's mystery passages (Rom. 16:25–26; 1 Cor. 2:6–10; Eph. 1:9–10; 3:2–9; 6:19; Col. 1:25–27;

---

32. See Paul Barnett, *The Second Epistle to the Corinthians*, NICNT (Grand Rapids: Eerdmans, 1997), 562.

33. See Craig S. Keener, *The IVP Bible Background Commentary: New Testament*, 2nd ed. (Downers Grove, IL: IVP Academic, 2014), 520–21.

2:2–3; 4:3; 1 Tim. 3:16). In two other passages, though, Paul labels more specific information as a mystery, implying that these insights could be the product of some additional revelation (Rom. 11:25; 1 Cor. 15:51).[34] In both passages, however, Paul provides supporting evidence from the Old Testament for his assertions (Rom. 11:26–27; 1 Cor. 15:54–55). This suggests that even these mysteries came to light through Jesus's fulfillment of the Old Testament story, even if Paul may have received special guidance to discern this and put all of the pieces together.[35]

Several other passages communicate similar ideas to the mystery passages without using mystery language. Information about the believer's bodily resurrection is attributed to "the Lord's word" (1 Thess. 4:15), in parallel to 1 Corinthians 15:51–52.[36] Paul's comment that the Spirit has foretold future apostasy (1 Tim. 4:1) corresponds to the idea of God uncovering the previously concealed mystery of Christ by means of the Spirit in 1 Corinthians 2:10. These two examples are not clear-cut instances of special revelation, however. The Lord's word could refer to Jesus's teachings while on earth (after all, much of 1 Thessalonians 4–5 alludes to Jesus's teachings from his Olivet Discourse). Likewise, Paul may have in mind some concepts derived from the Old Testament or Jesus's teachings (Matt. 24:10–11) when he refers to the Spirit's disclosure in 1 Timothy 4:1.[37] Though the source material for these two divine messages cannot be identified with certainty, it is still inconclusive that these are cases of new revelation to Paul.

Apart from these examples, Paul never explicitly claims that he received his information from special instances of divine communication.[38] I recommend exhausting other alternatives for the sources of Paul's ideas before resorting to the special revelation option. We frequently can explain and even defend Paul's ideas along one of two lines. First, his teachings could represent logical outgrowths of some combination of Old Testament theology, the recognition of Jesus as the promised Messiah and fulfillment of God's plans, the earthly teachings of Christ, and other familiar ideas that were well known in early Christian circles. Second, Paul's teachings could reflect judicious applications of those truths to problems within the church.

---

34. Bockmuehl, *Revelation and Mystery*, 170–75.
35. Ibid.
36. Ibid., 170–72.
37. Supporting a source in Jesus's teaching is George W. Knight III, *The Pastoral Epistles: A Commentary on the Greek Text*, NIGTC (Grand Rapids: Eerdmans; Carlisle: Paternoster, 1992), 188. Opting for a prophetic revelation given to Paul for other believers is Philip H. Towner, *The Letters to Timothy and Titus*, NICNT (Grand Rapids: Eerdmans, 2006), 287–88. Remaining undecided is William D. Mounce, *Pastoral Epistles*, WBC 46 (Dallas: Word, 2000), 234.
38. Two other references, to "the Lord's command" (1 Cor. 14:37) and commands given "through the Lord Jesus" (1 Thess. 4:2, ESV), could indicate specially obtained revelation but may also refer to the apostolic authority given to Paul by the Lord Jesus.

CONCLUSION

As readers we can glean insights into how we should view the Scriptures from the way Paul interacts with his sources. First, we should remember for our own studies that the Old Testament and the Gospels are important prerequisites for studying the letters of Paul. If Paul was assuming foundational knowledge of the Old Testament and the life and teachings of Christ as a starting point, we as readers should make sure that we are proficient in that content as well. Beyond this recognition, be on the lookout for connections between Paul's ideas and prior teachings from the Old Testament and Jesus. Try to see both Paul's obvious dependence on specific passages as well as the thoughtful ways that Paul builds upon existing material for new settings. We can treasure Paul's Spirit-inspired words as part of a greater whole—the Scriptures that include the Old Testament, Gospels, and other New Testament writings that speak with one voice about the wonders and saving mercies of God.

Paul draws upon other sources of knowledge in instructive ways as well. We can appreciate how Paul's life-changing encounter on the road to Damascus reshaped his understanding of God's unfolding work in the world. Paul spoke with firsthand assurance that the God of the Bible was "on the move" through his Son Jesus Christ, who had been raised from the dead. Accordingly, our experiences of walking with the living God should open our eyes even more to the rich truth that we read about in the pages of the Bible. Similarly, we can learn from the wisdom Paul demonstrated when he applied his deeply grounded theology to address specific problems in his churches. God's truth awaits practical implementation. The Bible doesn't supply us with exhaustive guidance for every specific challenge or opportunity. But we can follow Paul's lead in applying profound theological truth to the various decisions we face. God's Word and his Spirit work in tandem to guide us through every circumstance in life.

■ ■ ■

CHAPTER TWELVE

HOW DOES PAUL INTERACT WITH THE OLD TESTAMENT?

Few things are as exciting for me as seeing connections among different passages in Scripture. Such discoveries remind me of the basic unity of Scripture, arising from the fact that there is one Divine Author who speaks in each chapter and verse of the Bible. Sometimes the connections I detect are simply in my mind as a reader, but other times Spirit-inspired human authors such as Paul made the connections intentionally. Reading the Bible while on the lookout for the interplay between later passages and earlier ones helps us enjoy the coherence and progression of the Scriptures. In general, thoughtful readers of literature may recognize the significance of a writing's placement within an existing stream of other works, which may exert direct and indirect influence on the wording and content of the text under investigation. Paul's letters swim in a stream filled with Old Testament works and ideas. In Pauline studies Richard Hays has been especially ambitious in exploring inner-biblical relationships in Paul's letters.[1] Paul regularly calls upon the verses, passages, and broader narrative of the Old Testament to enrich the teachings he imparts to his readers. Hays has encouraged readers to be keenly attuned to the creative and insightful ways Paul integrates the Old Testament into his letters. Warning: This way of reading the Scriptures is addictive!

It is tempting to think of Paul's references to the Old Testament as scattered threads that hold two things together but could easily break under pressure. Didn't Paul just quote Old Testament passages as proof texts, to artificially bolster his arguments? It would be a big mistake to think of Paul's use of the Old Testament this way. It underestimates the significance of the Old Testament to Paul and other Jewish believers in the

---

1. See especially Richard B. Hays, *Echoes of Scripture in the Letters of Paul* (New Haven, CT: Yale University Press, 1989); Hays, *The Conversion of the Imagination: Paul as Interpreter of Israel's Scripture* (Grand Rapids: Eerdmans, 2005).

early church. We view the Old Testament as a distant skyscraper in our
peripheral vision as we drive by a city, on our way to our final destination
somewhere else. But Paul was standing in the middle of downtown, with
buildings looming over him and making their presence known. The Old
Testament wasn't something to nod to in passing, but was the setting in
which Jesus's ministry sprang up. The Old Testament, simply known as *the*
Scriptures in Paul's day, was the unrivaled account of what God had done
in the world so far, preparing for Jesus's entrance onto the scene.

In the last chapter I contended that Paul drew upon the Old Testament as a major source for his teachings. In this chapter we will investigate
further Paul's indebtedness to the Old Testament and the ways he sees the
Scriptures pointing towards a new era in Christ. Trying to interpret Paul's
letters without any awareness of his interaction with the Old Testament
leaves us with an impoverished view of what Paul is trying to say. In this
chapter we will find that Paul grasps the revelatory purpose of the Old
Testament and discerns covenantal dynamics of promise and fulfillment
alongside a contrast between the old and the new when he connects Christ
to the Scriptures. We will also examine how Paul delves into specific Old
Testament passages with varied and creative approaches that are nonetheless faithful to the unfolding story of Scripture. Finally, it will become
apparent that when Paul selects and arranges Old Testament material
he turns to certain passages multiple times and often gathers different
passages together at various points in his letters.

THE RELEVANCE OF THE OLD TESTAMENT TO PAUL

Paul embraces the Old Testament Scriptures as highly relevant to his
teachings and writings, but he knows that they are relevant only when
understood properly. The Old Testament on its own doesn't determine
what life with God should look like. Instead, the Old Testament points
primarily toward Jesus's fulfillment of God's saving plans. In other words,
the principal function of the Old Testament for New Testament believers
is revelatory, rather than regulatory.[2] For instance, in Romans 3:21 Paul
says, "But now apart from the law the righteousness of God has been made
known, to which the Law and the Prophets testify." Paul says a lot about his
view of the Old Testament from this one verse. In the first half of the verse
Paul refers to "the law" as a system initiated by God to govern his people
Israel. Paul reiterates his point from the previous verse that people cannot
"be declared righteous in God's sight by the works of the law" (Rom. 3:20).
But "the Law and the Prophets" (Rom. 3:21b) denotes the Old Testament

---

2. For the helpful language of the regulatory and revelatory functions of the law, see Wayne G.
Strickland, "The Inauguration of the Law of Christ with the Gospel of Christ: A Dispensational
View," in *Five Views on the Law and the Gospel*, ed. Wayne G. Strickland (Grand Rapids: Zonder-
van, 1996), 277–79.

in its revelatory function: it "testifies" about a new way of righteousness by pointing to Jesus. Luke characterizes Paul's teaching this way as well: "[Paul] witnessed to them from morning till evening, explaining about the kingdom of God, and from the Law of Moses and from the Prophets he tried to persuade them about Jesus" (Acts 28:23).

Paul's most basic yet most profound insight about the Old Testament is that it testifies to Jesus as the cornerstone of God's divine building program. In Romans, before Paul introduces any of the major topics of the letter, he announces a gospel "promised beforehand through his prophets in the Holy Scriptures regarding his Son" (Rom. 1:2–3; see also Gal. 3:8). Note also Paul's repetition in 1 Corinthians 15:3–4 (emphasis added): "For what I received I passed on to you as of first importance: that Christ died for our sins *according to the Scriptures,* that he was buried, that he was raised on the third day *according to the Scriptures.*" The pattern persists to the end of Paul's ministry: "You have known the Holy Scriptures, which are able to make you wise for salvation through faith in Jesus Christ" (2 Tim. 3:15). Paul declares a message that can be best understood against the backdrop of the Old Testament Scriptures. Trying to make sense of Jesus without the Old Testament would be like skipping to the final chapters of a novel without reading all of the chapters that came before them. According to plan, Jesus stepped into the story and brought resolution to God's epic script for the world.

A corollary to seeing Christ's ministry as the continuation and resolution of the Old Testament story is that believers in Christ become part of that unfolding story. Believers in Christ identify as the people of God, in continuity with God's chosen people from the Old Testament. For Paul, that means that believers embrace the Old Testament as their story as well, and that God continues to speak actively through the Old Testament Scriptures in believers' lives. Paul insists that the Old Testament as a whole has bearing on our lives (Rom. 15:4; 1 Cor. 10:11, 1 Tim. 3:16–17). He also contends that specific Old Testament verses were written for our benefit (Rom. 4:23–24; 1 Cor. 9:9–10). The enduring connections Paul sees between the Old Testament Scriptures and present life for the church leads Hays to characterize Paul's hermeneutic (philosophy of interpretation) as *ecclesiocentric* in addition to *Christocentric*.[3] Paul reads the Old Testament with his eyes on Christ and the church, and conversely, Christ and the church make the most sense against an Old Testament backdrop.

Paul's confidence in Scripture never wavered, since he perceived that all parts of the Old Testament testified to the eternal work of God in this world. Paul appreciated the revelatory power of Scripture and broadcast how God's saving plans that originated in the Old Testament came to fruition in Christ for the church. Paul acknowledges the full and enduring relevance of the Old Testament for the lives of believers. But as we will

---

3. See Hays, *Echoes of Scripture,* 120–21; Hays, *Conversion of the Imagination,* 186–87.

learn in the next section, the authority of the Old Testament takes shape within our new covenant setting in salvation history.

HOW PAUL'S TEACHINGS ARE GROUNDED IN THE OLD TESTAMENT STORY AS A WHOLE

We can consider how Paul understands Christ (and the church) as fulfilling the Old Testament story on both a macro level and a micro level. We can't skip hurriedly to the micro level, because the individual threads Paul weaves from the Old Testament to Jesus are part of a larger tapestry that displays how Paul saw Christ consummating Israel's story.

Paul's use of Old Testament ideas and texts was governed by an understanding of covenantal history, or God's revealed history of defined relationships with his people.[4] In certain places Paul demonstrates a keen awareness of the progressive unfolding of God's dealings with his people (Romans 9–11 and Galatians 3–4 stand out in this regard). Paul does not read the Old Testament as a flat and static collection of documents. He sees movement within the Old Testament. God is directing history, carrying out his plans in mysterious ways that can nonetheless be tracked by sensitive readers, especially in hindsight. Covenants are central to these plans.[5]

God made a series of interrelated covenants with Israel, moving from his covenant with Abraham, to his covenant with Israel (through Moses), to the Davidic covenant, and finally, to promises of a new covenant.[6] The Abrahamic covenant consists of gracious promises God announced to Abraham's family (Gen. 12:1–3; 15:1–21; 17:1–8), with the stipulation that Abraham and his descendants should walk faithfully with God (Gen. 17:9; 18:19).[7] Generations later, when God delivered Abraham's descendants the Israelites from Egypt, he set them apart as his special people, with a sacred mission to the rest of the world (Exod. 19:4–6). As part of the Mosaic covenant God forged with the Israelites, he gave them ceremonial, moral, and civil laws that would govern their practices as a holy nation. The Israelites would need to respond to God's gracious deliverance and ongoing presence by obeying his commands and carrying out his laws. Over the years and centuries that followed the Israelites consistently wandered from God and were unfaithful to these covenant obligations. They rejected God through idolatry, selfishness, and injustice. This covenantal failure created the need for a drastic intervention in the form of a promised new covenant (Jer. 31:31–34). God promised to forgive the Israelites' sins and give them the resources and

---

4. See also Helyer, *Jesus, Paul and John*, 394–95.
5. A covenantal framework corresponds to the idea of "a narrative of election and promise," which are the words of Hays, *Echoes of Scripture*, 183–84.
6. God's covenant with Noah, along with some other more minor covenants or covenant renewals, are less significant to the story Paul delves into.
7. These covenants were later confirmed to Abraham, Isaac, and Jacob.

motivation to be devoted to him in covenant relationship. Chief among these gifts would be the provision of his own Spirit (Isa. 44:3–4; 59:21; Ezek. 36:24–28; Joel 2:28–32). Meanwhile, God promised Abraham's descendant David that a dynasty, leading to an everlasting kingdom, would rise through his line (2 Sam. 7:4–29). This leads us to Jesus.

Paul understands that the promised new covenant comes to fruition in Jesus, as explained by Jesus at his last supper with his disciples (1 Cor. 11:23–25; see also Mark 14:22–25 and parallels). This inauguration of the new covenant gives God's new covenant people access to the blessings promised through the Abrahamic and Davidic covenants (Rom. 4:13–17; 15:12; Gal. 3:7–14, 29; Eph. 2:11–13; 2 Tim. 2:8). Moreover, Paul proclaims that all of God's promises are now "Yes" in Christ (2 Cor. 1:20). These promises are secured already in Christ, are guaranteed by the Spirit, and will be experienced in full when Christ returns (2 Cor. 1:21–22). What this means for Paul's use of the Old Testament is that he discerns a promise–fulfillment pattern from the Old Testament to Christ. The story that began in the Old Testament reaches its resolution in Christ, by the Spirit.

The significance of the arrival of the new covenant doesn't end with promise and fulfillment. Paul also sees some discontinuity between the old (Mosaic) covenant and the new covenant. The new covenant, though in some continuity with the old covenant, also replaces the old covenant. That means that the old covenant is no longer the governing system for a believer's life. Its comprehensive regulatory function (as law) for the people of God has ended (Rom. 3:21a; 7:1–6; 10:4; Gal. 3:23–24; 1 Tim. 1:8–10). The new covenant revealed in Christ becomes the means by which God relates to his people.[8] God's revelation throughout the Old Testament (since the time of Moses) was given as part of Israel's relationship with God as defined under the old covenant. Paul takes this into account when he appeals to teaching from the Old Testament, meaning that Old Testament teaching is not always *directly* applicable to new covenant believers. Paul still affirms the value of *all* of the Old Testament, which is clear from passages such as Romans 15:4, 1 Corinthians 10:11, and 2 Timothy 3:16–17. But the life relevance of the Scriptures is reconfigured within a new covenant context.

The move from old to new covenant also explains some of Paul's language of contrast in his letters. Condemnation under the law in the old covenant is contrasted with forgiveness and life in Christ in the new covenant (Rom. 3:19–24; 8:1–4). Bondage under the law in the old covenant is contrasted with freedom in Christ in the new covenant (Gal. 4:21–31). Circumcision in the old covenant is contrasted with new creation in the new covenant (Gal. 6:15). Veiled encounters with God in the old covenant

---

8. Not surprisingly, God requires the same general outcomes for both old and new covenant believers. Because of his unchanging character, he still loves kindness, mercy, justice, righteousness, and holiness. In the new covenant God delivers a recast vision for what the specific expressions of those values should look like.

are contrasted with direct access to God's glorious presence in the new
covenant (2 Cor. 3:7–18). Paul does not dismiss Old Testament Scripture
in these passages. Rather, he acknowledges the failure of the people of God
to be faithful under the old covenant, which brought about the need for a
transforming and liberating new covenant. The teachings of the Old Testament can now be honored and obeyed by people who have been forgiven
and set free in Christ and empowered by the Spirit.

The new covenant is marked by the ministry of the Son and the gift of
the Spirit. The definitive revelation of the Son and Spirit invite a fuller Trinitarian account of God's work in the world.[9] Like several other New Testament
authors Paul specifies that the world was created through Jesus, and that he
continues to actively hold all things together (Col. 1:15–17; see John 1:3, 10;
Heb. 1:1–3). At the other end of the story, as God's appointed king Jesus will
judge and reign over the world (Rom. 2:16; 1 Cor. 15:24–28; 2 Cor. 5:10;
2 Tim. 2:12; 4:1). In the meantime, Jesus sits at God's right hand, with all
authority over the world and the church (Rom. 8:34; Eph. 1:20–23; Col. 3:1).

Paul also highlights Jesus's divine authority and identity when he
seamlessly associates Jesus with the eschatological concept of the day of
the Lord (which becomes the day of Christ or the day of the Lord Jesus—1
Cor. 1:8; 2 Cor. 1:14; Phil. 1:6, 10; 2:16). Other Old Testament passages
that elevate the name of God become readily transferable to Jesus in the
new covenant era (Joel 2:32 and Rom. 10:13; Isa. 45:23–25 and Phil. 2:10–
11).[10] The same can be said for the divine title "Savior" (Eph. 5:23; Phil.
3:20; 2 Tim. 1:10; Titus 1:4; 2:13; 3:6).[11]

Even the fundamental affirmation of the Shema—"Hear, O Israel: The
LORD our God, the LORD is one" (Deut. 6:4) takes on richer expression in
Paul's letters. Paul confesses, "yet for us there is but one God, the Father,
from whom all things came and for whom we live; and there is but one
Lord, Jesus Christ, through whom all things came and through whom we
live" (1 Cor. 8:6; see also 1 Tim. 2:5). Paul proclaims the shared glory of
Father and Son as the necessary implication of Jesus's resurrection and
exaltation, in line with the worship practices of the early church.[12] Paul also
sees the recognition of God's exclusive reign, recounted in the Shema and
anticipated to overflow into all nations (Zech. 14:9) being accomplished
only through Jesus, who justifies both Jews and Gentiles (Rom. 3:29–31;

---

9.   Trinitarian language and concepts had not been crystallized at this point in church history, but
     Trinitarian judgments and assumptions are displayed in the writings of Paul and other apostles
     (see David S. Yeago, "The New Testament and the Nicene Dogma: A Contribution to the Redis-
     covery of Theological Exegesis," *ProEccl* 3 [1994]: 152–64).

10. See Larry W. Hurtado, *Lord Jesus Christ: Devotion to Jesus in Earliest Christianity* (Grand Rapids:
     Eerdmans, 2003), 112.

11. Titus 2:13 may even identify Jesus as God, in addition to Savior. The grammatical construction
     Paul uses points to this likelihood (Daniel B. Wallace, *Greek Grammar beyond the Basics: An
     Exegetical Syntax of the New Testament* [Grand Rapids: Zondervan, 1996], 276).

12. See Hurtado, *Devotion to Jesus in Earliest Christianity*, 134–53.

10:12). According to Paul the exclusive glory of God is not threatened by Christ but actually realizes its universal scope in Christ.[13]

Earlier we commented upon the Spirit's close association with the arrival of the new covenant in the Old Testament, and Paul retains and develops this pairing in his letters, highlighting the Spirit's permanent indwelling and empowering of believers in the new covenant era (1 Cor. 12:4–13; 2 Cor. 3:4–18). Paul also celebrates the Spirit's role in giving life (Rom. 8:2; 2 Cor. 3:6; Gal. 5:25), in step with Old Testament foundations connecting life and spiritual renewal with God's breath or Spirit (Gen. 1:2; 2:7; 6:3; 7:22; Ps. 33:6; 104:29–30; Ezek. 36:24–28). The Spirit who furnishes believers with spiritual life is the agent of resurrected life when Christ returns (Rom. 8:11; Eph. 1:13–14). In true Trinitarian fashion Paul recognizes the Spirit's distinct work but also preserves the indissoluble union within the Godhead in his language about the Spirit in relation to Father and Son (Rom. 1:2–4; 8:9–10; 1 Cor. 12:4–6; 2 Cor. 3:17; 13:14; Gal. 4:6; Eph. 2:21–22; 3:16–17; 2 Thess. 2:13–14; Titus 3:5–6).[14]

To summarize this section, Paul's sensitivity to the covenantal progression of salvation history helps him see both promise-fulfillment and old-new patterns from the Old Testament to Christ. Elements of both continuity and discontinuity are featured at the turning point of God's grand narrative for the world. That means that Paul affirms the Old Testament as revealed by God as valuable for Christian living, as long as it as seen as pointing to Christ and put into practice within the realities of the new covenant relationship between God and his people. It also means that a fuller Trinitarian vision emerges in Paul's recounting of God's story.

HOW PAUL INCORPORATES SPECIFIC OLD TESTAMENT PASSAGES INTO HIS LETTERS

Appreciating Paul's treatment of the Old Testament on a macro level is essential for reading his letters. Once the macro patterns are determined, we can delve into how Paul uses the Old Testament on a micro level.

Paul's inclusion of source material is not always as straightforward as directly quoting a prior work. This is true for Paul's interaction with specific Old Testament passages as well. Paul does quote passages, but he also frequently alludes to or even echoes Old Testament wording and ideas.[15] The quotations can be easy to identify, but detecting allusions and

---

13. See Gregory S. MaGee, "Paul's Gospel, the Law, and God's Universal Reign in Romans 3:31," *JETS* 57 (2014): 341–50.

14. See the discussion of Paul's Trinitarian view of the Spirit in Gordon D. Fee, *God's Empowering Presence: The Holy Spirit in the Letters of Paul* (Peabody, MA: Hendrickson, 1994), 834–42.

15. Scholars have been conversant with the difference between quotations and allusions for a long time, but Richard Hays helped popularize the notion of echoes more recently. Echoes are less obvious than allusions, and they may not even be conscious connections made by the author. See Hays, *Echoes of Scripture*, 25–33.

echoes requires a more careful reading. Lack of familiarity with the Old Testament hinders many readers, but the good news is that the more we read the Old Testament, the more readily we can pick up on allusions and echoes. Paul's own deep immersion in the Old Testament thought-world and language is why he so naturally implanted many Old Testament excerpts and ideas into his letters.

Each instance of Paul quoting, alluding to, or echoing Old Testament passages deserves its own consideration.[16] Paul doesn't follow a set pattern in his dealings with the Old Testament. Sometimes he appeals to Old Testament passages directly to support a principle or command (2 Cor. 8:15; Eph. 6:1–3). Other times he may recall specific wording as a nod to the entire Old Testament passage in which the wording is found (Rom. 10:16; 1 Cor. 10:7). Paul regularly refers to summaries of Old Testament ideas such as the kingdom of God, day of the Lord, the temple, or the law. Paul also reflects creative engagement with the Old Testament, similar to what is found in the practice of his Jewish contemporaries.[17] This can include discerning typological (Rom. 5:12–19; 1 Cor. 10:1–10) or even allegorical (Gal. 4:21–31) correspondences between old covenant and new covenant events, institutions, or characters.[18] A key point to remember is that however Paul does appeal to Scripture, he does so within his broader grasp of promise and fulfillment and the progression from old to new covenant. Otherwise, his references to Old Testament verses can at times sound arbitrary. We will present the interplay between macro level and micro level perspectives in two examples that follow.

First, Paul enlists passages regarding both Abraham and David in Romans 4:1–8. Abraham and David are especially significant as recipients of the covenant promises of God. From the vantage point of God's sweeping redemptive work, their experiences preview the forgiveness and righteousness believers receive through faith because of God's gracious provision of Christ. This larger agenda also accords with the finer details of the passages and why they are brought together in the first place. One regular Jewish exegetical practice known as *gezerah shewa* features linking together two otherwise unrelated passages because of key words and ideas that they share in common. In this case, the Septuagint translations of Genesis 15:6 (Rom.

---

16. An excellent resource for in-depth analysis of most occurrences of the New Testament use of the Old Testament is *Commentary on the New Testament Use of the Old Testament* (Beale and Carson).

17. Richard N. Longenecker, *Biblical Exegesis in the Apostolic Period*, 2nd ed. (Grand Rapids: Eerdmans; Vancouver: Regent, 1999), 6–35, 98–116.

18. The difference between typology and allegory is subtle. Typology is the tighter category. It discerns recurring patterns in salvation history, seeing earlier people, events, and institutions as preparatory for later ones, especially in the new covenant era. Allegory is a freer interpretation that explores the metaphorical significance of texts. Many scholars do not consider Galatians 4:21–31 to display pure allegorical interpretation because it reflects certain historical correspondences, even if rather creatively.

4:3) and Psalm 32:1–2 (Rom. 4:7–8) share the terms for "credit" ("count," ESV; from λογίζομαι), along with the similar concepts of righteousness and forgiveness. Moreover, in both cases it is God who credits his beloved servant with righteousness, or doesn't credit him with sin (by forgiving him). These cues signal to Paul that the passages belonged together in support of the new covenant truth of receiving forgiveness of sins through the work of Jesus.[19]

Second, two passages from 2 Timothy tap into the larger Scriptural narrative Paul operates within.[20] The promise-fulfillment structure of God's story means that God's kingdom is marching toward certain and total victory in our world. But until that final day, God's reign has been and will be sharply contested. This is a prominent theme throughout 2 Timothy. On a detailed level, Paul illustrates this with two nods to Old Testament events. First, he refers to wording from Numbers 16:5 (in the Septuagint)—Moses's foreboding comment to Korah and his followers that "the LORD will show who belongs to him." The story of Korah's uprising in general lurks behind the scenes in 2 Timothy 2:19.[21] In both settings resistance to God's work arises from within the community of faith (in Paul's case, from false teachers). Paul's conclusion that "everyone who confesses the name of the Lord must turn away from wickedness" (2 Tim. 2:19b) demonstrates that in order to live as God's holy people, on the march towards his kingdom, sometimes decisive action is needed. That was true for the Israelites in the days of Korah, and it remained true for the believers under Timothy's care. In a second location Paul's reference to Jannes and Jambres (2 Tim. 3:8–9),[22] who sought to oppose God by mimicking Moses's miraculous signs (Exod. 7:11–12, 22; 8:7, 18), further reinforces the division between God's servants and his enemies. The allusion to a well-known instance of opposition to God's work in the past helps Paul criticize false teachers while affirming that God's current work in the church carries on the legacy of God's great works from Israel's past. In both Korah's rebellion and the Egyptian magicians' resistance to God's work, Paul exposes the folly of opposing God's reign, since God's plans will certainly triumph over the resistance of his enemies. From this pair of accounts that Paul draws attention to in 2 Timothy 2–3 we see that Paul does not simply borrow language from the Old Testament when it is superficially convenient. He often recalls entire passages, using the specific wording or reference as a window into the broader event, in support of the points he emphasizes.

---

19. See this and other examples of Paul's use of *gezerah shewa* in Longenecker, *Biblical Exegesis in the Apostolic Period*, 100–101.
20. Many treatments of Paul's use of the Old Testament ignore the Pastoral Epistles altogether or give the letters just a cursory glance. Examples include Hays, *Echoes of Scripture*; Hays, *Conversion of the Imagination*; Steve Moyise, *Paul and Scripture: Studying the New Testament Use of the Old Testament* (Grand Rapids: Baker, 2010).
21. See Philip H. Towner, "1–2 Timothy and Titus," *CNTUOT* 906.
22. Ibid., 906–7. Jewish tradition identifies Jannes and Jambres as Pharaoh's magicians, who are unnamed in Exodus 7 and 8.

PAUL'S SELECTION AND ARRANGEMENT
OF OLD TESTAMENT PASSAGES

We can draw some tentative conclusions about Paul's perception of the Old Testament story and its relevance by observing some favorite Old Testament sources for Paul's letters and seeing how Paul arranged and integrated these sources into his writings. There are two ways of looking at this topic. First, the early Christians appear to have gravitated to a common collection of Old Testament passages that resonated especially well with Christ's agenda. Certain Old Testament passages surface on multiple occasions in different New Testament writings. Second, New Testament writers occasionally group related Old Testament passages together in one location to show the Old Testament basis and support for a theme they are emphasizing for a new era in Christ. We see both of these phenomena in Paul's letters.

Scholars speculate that certain Old Testament passages were formally or informally recognized as significant within the early church. They observe that passages such as Psalm 110:1–4, Psalm 118:22–26, Isaiah 6:9–10, Isaiah 53, and Habakkuk 2:4 are featured in writings from multiple Christian authors. Paul likewise draws upon select passages or sections of the Old Testament on more than one occasion. A pair of verses, Genesis 15:6 and Habakkuk 2:4, support Paul's teaching on being justified by faith in Christ, rather than by Jewish works of the law. Paul notices that Abraham's faith was credited as righteousness, and that this occurred before he was circumcised (Rom. 4:3, 9–12, 22; Gal. 3:6; see Gen. 15:6). Righteousness through faith thus becomes the way forward for all people, whether Jew or Gentile, and those who believe in Christ even now represent the fulfillment of the original words to Abraham (Rom. 4:22–25). Habakkuk 2:4 commends persevering faith (while waiting for God's promised deliverance) as the way the righteous one should live.[23] Paul sees this as paradigmatic for how people enter into and continue in God's family through Christ (Rom. 1:17; Gal. 3:11).

Paul also draws upon several passages from the generation of Israel's wilderness wanderings (1 Cor. 10:1–13; 2 Cor. 8:8–15; 2 Tim. 2:19). Paul may find this period to be particularly instructive for the early church because it required the people's extended patience, faith, and obedience between a time of initial deliverance (the exodus from Egypt) and an eventual promised payoff (entrance into the promised land). That mirrors believers' experience of exercising faith and perseverance between the time of Christ's initial ministry and his future return.

---

23. Paul's use of Habakkuk 2:4 in Romans 1:17 and Galatians 3:11 is filled with challenging textual and interpretive questions, but Paul's appropriate use of the passage can be defended. See Moisés Silva, "Galatians," *CNTUOT* 800–802.

Paul appears to lean heavily upon Isaiah 49–54 as well.[24] Paul sees his service to God along the lines of the chosen servant of Isaiah 49:1–7, since Paul was called "from the womb" (Gal. 1:15), carried out a ministry of both proclamation and suffering, was concerned that he had not "labored in vain" (Isa. 49:4; Gal. 4:11; Phil. 2:16; 1 Thess. 3:15; see also 1 Cor. 15:14; 2 Cor. 6:1; Gal. 2:2), and looked to God alone for marching orders and consolation. Paul finds special solace in the promise that God has believers' backs in the midst of opposition (Isa. 50:8–9; Rom. 8:32–34). Paul praises the messengers who bring the good news of God's reign (Isa. 52:7; Rom. 10:15; see also Eph. 6:15). As with many other New Testament authors, Paul quotes or alludes to the picture of the servant who suffered for the people's sins and was then exalted by God (Isa. 52:13–53:12; Rom. 4:25a; 10:16; 15:21; 1 Cor. 15:3; Phil. 2:6–11). Paul also quotes from additional verses from Isaiah 49–54 in various other places (Isa. 49:8 and 2 Cor. 6:2; Isa. 52:5 and Rom. 2:24; Isa. 52:11 and 2 Cor. 6:17; Isa. 54:1 and Gal. 4:27). Hays suggests that this section was fruitful ground for Paul because of its coherent vision of a gospel that promised to both restore Israel and radiate to all other nations, advanced by faithful servants who proclaimed this message of good news.[25]

In the reverse direction, sometimes Paul and other early Christian writers gathered a group of thematically related Old Testament passages into one densely packed section of a letter. This was a known practice even outside the Christian community at that time. Two of the Dead Sea scrolls consist of select Old Testament passages that are written out one after the other (or with minimal commentary interjected), with an identifiable theme linking them together. One scroll's verses appear to have Messianic interests (4QTest [4Q175]), while the other's verses are eschatologically oriented (4QFlor [4Q174]).[26] These scrolls testify to a tendency to group together thematically similar texts from the Old Testament. New Testament authors demonstrate a similar approach in passages such as Hebrews 1:5–13 and 1 Peter 2:6–8.

Paul too exhibits this method on several occasions.[27] In Romans 3:10–18 Paul works through a quick series of Old Testament verses that highlight thoroughgoing sinfulness and resistance to God.[28] A pair of passages from Hosea are set beside two excerpts from Isaiah to juxtapose the themes of God's surprising expansion of his people beyond Israel and the reduction of Israel to small remnant (Rom. 9:25–29). In Romans

---

24. See Hays, *Conversion of the Imagination*, 37–40.
25. Ibid., 39–40.
26. The Scriptural excerpts that are strung together one after another are known as *testimonia* (with the designation "Test" used in the Dead Sea scroll labeling), while the *florilegium* ("Flor") consists of a mix of collected texts and commentary.
27. Longenecker calls this method "pearl stringing" and includes a more comprehensive list of examples (*Biblical Exegesis in the Apostolic Period*, 99–100).
28. Some of the Old Testament verses in Romans 3:10–18 and other passages involve conflation, or the merging of wording from more than one verse into single clauses or sentences.

15:9–12 Paul rolls out Old Testament passages that celebrate the exposure of all nations to the glorious reign of God. In the compact section of 2 Corinthians 6:16–18 Paul calls upon passages that describe the blessings and responsibilities of living as God's holy people in God's holy presence. Finally, in 1 Corinthians 1:18–3:23, the Old Testament references are more spread out but all relate to the themes of pride and humility before God (1 Cor. 1:19 and Isa. 29:14; 1 Cor. 1:31 and Jer.. 9:23–24; 1 Cor. 2:9 and Isa. 64:4; 1 Cor. 2:16 and Isa. 40:13; 1 Cor. 3:19 and Job 5:13; 1 Cor. 3:20 and Ps. 94:11).[29]

CONCLUSION

Paul views the Old Testament as the crucial initial chapters of the epic story of God's redemptive love for the world. The ministry, death, and resurrection of Jesus constitute the climactic chapters of that story, while we await the conclusion to the story when Jesus returns. When we examine Paul's forays into the Old Testament, we should think of plunges into the story as a whole, not just dips into isolated passages. Though Paul typically shows awareness of the immediate contexts of the passages he recalls, even more he has in mind the Old Testament context as a whole and the story that it narrates.[30] Paul works with an enlightened understanding of the Old Testament story now that he perceives the trajectory of thought from the Old Testament to Jesus. The Savior who blinded Paul with light on the road to Damascus continued to illuminate Paul's understanding of how Jesus and the Old Testament fit together.

In turn, our study of Paul's letters and their indebtedness to the Old Testament can fortify our confidence in Jesus as the culmination of all of God's saving plans for this world and for our lives. Our spines can be stiffened when we see the intricate details of God's redemptive work spanning eras of history. This will also motivate us to read each passage in Paul's letters with an open ear to the influence of the Old Testament in Paul's teachings. The God of creation, history, redemption, and the future has left his mark throughout Scriptures that are remarkable in their depth and unity.

---

29.   See Hays, *Conversion of the Imagination*, 12–18. Jeremiah 9:23–24 is another example of a passage enlisted in multiple letters, since Paul incorporates it again in 2 Corinthians 10:17, though for a different purpose.

30.   Moyise (*Paul and Scripture*, 111) distinguishes between an "intertextual" vs. "narrative" model of how Paul uses the Old Testament. With the intertextual approach, Paul is more interested in the immediate literary context of Old Testament citations, while with the narrative method he consults Old Testament verses with the larger narrative trajectory of Scripture in mind. I see the immediate and canonical contexts as complementary pieces but suggest that interpreters allow the larger category of the Scriptural narrative to inform their understanding of how Paul is interacting with a verse in its narrower context.

■ ■ ■

CHAPTER THIRTEEN

WHAT ARE THE EXPERTS SAYING ABOUT PAUL THESE DAYS?

I
t may seem surprising that after nearly two thousand years, people are still debating the meaning of Paul's letters and theology. Some even come up with new ways of looking at Paul's overall perspective. Isn't Paul's agenda and viewpoint obvious by now? And yet, the conversations continue. The occasional nature of Paul's letters, along with the depth and complexity of his thought, makes Paul a difficult man to pin down. Another important consideration is that readers of any time and location have read Paul within their own cultural contexts. This practice is vital for churches, since God surely wants his words in the Bible to be relevant to the concerns of churches in any era, leading to meaningful application. But it also leaves us vulnerable to blind spots as readers. If certain topics aren't on our cultural radar, we will tend to overlook them when Paul talks about them, especially when he *indirectly* appeals to those concerns or assumes them as givens in his writings. Good scholarship continually asks, what could we notice or understand differently if we looked at this with fresh eyes?

We do not interpret Paul's letters from scratch. We rely, directly and indirectly, upon the insights passed down by interpreters who have gone before us. They share their observations, exegetical breakthroughs, and grasps of theological undercurrents in Paul's letters with us. They provide us with maps that we can use to help us find our way through Paul's letters. No map is perfect, and we may discover that some are more useful to us than others.[1] But the mapmakers, who frequently revise their maps in response to challenges and input from others, contend vigorously for the distinct symbols and representations they include in their maps. We can

---

1. See the discussion of "maps" in interpretation in Christopher J. H. Wright, "Mission as a Matrix for Hermeneutics and Biblical Theology," in *Out of Egypt: Biblical Theology and Biblical Interpretation*, eds. Craig Bartholomew, et al. (Grand Rapids: Zondervan, 2004), 138–39.

evaluate why they highlight what they do and gain greater clarity for our own study of Paul's letters.

SURVEYING THE LANDSCAPE

This chapter attempts to orient readers to the current landscape of scholarship on Paul and his letters, as opposed to giving a comprehensive recounting of the history of how we arrived here.[2] There are three primary spectra that scholars tend to organize themselves across. Each spectrum represents the range of ways that experts answer three important questions. First, is Paul's primary emphasis in his letters on an individual's salvation and relationship with God, or are individual concerns only one smaller part of a larger radical and comprehensive vision that Paul subscribes to? Second, just how new is God's work in the Christian era, and how unexpected was Jesus's arrival in view of the Old Testament story that preceded him? Third, how much knowledge, beyond what we see in the Bible itself, is required for truly understanding Paul's writings?

When we grasp how scholars answer these three debated questions we can begin to identify and differentiate between the current camps that people gravitate towards. Granted, there are more complexities and subtleties for any given author and his or her views beyond these three questions, but analyzing the contested issues along these three spectra will rather quickly get beginning students up to speed on what to look for when reading specific scholarly works. It will also help students to read Paul's letters with these three questions in mind and begin to form their own opinions on what Paul is all about.

In addition to the three major questions, you will also encounter in this chapter three labels for broad groupings of scholars. These groupings are known, somewhat simplistically, as the Old Perspective on Paul ("Old Perspective"), the New Perspective on Paul ("New Perspective"), and the Apocalyptic Perspective on Paul ("Apocalyptic Paul"). Scholars from these three perspectives have had some lively exchanges with one another over what shapes Paul's theological perspective, both in print as well as in person (at conference presentations and panel discussions).

Complicating matters somewhat with all of these discussions are two related methodological questions. First, which letters among the thirteen-letter Pauline corpus do individual scholars embrace as genuinely and directly from Paul?[3] One should not assume that an author accepts all thirteen letters as authentically Pauline, since that is the minority viewpoint. Second, even among the letters identified as genuine, which letters

---

2. Readers desiring a more comprehensive treatment of the recent history of Pauline studies should consult N. T. Wright, *Paul and His Recent Interpreters: Some Contemporary Debates* (Minneapolis: Fortress, 2015).

3. See the extended exploration of this question in an earlier chapter.

do specific experts prefer and draw upon most in constructing their own formulations of Paul's overall theological perspective? Pauline specialists usually have more experience in some letters than others. Experts in Galatians, for example, might privilege that letter over others in the Pauline corpus when they try to grasp Paul's overall thinking. Or, scholars may have some opinions about which letters best represent the heart of Paul's vision and spend more of their time in those letters. Answers to these two questions remain telling, and they should be considered alongside the answers to the three spectrum-location questions that follow.[4]

THE FIRST SPECTRUM:
INDIVIDUAL OR BROADER EMPHASIS?

The first major question readers of Paul must confront is the focus and scope of his teachings. Does Paul ultimately care about seeing individual sinners, whether Jew or Gentile, reconciled to a holy God, to experience eternal salvation? This has been the prevailing paradigm for understanding Paul in the Western world, at least since the Protestant Reformation. In the final decades of the twentieth century, though, a number of scholars who identify with what is now known as the New Perspective on Paul began to protest that this assumption was too shaped by the increasingly individualistic mindset of modern Western thought. According to them the so-called Old Perspective *feels* obvious to people when they read Paul, but that is because they have become too conditioned to see the world as a collection of individuals who independently seek to find their own way in this universe. New Perspective advocates also claim that the needs and concerns that sparked the Protestant Reformation and its views on salvation were not the same needs and concerns that Paul had in his setting. This led to slightly skewed, or at least overly narrow, interpretations of Paul by the Reformers and their successors.

Early pioneers in New Perspective thinking (before it was known as such) were Krister Stendahl and E. P. Sanders. Stendahl raised the question of whether Protestant preoccupation with individual feelings of guilt before God had clouded Christian readings of Paul.[5] This preoccupation creates a drift away from Christianity as a corporate enterprise and moves it more into the personal and psychological realm. Sanders sought to demonstrate that common scholarly readings of Paul incorrectly characterized the Judaism that Paul had supposedly set himself apart from in his theology.[6] In particular, the Jewish writings immediately before and after Paul's lifetime exhibit a belief in what Sanders called "covenantal nomism" rather than in some sort

---

4. See the related discussion in Wright, *Paul and the Faithfulness of God*, 56–61.
5. Krister Stendahl, "The Apostle Paul and the Introspective Conscience of the West," *HTR* 56 (1963): 199–215.
6. E. P. Sanders, *Paul and Palestinian Judaism* (Philadelphia: Fortress, 1977), 1–12.

of works-righteousness. For Sanders, this distinction makes all of the difference. Works-righteousness is a label for a belief that to be right with God, one
must faithfully abide by his laws and rest on one's own merit for righteousness.[7] For the Jew, this would mean observing the laws given to Moses on
Mt. Sinai. According to Sanders, attributing a belief in works-righteousness
to first-century Jews both unfairly describes their belief system and misses
what Paul is saying about how life under Christ is different.[8] Sanders puts
forward "covenantal nomism" as a better title for the typical Jewish perspective at the time of Paul's writings. Covenantal nomism is the belief that Jews
had relational access to God because he graciously initiated a covenantal
relationship (the Mosaic covenant) with them.[9] In response, the Jews sought
to carry out the responsibilities of the Mosaic covenant (the Mosaic law—
"nomism" comes from the Greek word for law) as a way of remaining on
good terms with God. They recognized that God had certain expectations of
them, but only as part of a covenantal relationship that he had already established (note the order of the words in covenantal nomism—the covenant
comes first, and then the law). Setting Paul's view of salvation against individualistic models of works-righteousness once again skews Paul's theology
in the direction of personal guilt and individual reconciliation with God,
missing the bigger picture of what Paul promoted. The idea of covenantal
nomism and its place within God's redemptive plans for Jews and Gentiles
helpfully frames Paul's teachings within corporate contexts.

A second generation of Pauline scholars, led by James Dunn and
N. T. Wright, has further developed the work of Sanders in particular
and has popularized the ideas of what they now call the New Perspective.
Dunn and Wright have explained in detail how they think that individual
passages in Paul's letters should be interpreted in light of a renewed understanding of the Judaism of Paul's day. The letters of Galatians and Romans
have taken center stage for this reevaluation of Paul's teachings, since in
those letters Paul spends much space addressing the purpose of the law,
as well as how life in Christ in some ways stands in contrast to life under
the law. The language of righteousness, justification, and justification by
faith, the latter of which was a hallmark of the Reformation, also shows
up most prominently in Galatians and Romans. Dunn and Wright read
these letters as Paul's advocacy for the incorporation of both of Jews and
Gentiles, through Christ, into God's chosen people.

In the wake of extensive work by Dunn, Wright, and others, many
scholars now believe that Paul did not set faith in Christ in opposition to
doing good works to earn God's approval. That way of framing things was
too abstracted from Paul's original missionary context. Paul was instead
concerned about specific laws—Jewish laws that were meant to separate Jews

7. Ibid., 53–54.
8. Ibid., 548–52.
9. Ibid., 75, 236, 422.

from Gentiles. Chief among these laws are circumcision, which Paul specifically targets in various places (Rom. 2:25–29; 3:30; 1 Cor. 7:19; Gal. 5:2–3, 11–12; 6:12–15; Col. 3:11), and dietary and Sabbath laws. Now that Christ has fulfilled these ceremonial laws, they no longer operate according to their original function of marking out God's chosen people from the rest of the world. Paul warned against the way these laws were still being used as "identity markers" to exclude Gentiles from full fellowship in God's family.[10] As an apostle to the Gentiles (Rom. 11:13), Paul was especially aware of the spiritual harm of convincing the Gentiles that they were somehow incomplete in Christ and his sacrifice for them. Paul also recognized how such a view created divisions in a body of Christ that should be perfectly united in Christ.

Some, but not all, New Perspective thinkers argue that both sides of Paul's "faith in Christ" vs. "works of the law" contrast (Rom. 3:20–31; Gal. 2:16) have been misunderstood.[11] According to them, the Greek behind "faith in Christ" (πίστις Χριστοῦ) and its related forms is better translated as "the faithfulness of Christ," which makes Christ instead of the believer the one who exercises the faith or faithfulness. Christ is thus the *subject* of that phrase rather than the *object*.[12] While the believer still embraces Christ through faith (as affirmed in other passages), in a few key passages this removes the sharp contrast between human faith and human works that had been pointed to traditionally to highlight the contrast between works-righteousness and trust and dependence in God's mercy through Christ.

Paul's uses of the terms justification and righteousness have also been reconfigured by New Perspective proponents. Justification, many argue, does not exist in a vacuum but within the environment of Paul's concerns about Gentiles being incorporated into God's family. Justification entails God's affirmation that Gentile believers belong in his family, in anticipation of the future day when he publicly vindicates their faith in him at the last judgment.[13] Righteousness, from the same word group as justification in the Greek, can often be linked to covenantal faithfulness—God's commitment to keep his promises to his covenantal people, and by extension (via Gen. 12:1–3), to the world.[14] Wright is insistent that righteousness is not an attribute of God that God somehow transfers to people, as held with the

---

10. This language, and much of the thinking behind it, originated with Dunn. See, for instance, James D. G. Dunn, *Jesus, Paul, and the Law: Studies in Mark and Galatians* (Louisville: Westminster John Knox, 1990), 191–98.

11. For instance, Dunn still supports the translation "faith in Christ" for πίστις Χριστοῦ (Dunn, *Theology of Paul*, 379–84), while Wright opts for "faithfulness of Christ" (Wright, *Paul and the Faithfulness of God*, 836–39).

12. Grammatically, these are interpretations of the genitive phrases as subjective genitives rather than objective genitives (see Wallace, *Greek Grammar beyond the Basics*, 113–19).

13. Dunn, *Jesus, Paul, and the Law*, 190; Dunn, *Theology of Paul*, 340, 385–89; N. T. Wright, *The Paul Debate: Critical Questions for Understanding the Apostle* (Waco, TX: Baylor University Press, 2015), 71–73, 88–91.

14. See Dunn, *Theology of Paul*, 342–44.

doctrine known as imputation (that God's own righteousness as possessed by Christ is imputed, reckoned, or credited to the believer through faith).[15] While most New Perspective advocates join Wright in rejecting the doctrine of imputation, not all have embraced "covenantal faithfulness" as a satisfactory substitute for "righteousness."[16] Still, by casting doubt on the centrality of concepts such as faith in Christ and an individual's justification before God in Paul's teachings, New Perspective supporters hope to build the case for a theology that orbits around more communal and global concerns.

In line with these global interests, New Perspective advocates, following Wright, also emphasize that salvation comes with a mission. Individuals are saved as part of a grander project to reclaim all of the created order for God. The church, made up of Jews and Gentiles, has been designed to take up the original mission of Israel: to be God's people and shine his light to the rest of the world in anticipation of Christ returning to claim his rightful place as ruler of all of creation. This has the effect of directing attention away from a believer's reconciliation to a holy God to a believer's missional calling, once reconciled.

In response to the advance of New Perspective ideas, other scholars (sometimes labeled "Old Perspective" for convenience) have protested that the shift away from God's salvation of individuals as the heart of Paul's theology has been too drastic.[17] Many Old Perspective scholars do acknowledge the benefits of a more nuanced and comprehensive understanding of Jewish perspectives on the place of good works and of seeing Paul's theology more situated within his missionary aims for a united Jewish and Gentile church. But Old Perspective scholars still caution that there is something timeless and universal about Paul's teachings about grace, faith, salvation, and works that should not be obscured.[18] Paul applied his teachings on these topics to the specific problem of Jew and Gentile relationships in the church in some of his letters, but on other occasions (Eph. 2:8–9; Titus 3:4–7) he spoke not specifically about works of the Jewish law but more broadly about the misguided human tendency to seek acceptance from God through righteous living. Even with the Jews in mind, Paul correlates adherence to the law with working or striving after righteousness, which is at odds

---

15. Wright, *Recent Interpreters*, 120–21.

16. Michael Bird, seeking to break the Old Perspective vs. New Perspective impasse, suggests that a doctrine of union with Christ serves the desired purposes of imputation without some of imputation's shortcomings (Michael F. Bird, "When the Dust Finally Settles: Coming to a Post-New Perspective Perspective," *CTR* n.s., 2 [2005]: 68).

17. Works sympathetic to an older perspective on Paul and responding to New Perspective challenges (though often modifying their interpretations with insights from the New Perspective) include Stephen Westerholm, *Perspectives Old and New on Paul: The Lutheran Paul and His Critics* (Grand Rapids: Eerdmans, 2004); D. A. Carson, Peter T. O'Brien, and Mark A. Seifrid, eds., *Justification and Variegated Nomism*, 2 vols. (Tübingen: Mohr Siebeck, 2001, 2004); John Piper, *The Future of Justification: A Response to N. T. Wright* (Wheaton, IL: Crossway, 2007).

18. See Westerholm, *Perspectives Old and New*, 440–45.

with receiving God's gift by faith (Rom. 4:4–8; 9:30–10:4; see also Phil. 3:9). God's bestowal of grace and righteousness through Christ's sacrificial death powerfully accomplishes what pious living cannot—bringing sinners into a right relationship with a holy God.

The spectrum that has been clarified from all of these discussions has on the one side Old Perspective proponents, who claim that when push comes to shove there is still a primary interest in the basic relationship between God and sinners in Paul's letters. They warn that the church risks too quickly brushing aside Paul's enthusiasm for the fundamental truth that God showers his grace on sinners through Christ's sacrificial death. On the other side are New Perspective advocates, who contend that while Paul values and even takes as a starting point God's salvation of sinners, the teaching in his actual letters spans a larger horizon. Paul more often addresses issues of how Gentile believers can be fully integrated into a church that was initially composed of Jewish believers alone, how the resulting church can be unified, and how the church needs to get in step with God's ultimate purpose. That purpose consists of Christ claiming the whole world—a newly and comprehensively transformed heaven and earth—as his kingdom. The discussions continue, even while some representatives of the two sides have modified positions in response to arguments and objections they have heard from the other side.[19]

THE SECOND SPECTRUM: CONTINUITY OR DISCONTINUITY WITH THE OLD TESTAMENT

A second spectrum has increasingly moved to the center stage of Pauline studies, regarding the question of just exactly how groundbreaking is the new era of Christ's saving work as portrayed in Paul's teaching. The spectrum has been brought into sharper focus with the emergence of what is known as the Apocalyptic Perspective on Paul, or the Apocalyptic Paul view. The Apocalyptic Perspective on Paul counts J. Louis Martyn, Beverly Gaventa, and Douglas Campbell as among its more prominent spokespersons.[20] Apocalyptic partisans underscore the radical newness of Paul's vision of God's intervention in the world through Christ. The arrival of Christ reveals the liberating love of God, which stands in contrast to any human-focused religious system.

According to the Apocalyptic Paul perspective, the dramatic invasion of God's grace into the world was not sufficiently previewed in the

19. I disagree with a recent popular perception that the debate between the Old and New Perspective is basically over, with the New Perspective "winning" the argument. While New Perspective insights have certainly supplemented and refined some readings of Old Perspective scholars, there are still some strong exegetical arguments from specific passages that suggest that the Old Perspective has a lot to offer to our understanding of Paul's aims.

20. See Wright, *Recent Interpreters*, 145–54, for an exploration of the origins of the Apocalyptic Paul view in the writings of Ernst Käsemann, J. Christiaan Beker, and others.

Old Testament or anticipated by even scripturally attuned Israelites. God surprised everyone and surpassed expectations about his goodness and power by sending Jesus his Son, not just to restore a covenant or fulfill a promise, but to defeat the mighty forces of Sin, Death, and Flesh (often written in capital letters to accentuate their enslaving powers).[21] Apocalyptic interpreters see God's intervention as both gracious and decisive against our world's greatest problems and enemies.[22] They highlight God's benevolent motivations and his effective work, apart from human response, even to the point that some apocalyptic proponents don't draw sharp distinctions between how believers and unbelievers benefit from that work. Christ, as the second Adam, directs his saving love to the whole world, and no one is left unaffected.

Apocalyptic interpreters differ from New Perspective scholars in the level of discontinuity they find between the Old and New Testaments.[23] Apocalyptic interpreters see a seismic shift in human relationships with God upon the transformative arrival of Christ. Accordingly, they see the incarnational life of Christ as the starting point for any theology of Christ, so that the Old Testament must be appreciated in the light of that revelatory moment. Apocalyptic Paul proponents put a strong accent on Christ being the turning point in history, and less so on the history as it unfolds throughout the Bible. New Perspective readers see more continuity from the Old to New Testament.[24] While acknowledging some profound newness in the revealed mystery of Christ, New Perspective adherents also point to how even the apostles and Jesus himself asserted that the Old Testament pointed forward to Jesus's appearing, and that spiritually sensitive readers should have been able to discern that trajectory towards fulfillment within the Old Testament Scriptures (Rom. 15:4; 1 Cor. 10:11; 2 Tim. 3:14–17). The Scriptures have a prospective force to them, and that forward-looking story reaches fruition in Christ. Paul's extensive and substantive interaction with so many parts of the Old Testament story suggests that Christ's work cannot be properly assessed apart from that unfolding account.

Apocalyptic and Old Perspective scholars both see significant contrasts between the Old and New Testament eras, but the two views are quite different in their focus and scope.[25] The Old Perspective sees

---

21. See Martyn's distancing of an apocalyptic vision of Paul from a salvation-historical portrayal of Paul (J. Louis Martyn, *Galatians*, AB 33A [New York: Doubleday, 1997], 347–50).

22. Martyn gives a summary of apocalyptic themes (ibid., 97–105).

23. Note the response to certain emphases within the Apocalyptic fold in Wright, *The Paul Debate*, 41–64. See also the online video of a forum at Duke Divinity School, in which Wright (New Perspective) and Douglas Campbell (Apocalyptic Paul), among others, interact about some of this discontinuity ("N. T. Wright: Panel Discussion on Pauline Theology with Faculty," Duke Divinity School, https://www.youtube.com/watch?v=mNzcwo6opqg).

24. Wright, *The Paul Debate*, 19–20.

25. See Stanley N. Gundry and Michael F. Bird, eds., *Four Views on the Apostle Paul* (Grand Rapids: Zondervan, 2012), especially the interaction between an older (Reformed) Perspective (Thomas

the contrast more on an individual level, organized around the themes of God's holiness, personal sin and guilt, and being justified through faith. Old Perspective thinkers believe that utter failure under the lofty standards of the Old Testament law highlighted the need for a new way of grace and faith through Christ. They often temper this contrast with a perspective of salvation history that sees the same God working in consistent ways across Old and New Testament eras to fulfill his promises to the world.

Apocalyptic Paul interpreters gravitate to themes such as enslavement, liberation, freedom, new life, and resurrection power, with these realities spanning more of a cosmic horizon for the world as a whole.[26] These joyful themes stand in stark contrast to dark, universal forces of Sin, Death, and Flesh. Individual sinners are not so much culpable failures under the law but victims of wider forces beyond their control. God enters into this dire state of affairs and delivers something strikingly new. Some Apocalyptic Paul advocates react quite negatively to what they observe as pronounced ideas of personal guilt, substitutionary atonement, and retributive judgment in Old Perspective models. In fact, Campbell, throughout Romans 1:18–3:20, quarantines certain excerpts that exhibit retributive justice from Paul's theology, by attributing them to Paul's characterizations of his *opponent's* views instead.[27]

Even though all three major camps acknowledge both continuity and discontinuity between the Old and New Testaments, they differ in how they balance the scale. New Perspective supporters put more weight on continuity, while Old Perspective sympathizers see significant discontinuity, on a personal level, within a broader coherent story, and Apocalyptic Paul thinkers emphasize features of discontinuity within their system.

THE THIRD SPECTRUM: KEYS WITHIN SCRIPTURE OR BEYOND SCRIPTURE

The third question that sorts scholars into different groups is whether interpreters need some proficiency in extrabiblical sources or fields of study such as noncanonical Jewish literature, Greco-Roman histories, or even modern sociological studies to be able to understand what Paul said in his letters.

R. Schreiner) and the Apocalyptic Paul view (Douglas A. Campbell). Also instructive is the debate between Douglas Moo (older Lutheran Perspective) and Douglas Campbell ("Is the Lutheran Approach to Pauline Justification 'Justified'?" Carl F. H. Henry Center for Theological Understanding, https://www.youtube.com/watch?v=KlujS-fH8R4).

26. See Martinus C. de Boer, "Paul's Mythologizing Program in Romans 5–8," in *Apocalyptic Paul: Cosmos and Anthropos in Romans 5–8*, ed. Beverly Roberts Gaventa (Waco, TX: Baylor University Press, 2013), 8–10. As a scholar with affinities for both Old Perspective and Apocalyptic Paul readings, Westerholm holds the cosmic and individual arenas together (Stephen Westerholm, "Righteousness, Cosmic and Microcosmic," in *Apocalyptic Paul*, 21–38).

27. Douglas A. Campbell, *The Deliverance of God: An Apocalyptic Rereading of Justification in Paul* (Grand Rapids: Eerdmans, 2009), 542–93. Martyn adopts a similar tactic, though in much more moderation, when he seeks to remove Paul's full endorsement of his own words in Galatians 1:4a (*Galatians*, 89–90).

In other words, are Paul's letters conditioned significantly by his context in the first-century Mediterranean world, or do they have more of a timeless quality to them? As mentioned elsewhere in this book, readers of Paul's letters must determine the original occasion of a letter, and the argument Paul was making in response to that occasion. Good interpretation means first ascertaining the intended meaning of discourse, in its original setting. But the procedure for doing this begins with the letter itself, using a mirror-reading strategy for identifying the occasion, and then tracing the letter's argument through a careful reading of the text. Is additional help needed from information beyond the text as well? Scholars sometimes distinguish between a *close* reading of a text and a *thick* reading of a text. A close reading requires detailed alertness to the cues within the text. A thick reading leverages outside information that is not evident from the text itself. How much should a student of Paul's letters aspire to attain a thick reading of his letters, on top of a close reading?

While most scholars recognize that there is some value to being well-informed on various background topics, they differ on the degree of familiarity needed. Some appeal to the Protestant idea of the perspicuity of Scripture, which claims that the primary meaning of a passage should be evident to any careful and spiritually sensitive reader, or more simply, that God wrote the Bible in order to be understood. If a high level of specialized knowledge is necessary to correctly interpret Scripture, wouldn't that take Scripture out of the hands of the average believer? On the other side of the spectrum, some scholars use extra biblical information as a controlling grid for understanding Paul's letters. An approach shaped by comparative religions, sociology, or any number of ideologies can become the dominant paradigm for interpreting Paul's discourse.

Examples of relying heavily on extra biblical resources are not hard to find. N. T. Wright appeals to various second-temple Jewish texts to demonstrate concepts such as common Jewish expectations about the kingdom of God in the years leading up to the ministry of Christ.[28] He then explores how Paul's outlook on Christ's work both takes shape within and exerts pressure against those expectations. Some interpreters consult knowledge about the Roman political system and especially the phenomenon of the imperial cult when reading Paul's letters. They hope to show how Paul's writings subtly subvert the Roman claims to supreme devotion and construct a countercultural community of believers loyal to Christ first.[29] *The First Urban Christians,* by Wayne Meeks, draws upon sociological concepts and historical insights to fill in biblical gaps of what the early Christian individuals and communities looked like in their common,

28. Wright, *Paul and the Faithfulness of God,* 621–24.
29. As an example, see Richard A. Horsley, ed., *Paul and the Roman Imperial Order* (Harrisburg, PA: Trinity Press, 2004), and especially Horsley's introduction to the book on pages 6–19. Another book of this type is Horsley, *Paul and Empire.*

day-to-day lives. Guided by historical sources Meeks makes educated guesses about the social and economic backgrounds of those believers and then considers how those believers would have been socially reconstructed as members of new and unified church communities that saw themselves as belonging to a new order.[30] Others have similarly advocated for and applied social-scientific criticism to Paul's letters.[31]

Among the three major groups of scholars today, New Perspective scholars typically rely more upon outside sources, while Old Perspective and Apocalyptic Paul advocates resort more to theological systems for their overall grids.[32] The differences between groups are not always as pronounced as with the first two spectra. Still, New Perspective scholars seek to understand the Jewish world as a first priority, since Jesus's ministry fulfills Israel's story.[33] But New Perspective scholars such as Wright also champion examining the way that Christian communities sprouted up within their social and political environments.[34] For these thinkers, the more information, the better. The question this raises, however, is whether this excludes the average reader from a place at the table. Can a relatively unsophisticated approach to Paul's letters yield accurate readings? Or must such readers simply defer to the experts?

Another concern about leaning too heavily on outside sources is that one can become so immersed in the ancient history that the actual text of Paul's letters can be nudged from the spotlight. Especially given that Paul conveys God's revelation of his nature and his saving works through his letters, and that God's Word never returns void but accomplishes the purpose God intends for it in our lives (Isa. 55:10–11), we should commit ourselves over and over to regular, firsthand, and prayerful interaction with Paul's letters themselves. Any powerful movie is best enjoyed without the distractions of constantly checking our phones for information related to the movie, its plot, characters, settings, etc. Once we have seen the movie (or perhaps before we do), we can consult other sources for additional background. But the movie itself is the star attraction. This is true even more so for the God-breathed letters of Paul.

On the other hand, with so much additional information at our fingertips today, shouldn't readers be willing to at least explore its potential? Widely available resources such as study Bibles and commentaries sort through the relevant extra biblical material and guide believers in applying

---

30.   Meeks, *First Urban Christians*, 190–92.

31.   See for instance David G. Horrell, ed., *Social-Scientific Approaches to New Testament Interpretation* (Edinburgh: T&T Clark, 1999). Horrell's introduction to the book looks at the history and potential of social-scientific perspectives, while examples of application of the methods to Paul's letters are found in chapters 7–10.

32.   Martin Luther and John Calvin exert strong influences in the way that some Old Perspective scholars interpret Paul, while Karl Barth's writings sometimes inform Apocalyptic Paul adherents.

33.   Wright, *Paul and the Faithfulness of God*, 75–196.

34.   Ibid., 197–348.

insights from it to their understanding of different passages. If judicious appeals to credible background studies generate more compelling readings of Paul's letters, why shouldn't we welcome those contributions?

CONCLUSION

The existence of different schools of thought on Paul ensures that all parties continue to return to Paul's letters with curiosity, openness, and attention to detail. The chart below (see table 1) sums up some of the information about three main movements within Pauline studies today and the way that each group views relevant topics. Undoubtedly, contributions from all three perspectives can be added to the maps that we use to navigate our way through Paul's letters. But we want to choose wisely what we rely upon for the journey. In the end, our own answers to these questions should assist us in understanding and responding to Paul's letters as divinely revealed truth about the most pressing and enduring questions of life.

Table 1—Comparison of Perspectives

	Old Perspective	New Perspective	Apocalyptic Paul
Focus of Christ's saving work	Individuals	Corporate: Jews *and* Gentiles	Cosmic: individuals, but collectively, within a larger, unseen arena
Key problem addressed	Sinners' guilt before God	Exclusion of Gentiles from the people of God	Enslaving powers of sin, Satan, and death
Continuity or discontinuity with the Old Testament	Some discontinuity: Mosaic law vs. grace, within a larger unified story	Continuity: covenants of grace and obedience in Old and New Testaments	Discontinuity: dramatic arrival of new creation; discontinuity between human-based "religion" and divinely enacted revelation
Proponents	Martin Luther, John Calvin, D. A. Carson, John Piper	Krister Stendahl, E. P. Sanders, James Dunn, N. T. Wright	Ernst Käsemann, J. Louis Martyn, Beverly Gaventa, Douglas Campbell

What insights will help us overcome the limitations we face from being immersed in our own cultures and rediscover some overlooked truths in Paul's letters? This chapter oriented us to three major questions that occupy interpreters of Paul's letters. I hope that, if anything, this chapter has further inspired you to question your own assumptions and reengage with Paul's letters with a greater sense of eagerness and wonder.

■ ■ ■

CHAPTER FOURTEEN

WHAT IDEAS WERE ESPECIALLY IMPORTANT TO PAUL?

Part of the fun of reading Paul's letters is trying to fathom the depths of his ideas. Paul's writings, with their vivid style and inspiring, provocative content, leave a strong first impression. Even over time the intricacies and subtleties of Paul's ideas and their application to diverse situations keep readers coming back to gain more insight and attempt synthesis of Paul's beliefs about Christ. Paul's compelling teachings and writings helped Christianity become a worldwide movement, and they have helped spark reformations and renewals in church history. Believers and skeptics alike recognize the indelible mark that Paul's teachings have left on the church.

While Paul has not provided us with a comprehensive textbook of systematic theology, even his occasional letters to churches and individuals present us with profound and majestic theological truths. But since Paul doesn't write as a systematic theologian, we won't walk through Paul's teachings by appealing to typical categories from systematic theology (Christology, soteriology, ecclesiology, eschatology, etc.). We will instead identify the theological assumptions that rest at the heart of Paul's teachings and that help explain why he emphasizes the themes he does in his occasional letters.[1]

As we saw in the last chapter, there are still lively debates about the focus of Paul's theology. But beyond the disagreements between Old Perspective, New Perspective, and Apocalyptic Paul, there are some shared perspectives about what makes Paul tick.[2] The five big ideas that follow just begin to

---

1. Beker notes that in Paul's letters we see both coherence and contingency (J. Christiaan Beker, *The Triumph of God: The Essence of Paul's Thought*, trans. Loren T. Stuckenbruck [Minneapolis: Fortress, 1990], 15–19). In other words, even though Paul addresses specific occasions in his letter, we can still discern a coherent theology holding his various instructions together.
2. To the list that follows, we could also add much of Paul's substantive interaction with the Old Testament, but that territory has already been covered in a different chapter.

scratch the surface of Paul's distinctive views, but they represent some of the genius of the way he understood and communicated God's truth.

THE GOSPEL

We start where Paul prefers to start. Do you know people who seem to constantly talk about an issue that they care deeply about? They mention the topic over and over, and their excitement about the topic shines through. Paul regularly talks about the gospel and expresses his passion for the gospel. The idea of the gospel or proclaiming the gospel is featured prominently in most of Paul's letters, especially Romans, 1 and 2 Corinthians, Galatians, and Philippians.

The term gospel comes from the Greek word εὐαγγέλιον, which means "good news." The cognate verb form εὐαγγελίζω is rendered "to preach or proclaim the gospel or good news." Paul's highlighting of the gospel is inspired by passages such as Isaiah 40:9–11 and 52:7–10 (see Rom. 10:14–15). These passages triumphantly proclaim the promised arrival of God's saving reign, using εὐαγγελίζω in the Septuagint's Greek translation to talk about the heralding of this good news. Paul employs the term gospel as a convenient summary label for the news that God is bringing that saving reign to fruition in Christ. The gospel is the hope-filled message about Christ that Paul proclaimed to his hearers and readers.

For Paul, the gospel is a message about events and their significance. The central events of the gospel are the death and resurrection of Christ.[3] Paul articulates this the most clearly in 1 Corinthians 15:1–5, where he reminds readers that the gospel he preaches is the same one he received as a new follower of Christ. The gospel is about Christ's death for our sins and his resurrection, both of which are the fulfillment of the Old Testament Scriptures.[4] Paul clarifies that believers embrace a message of good news that makes claims about actual events in history. The gospel is no mere philosophy based on human reasoning. It is the joyful conviction that God has acted in history, especially through the death and resurrection of Jesus, God's Son and promised Messiah. These central events fit within the larger unfolding story that began in Genesis. God has been at work throughout history, but now he has acted definitively in Christ.

Paul announces the joyful reality of Christ's death and resurrection, but he also proclaims the resulting significance of those events. The events

---

3. Christ's death and resurrection are the focus of Paul's gospel, even if the entire ministry of Christ's first advent, his current reign at the right hand of God, and his promised return are all interconnected as parts of the good news about Christ. See this point in Ladd, *Theology of the New Testament*, 391–92.

4. Paul directly links the gospel to the resurrection of Christ, in fulfilment of the Old Testament story, in Romans 1:2–4 and 2 Timothy 2:8. He connects the gospel to Jesus's death on the cross in 1 Corinthians 1:17–18.

have had reverberating effects throughout history.[5] Romans 1:16–17 and 1 Corinthians 15:2 talk about the saving power of God at work in the gospel. Paul learned for himself that a life can be transformed when confronted with the truth of the resurrected Christ. He had also seen believers in various cities changed by the power of the gospel. Throughout his letters Paul uses assorted terms to describe the far-reaching effects of the gospel:[6]

- *Salvation* (rescue) from condemnation and judgment (Rom. 1:16; 5:9–10; 10:9–13; 13:11; 1 Cor. 1:18–21; Eph. 2:4–9; 1 Thess. 5:9; 1 Tim. 1:15; 2 Tim. 2:10; Titus 3:5).
- *Reconciliation* (restoration of a right relationship) to God (Rom. 5:10–11; 2 Cor. 5:18–20; Eph. 2:16; Col. 1:20–22).
- *Justification* (pronouncement of a right standing) before God (Rom. 3:24–30; 4:25; 5:9, 16–18; 1 Cor. 6:11; Gal. 2:16–17; Titus 3:7).
- *Forgiveness* of sins through sacrificial *atonement* for those sins (Rom. 3:25; 4:7; 8:3; Eph. 1:7; 4:32; Col. 1:14; 2:13; 3:13).
- *Redemption* (purchased freedom) from slavery, so that believers now belong to God (Rom. 3:24; 8:23; 1 Cor. 1:30; 6:19–20; Eph. 1:7; Col. 1:14; Titus 2:14).
- *Adoption* into God's family, allowing believers to relate to God as father and receive his inheritance (Rom. 8:15–17, 23; Gal. 4:5–7; Eph. 1:5).
- Reception of *new, eternal life* in Christ (Rom. 5:21; 6:22–23; 2 Cor. 5:17; 1 Tim. 1:16; 6:12; Titus 1:2; 3:7).

In 2 Corinthians 5:14–21 we can observe in detail how robust Paul's gospel and its benefits are. The first half of the passage sets up Christ's death and resurrection as an axis around which the whole passage revolves. The sacrificial death and resurrection of Christ lays the groundwork for believers' death and resurrection. Christ *represents* believers by dying for them ("one died for all"), as an act of God's love (5:14). Christ not only dies for believers but is also raised again (5:15). Christ represents believers, but believers also *participate* in Christ's death and resurrection, dying with him ("therefore all died") and being raised with him to experience a life of new creation in Christ (5:17). Being raised to new life brings *transformation*, since the old self is gone and the new self is here. Believers' reception

---

5. Contrary to popular understanding, the effects themselves are not the totality of the gospel. The gospel starts with God's sending his Son to die for sinners and conquer the grave. Believers' response to that good news unleashes the blessings of salvation in their lives. See this helpful distinction in Scot McKnight, *The King Jesus Gospel: The Original Good News Revisited* (Grand Rapids: Zondervan, 2011).

6. I first encountered this idea of the multi-faceted gospel in Mark McCloskey, *Tell It Often, Tell It Well* (San Bernardino, CA: Here's Life Publishers, 1985), 20–27. See also Michael J. Gorman, *Apostle of the Crucified Lord: A Theological Introduction to Paul and His Letters* (Grand Rapids: Eerdmans, 2004), 111–13; Matera, *Paul's Saving Grace*, 102–23.

of a transformed life means that they no longer live as selfish people but live for Christ (5:15). They also view other people differently. Since God has revealed Jesus in his "new creation" form (resurrected and glorified), that same opportunity of transformed, new creation existence has been opened up to other people that believers will encounter (5:16). The second half of 2 Corinthians 5:14–21 again stresses God's grace as the catalyst for reconciliation in believers' lives (5:18). This reconciliation consists of God no longer counting sins against believers (5:19) because of his death for them. Both representation and transformation are again highlighted in 5:21, where Paul describes Jesus sacrificially taking on human sin "for us" (representation) so that believers can experience "the righteousness of God" (transformation).

This talk of new creation in 2 Corinthians 5:17 hints at a larger dimension of Paul's conception of the gospel. Paul sees the scope of the gospel's effects as encompassing individuals, churches, and the entire created order.[7] This can be observed in the argument of Ephesians. Believers transformed personally by the gospel (Eph. 2:1–10) become incorporated into radically reconstituted communities governed by Christ and empowered by the Spirit (Eph. 2:11–22). These communities (comprising the universal church) then put Christ's restoring and unifying power on display for the whole universe to see (Eph. 3:10–11). All of this fulfills God's ultimate plans for a future age in which all things in heaven and earth will be renewed and ordered under Christ's perfect leadership (Eph. 1:9–10). Paul similarly ties the fate of the whole created order together with the fate of believers in Romans 8:18–25. Creation (8:22) and believers (8:23) groan together for a promised liberation (8:21) from the sin and brokenness of this world. The gospel's effects, while focused on individual lives, expand to touch even the entire cosmos.

Paul both preaches and defends (Phil. 1:7, 16) this potent gospel. Though at its core Paul's gospel is about a person, God's Son (Rom. 1:2–3), it is also a message with content that can be proclaimed (Rom. 15:20; 1 Cor. 1:17; 9:16; 2 Cor. 10:16; Gal. 2:2; Eph. 6:19; 1 Thess. 2:2; 2 Tim. 2:8), distorted (2 Cor. 11:4; Gal. 1:6–9), received (1 Cor. 15:1; Eph. 1:13), or rejected (Rom. 10:16; 2 Thess. 1:8). Paul makes no apologies when he condemns false teachers who undercut the power of the gospel or blur its meaning. The gospel meant everything to Paul.

UNION WITH CHRIST

Paul's discourse throughout his letters reveals a rich and pervasive belief that believers have been joined with Christ in the most intimate relationship imaginable, allowing them to share in the divine life and blessings that reside in Christ. This fascinating biblical doctrine, featured most

---

7. See also Helyer, *Jesus, Paul and John*, 388, 400–402.

prominently in Paul's letters, is popularly known as union with Christ.[8] First, Christ identifies himself with humanity in his incarnation and atones for human sin through his sacrificial death on the cross (Rom. 8:3; 2 Cor. 5:14–21; Phil. 2:6–11). Just as humanity had been united with Adam in sin and death, Christ offers a way to be united with him in righteousness and life (Rom. 5:12–21; 1 Cor. 15:20–22, 45). Then, when believers are baptized or integrated fully into Christ through faith, they enter into relational communion and oneness with Christ (Rom. 6:3–4; 1 Cor. 12:13; Gal. 3:27; Col. 2:12).[9] They become identified with Christ, and he becomes definitive for their identity. Though they had been engulfed in Adam's existence and destiny, now they share in Christ's life and destiny. Finally, through believers' union with Christ, all of the present and future saving effects of the gospel are applied to them (Eph. 1:3).[10]

Paul expresses the reality of being united with Christ in several different ways. Most succinctly, Paul employs the phrase "in Christ" or its equivalents to show that believers appropriate all of God's blessings by virtue of their union with Christ (most notably in Romans, Ephesians, and Colossians).[11] Elsewhere, but less frequently, Paul talks about Christ living in believers (Gal. 2:20; 4:19; Col. 1:27; 3:11), showing the flip side of that relational union.[12] Other prepositions such as "with" (Rom. 6:8; Col. 3:3), "into" (Gal. 3:27), and "through" (2 Cor. 1:5),[13] along with the prefix συν-, which means "together with" (Rom. 8:17; Gal. 2:19–20; Eph. 2:5; Col. 3:1) also help convey the notion of union with Christ in Paul's letters.[14]

A corollary to union with Christ is the practice of dying and rising with Christ, or sharing in Christ's suffering and glory. Paul often enlists this imagery to characterize his own experience in ministry. He welcomes countless hardships as opportunities to share in Christ's sufferings—to

---

8. Though Paul develops the concept of union with Christ more extensively than anywhere else in the New Testament, there are still some complementary ideas featured elsewhere. In the Gospels Jesus identified himself fully with his persecuted disciples (Matt. 10:16–25; 24:9; 25:31–46; Mark 8:31–9:1; John 15:18–21; 17:14–18). John 17:20–23 describes the Father and Son mutually indwelling one another and extending that unbreakable relational communion to believers. In Acts, persecuted believers apply words of the Messiah's vindication to themselves (Acts 4:23–31). Jesus also confronts Saul's opposition to his disciples with "why do you persecute *me*" (Acts 9:4; 22:7; 26:14). Finally, 1 Peter talks about believers participating in Christ's suffering and glory (1 Peter 4:12–14, 5:1).

9. While Paul uses baptism to describe a spiritual assimilation into relational union with Christ, the physical practice of baptism typically accompanied and demonstrated the reality of this incorporation into Christ and his body, the church.

10. See also Schnelle, *Apostle Paul*, 479–81.

11. See the meticulous treatment of each occurrence of "in Christ" or its equivalents in the Pauline Epistles in Constantine Campbell, *Paul and Union with Christ: An Exegetical and Theological Study* (Grand Rapids: Zondervan, 2012), 73–199. The instances of "in Christ" vary in their theological significance to Paul's doctrine of union with Christ.

12. On this point, see also Dunn, *Theology of Paul*, 400–401.

13. See Campbell, *Paul and Union with Christ*, 200–266.

14. For a full list of συν- prefixed words in Paul's letters, see Dunn, *Theology of Paul*, 402–3.

die with Christ, in anticipation of one day sharing in Christ's resurrected life (2 Cor. 4:7–12; Phil. 3:10–11). Paul extends this to all believers when he talks about sharing in the death and life or suffering and glory of Christ (Rom. 6:3–5; 2 Tim. 2:11–12). Believers participate in the suffering and shame of Christ on the path towards reigning with Christ as co-heirs in God's kingdom (Rom. 6:3–5; 8:17; Gal. 4:7; Eph. 3:6; 2 Tim. 2:11–12; Titus 3:7).

Paul charges believers to act upon the truth of having died and been raised with Christ.[15] Paul exhorts believers who are united with Christ to put off the enslaving old self that they have died to, and to put on the new self that they have been raised into (Rom. 6:1–14; 13:14; Eph. 4:20–24). Believers' actions should match the reality of their union with Christ, in his new life. This starts with adopting the cross-shaped, or cruciform, nature of Christ's incarnational ministry.[16] But believers can also draw upon the power of Christ's resurrected life to equip them to grow into this new life (Eph. 1:18–20). The move from the old life to the new life reflects the transfer of ownership Christ has brought about. Believers no longer answer to themselves or the sin that enslaved them. They answer to Christ, who purchased them with his sacrificial shedding of blood (Rom. 14:7–8; 1 Cor. 6:19–20; 2 Cor. 5:14–15).

Since all believers are equally invited into fellowship with Christ, they become one in Christ, as part of his body, the church. Paul proclaims a radical leveling of status in Christ. Union with Christ produces unity in Christ. Any distinguishing traits between people become secondary in the light of Christ's saving work. Paul says, "There is neither Jew nor Gentile, neither slave nor free, nor is there male and female, for you are all one in Christ Jesus" (Gal. 3:28; see also 1 Cor. 12:12–13). This unity in Christ does not eradicate differences but rather puts them in perspective. Believers in Christ are drawn together with a force more dominant than any difference that would pull them apart. Celebrating the Lord's Supper together powerfully reminds believers of this unity in Christ (1 Cor. 10:16–17).

One passage that captures several of these interrelated features of union with Christ is Colossians 3:1–11. The passage roots believers' identity in Christ, describing their lives as "hidden with Christ in God," so that Christ "is your life" (Col. 3:3–4). Believers who are united with Christ have died with Christ and are now raised with him (Col. 3:1–4). As an extension of this participation in Christ, believers must leave behind their old ways of life and live consistently with their new life in Christ, which is in the process of being reshaped into the image of God (3:5–10). The shared experience of being totally defined by Christ and his indwelling

---

15. This follows an indicative–imperative pattern that we will examine in the next section.
16. The language and concept of cruciform living has been popularized by Michael J. Gorman, *Cruciformity: Paul's Narrative Spirituality of the Cross* (Grand Rapids: Eerdmans, 2001). See also the summary in Gorman, *Apostle of the Crucified Lord*, 120–24.

presence means that "there is no Gentile or Jew, circumcised or uncircumcised, barbarian, Scythian, slave or free" for those who are in Christ (Col. 3:11a). The reason for this fundamental equality of all believers is stressed once more: "Christ is all, and is in all" (Col. 3:11b). Thus, the passage ends with a strong note of believers' shared identity.

We could continue to pursue the depth and reach of the idea of union with Christ in Paul's teachings, and we would have plenty of material to work with. One scholar calls this doctrine the "webbing" of Paul's theology, since it spreads out into so many other areas of Paul's teachings.[17] As we add more themes to the list of Paul's important ideas in this chapter, we will probably notice how they all seem to interrelate and overlap with one another.

GRACE, FAITH, AND OBEDIENCE

The topics of grace, faith, and obedience, all frequent and overt in Paul's letters, tap into questions of how God's plans and human freedom fit together. Paul expresses his conviction that God is always at work in perfect but mysterious ways that stretch beyond human comprehension (Rom. 11:33–36). Still, Paul has no problem with the compatibility between God's sovereign orchestrations and the genuine call for human response. The pattern Paul does adhere to over and over is the consistent order of God's initiative preceding human response.

Paul regularly pinpoints the grace, mercy, and love of God as motivations for God's saving works. Christ's arrival to our world set in motion the benevolent plans that God had crafted before the beginning of time, for the praise of his glory (Eph. 1:3–14; 2 Tim. 1:9–10). God's grace consists of his loving determination to reach out to helpless sinners (Rom. 3:23–24; 5:6–8; Eph. 2:4–9; Titus 3:4–7). The emphasis on God's grace and mercy underscores the fact that God's saving interventions in our world are undeserved and unprovoked by human goodness.

Paul is adamant that faith is the essential response to God's grace. Those who hear and believe the message about Christ gain access into the grace of God (Rom. 5:1–2). Through faith believers become united in Christ's death and resurrection (Col. 2:12). Paul sometimes contrasts faith with works, or believing with achieving (Rom. 4:4–5; 9:32; Eph. 2:8–9; Phil. 3:9; Titus 3:4–7). God's gift of Christ and forgiveness is received rather than earned.[18]

Saving faith is the entryway into an ongoing life with Christ.[19] In this arena of ongoing life Paul continues to respect the order of God's

---

17. Campbell, *Paul and Union with Christ*, 441–42.
18. This appears to be true in a universal sense, from the passages listed, even if Paul contrasts faith with works of the Jewish law in particular in several contexts (especially Rom. 3:27–31 and Gal. 2:11–21).
19. Of course, faith plays a central ongoing role in the Christian life as well.

work and the believer's response. A language pattern known as "the indicative-imperative" construction puts this sequence on full display.[20] In grammar, indicative sentences typically communicate the way things are, while imperative sentences present the way things ought to be.[21] When Paul describes what God has done in believers' lives, he uses indicative sentences, because he is asserting that these divine actions in the lives of believers are settled matters. Believers have already been united with Christ, they have new life in him, and they are no longer slaves to sin (Rom. 6:5–10). When Paul commands and exhorts believers he usually employs imperative sentences. When he tells them to count themselves dead to sin and offer themselves to God in righteousness (Rom. 6:11–13), Paul uses imperative sentences to entreat believers to rise to this standard.

The key in the indicative-imperative pattern is that Paul launches his imperative commands from the base of the indicative truths that correspond to them. In other words, Paul challenges believers to act upon what is already true about them (see Phil. 3:12b, 16). Christian obedience is not expected in a vacuum but as a natural extension of the change God has already secured for us in Christ. God has made believers a new creation, so believers need to appropriate that fact and live accordingly.[22] I once saw a young boy fall into a lake and begin yelling for help. As he was flailing about in the water I prepared to jump in to help him. But suddenly he stopped wailing and simply stood up in the shallow lake. The water came up to his chest. There had been solid ground beneath him all along, so he just needed to stand on that ground. Paul's indicative–imperative concept likewise calls believers to stand on the solid ground that Christ has placed them on.

As seen from the indicative–imperative pattern, believers aren't expected to drum up the will to obey God apart from the spiritual resources he has already given them. But knowing that believers possess these divine resources, Paul does expect them to obey God. Grace, faith, and obedience belong together. For believers who are tempted to abuse grace by slipping into spiritual and moral laxity, Paul exclaims, "May it never be!" (Rom. 6:1–2, 15, NASB). Paul connects faith and obedience closely together (Rom. 1:5; 16:26; Col. 2:6–7), so that faith can't be viewed as essential while obedience is optional. In fact, while Paul never views obedience as a precondition for salvation, its absence after a profession of faith calls into question the legitimacy of faith. On

---

20. For a more extensive discussion of this indicative–imperative pattern, see Herman Ridderbos, *Paul: An Outline of His Theology*, trans. John R. DeWitt (Grand Rapids: Eerdmans, 1975), 253–58; Dunn, *Theology of Paul*, 626–31.

21. This is a simplification of the subtler nuances of the indicative and imperative mood in Greek. See Wallace, *Greek Grammar beyond the Basics*, 443–45, 485.

22. The indicative and the imperative relationship applies to the church as a whole as well. For instance, Paul challenges believers to "keep" rather than create "the unity of the Spirit" (Eph. 4:3).

occasion Paul upholds continuing or persevering in the faith as a necessary consequence of a life changed by God (2 Cor. 13:5; Col. 1:23). Similarly, he voices the hope that his ministry to his readers won't have been in vain, indicating his concern about their endurance in following Christ (1 Cor. 15:2; 2 Cor. 6:1; Gal. 4:11; Phil. 2:16; 1 Thess. 3:15). This language suggests Paul's understanding that initial faith must be accompanied by ongoing perseverance in that faith.

On the flip side, Paul's view of God's faithfulness and power is high enough to give him confidence that God finishes what he starts (Rom. 8:28–30; 1 Cor. 1:8–9; 2 Cor. 1:21–22; Phil. 1:6; 1 Thess. 5:23–24; 2 Tim. 1:12). In order to finish the race, believers depend upon a divine enablement that is much more reliable than their own strength and willpower. As we will see in the next section, the Holy Spirit who activated believers' faith continues to supply the resources needed for growth. This doesn't completely alleviate the tension between God's work and human accountability, but it shows that Paul himself was not uncomfortable holding these ideas together in harmony.[23]

THE HOLY SPIRIT

Paul operated with a hearty doctrine of the Holy Spirit. His understanding of the Holy Spirit fed into the ideas of gospel, union with Christ, and grace, faith, and obedience that we have already examined in this chapter. As was the case with union with Christ, the Holy Spirit is another theme that seems to weave its way into most areas of Paul's thought.[24]

Paul recognized the permanent endowment of the Holy Spirit as the defining mark of the new covenant era. Paul likely perceived that God's bestowal of the Spirit fulfilled Old Testament prophecies that God would lavish his Spirit on his people in a new era of salvation. In Israel's experience under the old covenant, the Spirit was given only to certain leaders for special tasks (Exod. 31:2–5; 35:30–33; Num. 11:16–30; Judg. 3:10; 6:34; 11:29; Zech. 7:12).[25] The Spirit was not a permanent gift even for those anointed leaders (see 1 Sam. 16:13–14; John 7:39). But Joel 2:28–32 promised a drastic change. Joel depicts the widespread outpouring of the Spirit on all of God's people, regardless of gender, age, or social status. Ezekiel 36:24–28 foretold a day in which the Spirit would transform God's people internally, changing their resistant "hearts of stone" to responsive "hearts of flesh." This inward renewal would give God's people the motivation and

---

23. For one careful discussion of Paul's view of perseverance, see Thomas R. Schreiner, *Paul, Apostle of God's Glory in Christ* (Downers Grove, IL: InterVarsity; Leicester: Apollos, 2001), 271–305.

24. See Fee, *God's Empowering Presence*. Also emphasizing the Spirit's importance is Dunn, *Theology of Paul*, 419, 425.

25. See also Moses's desire for a more widespread reception of the Spirit among the people of God in Numbers 29:11.

ability to please God and obey his commands. These promises came to fruition when Jesus launched the new covenant and poured out his Spirit on Jews (Acts 2), Samaritans (Acts 8), Gentiles (Acts 10), and all subsequent believers in Christ (Eph. 1:13).

In 2 Corinthians 3:6–18, Paul contrasts the glorious ministry of the old, Mosaic covenant with the even greater ministry of the new covenant. The Spirit is the difference-maker. The new covenant is the covenant of the life-giving Spirit (3:6). The Spirit gives believers freedom for direct access to God's presence, and as the Spirit mediates access to God, believers are supernaturally transformed by that encounter (3:17–18).[26]

Paul uses vivid imagery to depict the Spirit as the initial guarantee of a greater salvation to come. The Spirit is a deposit or down payment of a full, eschatological inheritance (2 Cor. 1:22; 5:5; Eph. 1:14). Believers are sealed by the Holy Spirit, showing that they are claimed by God and belong to him (Eph. 1:13; 4:30). The same Spirit who resides in the lives of believers now will be the agent of believers' future bodily resurrection (Rom. 8:11). The Spirit's presence in believers' lives is the first fruits of a greater harvest that will come in the form of resurrection and a creation-wide renewal (Rom. 8:23).

The Spirit empowers the ministry and growth of Christ's church. Paul recalls how observable manifestations of the Spirit's work accompanied his preached message (1 Cor. 2:4–5; 1 Thess. 1:4–5). The same Spirit who powerfully confirms the gospel message incorporates new believers into the body of Christ (1 Cor. 12:13). The Spirit dwells in this body of believers, which functions as a holy temple for God's divine presence (1 Cor. 3:16–17; Eph. 2:18–22).

The Spirit who dwells in the church congregation equips believers with manifold gifts, so that believers can use these gifts for the edification and strengthening of the church body (Rom. 12; 1 Cor. 12–14). Paul explains that each believer receives gifts for the common good (1 Cor. 12:7–11). Paul also instructs people in the corporate use of these gifts. Paul envisions Spirit-guided, truth-centered, orderly worship gatherings that invite the participation of all types of people and result in growth towards maturity in the congregation (see 1 Cor. 14:26–33; Eph. 4:11–16; 5:18–20; Col. 3:15–16).

As mentioned earlier, Joel 2:28–32 specifies that God will shower his Spirit on both men and women, enabling them to prophesy. Not surprisingly, Paul accepts prophecy by both males and females as a common practice in his churches, giving instruction on how this should be carried out rather than revisiting whether it is legitimate or not (1 Cor. 11:4–5).[27] The

---

26. Connecting the Spirit strongly to God's presence is Fee, *God's Empowering Presence*, 843–45.
27. Ibid., 885. The debated passage 1 Corinthians 14:34–35 may introduce some restrictions on women publicly critiquing the prophecies of men, though it does not appear to mean that women were prevented from contributing to public worship, in view of Joel 2:28–32, 1 Corinthians 11:4–5, and examples from Paul's ministry team.

Spirit's gifting of both men and women in many other areas of ministry is also observed in Paul's circles with the numerous female coworkers he mentions in his letters.

Paul sprinkles references to the Spirit throughout his letters, rather than concentrating the discussion in one longer passage. Galatians is a good example of this tendency. Throughout Galatians Paul reiterates the significance of the Spirit to the commencement and progression of life with Christ. Believers receive the Spirit by faith, which marks the beginning of their life with Christ (Gal. 3:2–3). Paul identifies the Spirit as the gateway through which God's promises to Abraham are delivered (Gal. 3:14). As an ongoing privilege of possessing the Spirit of God's Son, believers can address God with the intimacy of a child to a father (Gal. 4:4–6). Through the Spirit (in active dependence upon him), believers faithfully live for God while waiting for Christ to return (Gal. 5:5; see also 6:8). This Spirit-led living involves walking with the Spirit, or letting the Spirit guide one's conduct, and allowing the Spirit to produce fruit or Christ-like virtues in one's life (Gal. 5:16–18). Paul reiterates this idea by encouraging believers to allow the same one who gave them new life (the Spirit) to guide them in their steps (Gal. 5:25).[28] From Galatians, and the rest of Paul's letters, we can observe the essential transforming, liberating, relational, and empowering role of the Spirit in a believer's life.

AN ETERNAL KINGDOM PERSPECTIVE

Eternity mattered to Paul. The hope of eternal life and eternal reward in God's kingdom propelled him through many thorny obstacles and setbacks in life. Many readers today fail to fully grasp Paul's vision in his letters because they lack this eternal perspective. Paul's actions and theology cannot be appreciated apart from the eternal horizon he has in view. Because of his eternal perspective he invested more deeply in life and ministry, rather than withdrawing from the world.

Paul believed in eternity because he was tapped into the promise of God's eschatological kingdom. This kingdom was previewed and longed for throughout the Old Testament as the culmination of God's plans for this world. The promised kingdom of God would be implemented by his anointed one (Ps. 2), the Davidic king (Isa. 9:2–7; 11:1–10), the Son of Man (Dan. 7:13–14), who would visit the world in judgment and salvation. In the Gospels Jesus announces the imminent arrival of the kingdom of God at the outset of his ministry (Mark 1:14–15) and inaugurates the kingdom

---

28. The English translations of this verse do not always do justice to the profundity of this verse. The first half of the verse in many versions is translated as "live by the Spirit," which obscures the idea of the life-giving work of the Spirit (as in 2 Cor. 3:6). A few translations capture the intended meaning well: "If the Spirit is the source of our life, let the Spirit also direct our course" (NEB); "The Spirit has given us life; he must also control our lives" (GNT).

of God through his authoritative ministry of teaching, healing, and exorcisms (Matt.. 12:28). Jesus also promises a day when he would return as victorious king over the entire world (Matt. 8:11; 19:28; 25:34; Luke 13:28–29; 22:29–30). When Jesus appears with full glory he will demonstrate his comprehensive power, authority, and sovereignty over the world through enacting a final judgment on his enemies (Matt. 25:31–33, 46a; John 5:22, 27, 29b) and giving rewards and resurrected life to his faithful servants (Matt. 5:3, 10; 16:27; 25:46b; John 5:24–26, 29a).

Paul adopts Jesus's teaching that the kingdom of God has already broken into the current world, even though believers still await its complete, comprehensive manifestation on earth as it is in heaven. The Jewish understanding of salvation history (as attested in Jewish literature from the centuries surrounding Paul's time) was that humanity lived in a present, corrupted age, and that God's people were awaiting an age to come, the age of God's installment of his kingdom on earth.[29] For the early church and Paul, Jesus changes the picture. He arrives to this world as God's anointed Son and King, inaugurating the age to come and kingdom of God. But Jesus does not immediately judge the current evil age. That day of judgment is delayed until his future return (Rom. 5:9; 1 Thess. 1:10; 5:9; 2 Thess. 1:6–10; 2 Tim. 4:1), as is the blessing of bodily resurrection (1 Cor. 15:50–57; Phil. 3:20–21; 1 Thess. 4:14–17) and "the life that is truly life" (1 Tim. 6:19). In the meantime, believers live in overlapping ages. They live within the realities of the broken present age while being a small colony of kingdom citizens who begin to experience life under God's reign even now, as a taste of the world to come (1 Cor. 6:2–3; 10:11; 2 Cor. 5:17; Gal. 1:4; Col. 1:13–14). For Paul, this preview of the perfect kingdom of God, along with the painful realities of life in the current world, whetted his appetite for the full arrival of God's reign (Rom. 8:22–23; 1 Cor. 15:22–28; Eph. 1:9–10; Phil. 3:20–21).

Paul fixed his gaze unwaveringly on the future return of Christ as victorious king of the world. Paul looked forward to the return of Christ even as he remained anchored in the past events of Christ's death and resurrection. In fact, he knows that the return of Christ is tethered to the prior events of the cross and resurrection (1 Thess. 4:14–17). The victory secured in Christ's first advent points towards a future victory in his second advent. A famous analogy inspired by World War 2 captures this connection. The dramatic victory of D-Day set in motion events that culminated in V(E)-Day. Christ's sacrificial death and resurrection represents D-Day, while his promised return will correspond to V(E)-Day.[30]

Paul's hope for the future consummation of God's kingdom shaped his outlook thoroughly. For one, he understood that the gospel's eternal

29. See Ladd, *Theology of the New Testament*, 364–65, 550–52.
30. See Oscar Cullmann, *Christ and Time: The Primitive Christian Conception of Time and History*, trans. Floyd V. Filson (Philadelphia: Westminster, 1950), 87, 145–46.

ramifications take precedence over any worldly cause. He was an eternally minded minister, as reflected in his priorities of preaching the gospel and planting and nurturing churches. This eternal focus made him single-minded and relentless in his ministry service (Phil. 3:10–14; Col. 1:28–29). He knew that every instance of gospel ministry he invested in was worth it because of the eternal stakes (1 Cor. 15:58).[31]

Paul's eternal hope freed him to serve God recklessly, holding nothing back. He knew that any sacrifice now paled in comparison to the divine rewards awaiting him at Jesus's return. Paul endured his trials with an unshakable hope: "Therefore we do not lose heart. Though outwardly we are wasting away, yet inwardly we are being renewed day by day. For our light and momentary troubles are achieving for us an eternal glory that far outweighs them all. So we fix our eyes not on what is seen but on what is unseen, since what is seen is temporary but what is unseen is eternal" (2 Cor. 4:16–18). Paul's longing for an unseen but certain future spurred him to live by faith rather than sight (Rom. 8:24–25; Gal. 2:20; 2 Cor. 5:7). Paul's future orientation shaped his daily living. He kept his eyes fixed on the one who will reward him on the last day (Phil. 3:12–14; 2 Tim. 1:12; 4:6–8).

Paul was even willing to cause temporary sorrow within his churches when he confronted sin (2 Cor. 7:8–10). Because he correctly valued the eternal benefits of being reconciled to God, he approached unrepentant sinners with the tough love of church discipline (1 Cor. 5:1–13; 1 Thess. 5:14; 2 Thess. 3:14–15; 1 Tim. 1:19b–20; see also Matt. 18:15–17). He was ready to remove them from the present comforts of shared life in the church in order to provoke repentance and restoration to fellowship with God and other believers (2 Cor. 2:5–11; Gal. 6:1). Such a drastic approach to wayward believers makes sense only from an eternal kingdom perspective.

A future kingdom that believers already belong to brings ethical implications for our current lives as well. Paul highlights love and holiness in particular. Paul often boils down the ethical obligations of God's commands to the principle of love (Rom. 13:8–10; 1 Cor. 13:1–13; Gal. 5:6, 14). This emphasis preserves the teachings of the Old Testament (Lev. 19:18) and Jesus himself (Mark 12:29–31 and parallels). Self-giving love consists of putting others' interests above one's own, just as Jesus modeled in his incarnation, life, and death (Phil. 2:1–11). In Ephesians 5:2 and 5:25 Paul similarly appeals to God's love for believers as the motivation for our love for one another.

Paul presents holiness as the way of life that anticipates meeting with the Lord one day in the future (Rom. 13:11–14; 2 Cor. 7:1; Phil. 1:10; 1 Thess. 5:1–10; Titus 2:11–14). This joyful gathering is likened to a groom

---

31. Paul thus perfectly captures Jesus's admonition to store up treasures in heaven rather than on earth (Matt. 6:19–21).

meeting his bride for a union in marriage (Eph. 5:25–27; see also the faint echoes of this in Col. 1:22; 1 Thess. 3:13; 5:23–24). A central idea of biblical holiness is being set apart for God. God chose Israel to be his special people (Exod. 19:4–6). He called them to remove themselves from allegiance to false gods and sinful entanglements so that they could be wholly devoted to him and even imitate his holiness (Lev. 11:44–45). Paul affirms a similar idea of twofold holiness in his letters. Believers are called to be set apart *from* sin and the old way of life and become set apart *to* God alone (2 Cor. 6:14–7:1). Holiness thus reflects believers' loyalty to God and his kingdom, over the gods and values of this world.

One final important point about the ethical consequences of Paul's eternal mindset is that his belief in the certain arrival of God's coming kingdom sparked action, not passivity. Paul encouraged productive work and chastised lazy believers who shirked their responsibilities in life (1 Thess. 4:11–12; 5:14; 2 Thess. 3:6–12; 1 Tim. 5:13–14). Paul himself set an example of being "all in" for the gospel by serving fervently and being willing to work to provide for himself when necessary (1 Cor. 4:12; 9:19–27; 1 Thess. 2:9; 2 Thess. 3:7–9). For Paul, the reality of God's eternal kingdom created the need to make the most of the window of opportunity in this life.

CONCLUSION

Many of Paul's actions make more sense when illuminated by the ideas in this chapter. Paul made his dedication to the ministry of the gospel overt in most of his letters. He knew that the gospel of God's Son entailed both the defining moments of Jesus's ministry (especially his death and resurrection) as well as the resulting effects of those events. The gospel opened the way for people to enjoy a relational union with Christ, through whom believers die to their old selves and are raised to live a new life in Christ. God graciously extends his love through Christ to those who have faith in Christ. Those who believe also obey, by learning to live in a way that is consistent with their new identity in Christ, which Paul reflects in his indicative-imperative pattern of instruction and exhortation. The Spirit who gives believers new life also empowers them to be fruitful for God and use their God-given spiritual gifts to serve the church. All of these initial blessings of salvation are a foretaste of the full package of divine gifts that God will give to believers when Christ returns. Paul was keenly aware of the weight of these eternal blessings, and he lived his life and ministered to others with the reality of God's eternal kingdom ever before him. These and other related theological convictions guided Paul and shaped his outlook on his own life and the lives he invested in.

The God of Israel and Lord of the universe took a man who was stubbornly opposed to his redemptive plans in Christ and graciously called him to be an apostle. Paul drew upon a rich Jewish background and wide-ranging exposure to a broader world to serve God over the course of three decades. Paul tirelessly ventured out into unreached regions of the Roman world, nurtured existing churches, and still made it a priority to write the thirteen letters that survive to this day. It is our privilege and joy to read, study, meditate over, and implement the teachings from these letters. When we read Paul's letters with both the mind and heart, we emerge with glimpses into the radical but indispensable theological convictions that shaped Paul and steered him in his writings. As the Thessalonians once learned, when we approach Paul's letters as God's communication to us, we find that his word truly is at work in us, pointing us to Christ and molding our lives into his image.

> And we also thank God continually because, when you received the word of God, which you heard from us, you accepted it not as a human word, but as it actually is, the word of God, which is indeed at work in you who believe (1 Thess. 2:13).

■ ■ ■

EPHESIANS

Title: The united church's riches and calling in Christ

Sender/Recipients: Paul, an apostle (1:1) and prisoner (3:1; 4:1) of Christ, to the church at Ephesus and other churches in the province of Asia (1:1).

Date and place of writing: around AD 60 or 61, during Paul's first Roman imprisonment (3:1; 4:1; 6:20).

Occasion: Paul knew of churches in Asia Minor that needed prayer and encouragement, but he could not visit them personally (1:15–16). After writing Colossians, he realized that a similar letter could meet the needs of many churches in that region. Perhaps the churches were at risk of losing their sense of confidence in the midst of a hostile spiritual environment (6:10–18).

Purpose: Paul wants to further establish the believers in their individual and corporate identity in Christ (1:3–14; 2:1–22), to instruct the readers about how to grow as a unified and holy body of believers (2:14–18; 4:1–6), and to help them depend on Christ's authority for spiritual battle and spiritual strength (1:15–23; 6:10–18).

Tone: Lofty; not very personal; positive.

Outline:

I.   God has richly blessed Jews and Gentiles by making them alive and united in Christ (1:1–2:22)
    A.   Paul the apostle greets faithful believers with grace and peace (1:1–2)
    B.   God has a plan to bless believers through the Son and by the Spirit (1:3–14)
        1.   The Father has an eternal plan to bless believers, in Jesus Christ (1:3–6)

2. Believers are forgiven through Christ's blood, in preparation for Christ's reign over all things (1:7–10)

3. The Spirit's presence ensures that believers will receive all blessings (1:11–14)

C. Paul prays that believers would grasp their riches in Christ, who rules over all (1:15–23)

D. Formerly "dead" believers have been made alive in Christ (2:1–10)

E. God has made formerly divided Jews and Gentiles into a new, unified, holy people in Christ (2:11–22)

    1. Formerly excluded Gentiles have been included in God's people by Christ's sacrifice (2:11–13)

    2. Formerly divided believers (Jews and Gentiles) have been made one in Christ (2:14–18)

    3. Jewish and Gentile believers who are united in Christ are God's new temple (2:19–22)

II. Paul fulfills his calling to instruct and pray for Christ's united church (3:1–21)

A. Imprisoned Paul recalls his divine mandate to reach the Gentiles (3:1–13)

B. Paul prays that believers would grasp the abundant love of Christ (3:14–21)

III. The united church should grow together in love and shine as Christ's holy people in a dark world (4:1–6:24)

A. Diverse believers united in Christ should grow together towards maturity (4:1–16)

    1. Believers should humbly unify around their common confession of faith (4:1–6)

    2. Christ has equipped diverse believers to grow together towards maturity (4:7–16)

B. Believers should put off the old and put on the new in practical ways (4:17–32)

    1. Believers should put off their old, corrupted selves and put on their new identity in Christ (4:17–24)

    2. Believers should live as new people in their speech, conduct, and attitude (4:25–32)

C. Loving and holy believers should shine Christ's light in a dark world (5:1–14)

    1. Believers should live as imitators of God, with sacrificial love and holiness (5:1–5)

    2. Believers should aspire to shine Christ's light in a dark world (5:6–14)

D. Believers should pursue Spirit-filled lives and relationships (5:15–6:9)

    1. The Spirit should guide believers in discernment and corporate worship (5:15–21)

    2. The Spirit should shape relationships between wives and husbands (5:22–33)

    3. The Spirit should shape relationships between children and parents (6:1–4)

    4. The Spirit should shape relationships between servants and masters (6:5–9)

E.   Believers should be equipped in Christ for spiritual battle (6:10–20)
F.   Paul shares final greetings of peace and grace (6:21–24)

Key verses

Ephesians 1:3—"[He] has blessed us in the heavenly realms with every spiritual blessing in Christ"—sets agenda for chapters 1–3, especially the "in Christ" theme.

Ephesians 1:9–10—"[H]e made known to us the mystery of his will . . . to bring unity to all things in heaven and on earth under Christ"—God's divine disclosure and Christ's authority over all things are both major themes in the letter.

Ephesians 4:1—"I urge you to live a life worthy of the calling you have received"— introduces the letter's shift from theology to practice while showing the logical connection between theology and practice.

Repeated words, phrases, topics: *In Christ* and its equivalents (*in him* and *in whom*, etc.), *the heavenly realms, walk* (ESV) or *live* (NIV), body (of Christ), *mystery, grace, love,* God the *Father,* unity/oneness, the authority of Christ, and the Holy Spirit as a *seal/pledge.*

Application for life and ministry

Praise God for the spiritual blessings he has given me and will give me	1:3–14
Pray for spiritual depth, growth, and boldness for myself and others	1:15–19; 3:14–21; 6:19–20
Thank God for his transforming salvation, all by grace	2:1–10
Reconciliation with Christ brings diverse people together	2:14–18
There are nonnegotiable doctrines that Christians must rally around	4:4–6
Various spiritual gifts should lead to unity and growth	4:11–13
New life must show itself in tangible ways	4:20–32
Encouragement should mark my speech	4:29
A loving husband should care for and sacrifice for his wife	5:25–30
Identify the correct enemy and resist through prayer, Christ's strength	6:10–13

Areas for further investigation:

- What does the language of "chosen" and "predestined" mean in the context of chapter 1?
- What is the significance of the idea of "mystery," mentioned in chapters 1, 3, and 6?

- How does the church display God's wisdom to the rulers and authorities of the heavenly realms (3:10)?
- What is the relationship and/or difference between being sealed and filled with the Holy Spirit (1:13–14; 4:30; 5:18)?
- What does it mean that Christ descended to the "lower, earthly regions" (NIV) or "lower parts of the earth" (NASB)?
- What is the meaning of 5:14 ("Wake up, sleeper . . .")? Is there a link to Romans 13:11–12?

BIBLIOGRAPHY

Agnew, Francis H. "The Origin of the NT Apostle-Concept: A Review of Research." *JBL* 105 (1986): 75–96.

Alexander, Loveday C. A. "Chronology of Paul." *DPL* 115–23.

Arnold, Clinton E. *The Colossian Syncretism: The Interface between Christianity and Folk Belief at Colossae.* Grand Rapids: Baker, 1996.

Barnett, Paul. *The Second Epistle to the Corinthians.* NICNT. Grand Rapids: Eerdmans, 1997.

Barr, George K. *Scalometry and the Pauline Epistles.* JSNTSup 261. London: Clark, 2004.

Barrett, C. K. *A Commentary on the Second Epistle to the Corinthians.* HNTC. New York: Harper & Row, 1973.

Bauckham, Richard. *Jesus and the Eyewitnesses: The Gospels as Eyewitness Testimony.* Grand Rapids: Eerdmans, 2006.

Baum, Armin D. "Semantic Variation within the *Corpus Paulinum*." *TynBul* 59 (2008): 271–92.

Beale, G. K., and D. A. Carson, eds. *Commentary on the New Testament Use of the Old Testament.* Grand Rapids: Baker; Nottingham: Apollos, 2007.

Beker, J. Christiaan. *The Triumph of God: The Essence of Paul's Thought.* Translated by Loren T. Stuckenbruck. Minneapolis: Fortress, 1990.

Bible Gateway. "Scripture Engagement." https://www.biblegateway.com/resources/scripture-engagement.

Bird, Michael F. *Romans.* SGBC. Grand Rapids: Zondervan, 2016.

_____. "When the Dust Finally Settles: Coming to a Post-New Perspective Perspective." *CTR* n.s., 2 (2005): 57–69.

Blomberg, Craig L. "Quotations, Allusions, and Echoes of Jesus in Paul." Pages 129–43 in *Studies in the Pauline Epistles: Essays in Honor of Douglas J. Moo*. Edited by Matthew S. Harmon and Jay E. Smith. Grand Rapids: Zondervan, 2014.

Bockmuehl, Markus. *Revelation and Mystery in Ancient Judaism and Pauline Christianity*. Grand Rapids: Eerdmans, 1990.

Boer, Martinus C. de. "Images of Paul in the Post-Apostolic Period." *CBQ* 42 (1980): 359–80.

_____. "Paul's Mythologizing Program in Romans 5–8." Pages 1–20 in *Apocalyptic Paul: Cosmos and Anthropos in Romans 5–8*. Edited by Beverly Roberts Gaventa. Waco, TX: Baylor University Press, 2013.

Boers, Hendrickus. "The Form Critical Study of Paul's Letters: 1 Thessalonians as a Case Study." *NTS* 22 (1975): 140–58.

Bruce, F. F. *New Testament History*. New York: Doubleday, 1971.

_____. *Paul: Apostle of the Heart Set Free*. Grand Rapids: Eerdmans, 1981.

_____. *The Book of Acts*. Rev. ed. NICNT. Grand Rapids: Eerdmans, 1988.

Campbell, Constantine. *Paul and Union with Christ: An Exegetical and Theological Study*. Grand Rapids: Zondervan, 2012.

Campbell, Douglas A. *The Deliverance of God: An Apocalyptic Rereading of Justification in Paul*. Grand Rapids: Eerdmans, 2009.

Carson, D. A., and Douglas Moo. *An Introduction to the New Testament*. 2nd ed. Grand Rapids: Zondervan, 2005.

Carson, D. A., Peter T. O'Brien, and Mark A. Seifrid, eds. *Justification and Variegated Nomism*. 2 vols. Tübingen: Mohr Siebeck, 2001, 2004.

Cassidy, Richard J. *Paul in Chains: Roman Imprisonment and the Letters of Saint Paul*. New York: Herder & Herder, 2001.

Clark, Andrew. "Apostleship: Evidence from the New Testament and Early Christian Literature." *VE* 19 (1989): 49–82.

Conzelmann, Hans. "Paulus und die Weisheit." *NTS* 12 (1965–1966): 231–44.

Cullmann, Oscar. *Christ and Time: The Primitive Christian Conception of Time and History*. Translated by Floyd V. Filson. Philadelphia: Westminster, 1950.

Duke Divinity School. "N. T. Wright: Panel Discussion on Pauline Theology with Faculty." YouTube video, 1:33:03. Posted Nov. 12, 2014. https://www.youtube.com/watch?v=mNzcwo6opqg.

Dunn, James D. G. *Jesus, Paul, and the Law: Studies in Mark and Galatians*. Louisville: Westminster John Knox, 1990.

_____. "Pauline Legacy and School." *DLNT* 887–93.

_____. *The Theology of Paul the Apostle*. Grand Rapids: Eerdmans, 1998.

Ehrman, Bart D. *Forged Writing in the Name of God—Why the Bible's Authors Are Not Who We Think They Are*. New York: HarperOne, 2011.

_____. *Forgery and Counterforgery: The Use of Literary Deceit in Early Christian Polemics*. Oxford: Oxford University Press, 2013.

Elliott, J. K. *The Apocryphal New Testament: A Collection of Apocryphal Christian Literature in an English Translation*. Oxford: Clarendon, 1993.

Ellis, E. Earle. "Coworkers, Paul and His." *DPL* 183–89.

_____. "Pastoral Letters." *DPL* 658–66.

Fee, Gordon D. *God's Empowering Presence: The Holy Spirit in the Letters of Paul*. Peabody, MA: Hendrickson, 1994.

_____. *Paul's Letter to the Philippians*. NICNT. Grand Rapids: Eerdmans, 1995.

Fee, Gordon D., and Douglas Stuart. *How to Read the Bible for All Its Worth*. 3rd ed. Grand Rapids: Zondervan, 2003.

Ferguson, Everett. *Backgrounds of Early Christianity*. 3rd ed. Grand Rapids: Eerdmans, 2003.

Flanagan, Neil M., and Edwina H. Snyder. "Did Paul Put Down Women in First Corinthians 14:34–36?" *Foundations* 24 (1981): 216–20.

Foster, Paul. "Who Wrote 2 Thessalonians? A Fresh Look at an Old Problem." *JSNT* 35 (2012): 150–75.

Garland, David E. *1 Corinthians*. BECNT. Grand Rapids: Baker, 2003.

Gill, David W. J. "Behind the Classical Façade: Local Religions of the Roman Empire." Pages 72–87 in *One God, One Lord in a World of Religious Pluralism*. Edited by Andrew D. Clarke and Bruce W. Winter. Cambridge: Tyndale House, 1991.

Gombis, Timothy G. "A Radically New Humanity: The Function of the *Haustafel* in Ephesians." *JETS* 48 (2005): 317–30.

Gorman, Michael J. *Apostle of the Crucified Lord: A Theological Introduction to Paul and His Letters*. Grand Rapids: Eerdmans, 2004.

_____. *Cruciformity: Paul's Narrative Spirituality of the Cross*. Grand Rapids: Eerdmans, 2001.

Gundry, Stanley N., and Michael F. Bird, eds. *Four Views on the Apostle Paul*. Grand Rapids: Zondervan, 2012.

Hafemann, Scott J. "Corinthians, Letters to the." *DPL* 164–79.

Hays, Richard B. *Echoes of Scripture in the Letters of Paul.* New Haven, CT: Yale University Press, 1989.

_____. *The Conversion of the Imagination: Paul as Interpreter of Israel's Scripture.* Grand Rapids: Eerdmans, 2005.

Helyer, Larry R. *The Witness of Jesus, Paul and John: An Exploration in Biblical Theology.* Downers Grove, IL: InterVarsity, 2008.

Hemer, Colin J. *The Book of Acts in the Setting of Hellenistic History.* Edited by Conrad H. Gempf. WUNT 49. Tübingen: J. C. B. Mohr (Paul Siebeck), 1989.

Henry Center for Theological Understanding. "Is the Lutheran Approach to Pauline Justification 'Justified'?" YouTube video, 1:57:27. Posted Feb. 25, 2015. https://www.youtube.com/watch?v=KlujS-fH8R4.

Hirsch, E. D., Jr. "Meaning and Significance Reinterpreted." *Critical Inquiry* 11 (1984): 202–25.

Horrell, David G., ed. *Social-Scientific Approaches to New Testament Interpretation.* Edinburgh: T&T Clark, 1999.

Horsley, Richard A., ed. *Paul and Empire: Religion and Power in Roman Imperial Society.* Harrisburg, PA: Trinity Press International, 1997.

_____, ed. *Paul and the Roman Imperial Order.* Harrisburg, PA: Trinity Press, 2004.

Hovhanessian, Vahan. *Third Corinthians: Reclaiming Paul for Christian Orthodoxy.* Studies in Biblical Literature 18. New York: Lang, 2000.

Hurtado, Larry W. *Lord Jesus Christ: Devotion to Jesus in Earliest Christianity.* Grand Rapids: Eerdmans, 2003.

James, Montague Rhodes. *The Apocryphal New Testament.* Oxford: Clarendon, 1924.

Johnson, Luke Timothy. *The First and Second Letters to Timothy.* AB 35A. New York: Doubleday, 2001.

Johnston, J. William. "Grammatical Analysis: Making Connections." Pages 135–53 in *Interpreting the New Testament Text: Introduction to the Art and Science of Exegesis.* Edited by Darrell L. Bock and Buist M. Fanning. Wheaton, IL: Crossway, 2006.

Kaiser, Walter C., Jr., and Moisés Silva. *Introduction to Biblical Hermeneutics: The Search for Meaning.* Rev. and exp. ed. Grand Rapids: Zondervan, 2007.

Keener, Craig S. *Paul, Women & Wives: Marriage and Women's Ministry in the Letters of Paul.* Peabody, MA: Hendrickson, 1992.

_____. *The IVP Bible Background Commentary: New Testament.* 2nd ed. Downers Grove, IL: IVP Academic, 2014.

Kenny, Anthony. *A Stylometric Study of the New Testament.* Oxford: Clarendon, 1996.

Kim, Seyoon. "Jesus, Sayings of." *DPL* 474–92.

_____. *The Origin of Paul's Gospel.* Grand Rapids: Eerdmans, 1981.

Knight, George W., III. *The Pastoral Epistles: A Commentary on the Greek Text.* NIGTC. Grand Rapids: Eerdmans; Carlisle: Paternoster, 1992.

Ladd, George Eldon. *A Theology of the New Testament.* Grand Rapids: Eerdmans, 1974.

Ledger, Gerard. "An Exploration of Differences in the Pauline Epistles Using Multivariate Statistical Analysis." *Literary and Linguistic Computing* 10 (1995): 85–97.

Lightfoot, J. B. *St. Paul's Epistles to the Colossians and to Philemon.* London: Macmillan, 1892.

Longenecker, Richard N. *Biblical Exegesis in the Apostolic Period.* 2nd ed. Grand Rapids: Eerdmans; Vancouver: Regent, 1999.

_____. *The Epistle to the Romans.* NIGTC. Grand Rapids: Eerdmans, 2016.

Lowery, David K. "Validation: Exegetical Problem Solving." Pages 155–66 in *Interpreting the New Testament Text: Introduction to the Art and Science of Exegesis.* Edited by Darrell L. Bock and Buist M. Fanning. Wheaton, IL: Crossway, 2006.

MaGee, Gregory S. "Paul's Gospel, the Law, and God's Universal Reign in Romans 3:31." *JETS* 57 (2014): 341–50.

_____. *Portrait of an Apostle: A Case for Paul's Authorship of Colossians and Ephesians.* Eugene, OR: Pickwick, 2013.

Mansoor, Menahem. "Pharisees." *EncJud* 16:30–32.

Martin, Ralph P. "Hymns, Hymn Fragments, Songs, Spiritual Songs." *DPL* 419–23.

Martyn, J. Louis. *Galatians.* AB 33A. New York: Doubleday, 1997.

Matera, Frank. *God's Saving Grace: A Pauline Theology.* Grand Rapids: Eerdmans, 2012.

McCloskey, Mark. *Tell It Often, Tell It Well.* San Bernardino, CA: Here's Life Publishers, 1985.

McKnight, Scot. *The King Jesus Gospel: The Original Good News Revisited.* Grand Rapids: Zondervan, 2011.

Mealand, D. L. "The Extent of the Pauline Corpus: A Multivariate Approach." *JSNT* 59 (1995): 61–92.

Meeks, Wayne A. *The First Urban Christians: The Social World of the Apostle Paul.* New Haven, CT: Yale University Press, 1983.

Miller, Colin. "The Imperial Cult in the Pauline Cities of Asia Minor and Greece." *CBQ* 72 (2010): 314–32.

Mommsen, Theodor, and Paul Krueger, eds. *The Digest of Justinian.* Translated by Alan Watson. Vol. 4. Philadelphia: University of Pennsylvania Press, 1985.

Moo, Douglas J. *The Epistle to the Romans.* NICNT. Grand Rapids: Eerdmans, 1996.

_____. *Galatians.* BECNT. Grand Rapids: Baker, 2013.

Moule, Handley Carr Glyn. *Charles Simeon.* London: Methuen & Co., 1892.

Mounce, William D. *Pastoral Epistles.* WBC 46. Dallas: Word, 2000.

Moyise, Steve. *Paul and Scripture: Studying the New Testament Use of the Old Testament.* Grand Rapids: Baker, 2010.

Murphy-O'Connor, Jerome. *Paul the Letter-Writer: His World, His Options, His Skills.* Good News Studies 41. Collegeville, MN: Liturgical Press, 1995.

Neumann, Kenneth J. *The Authenticity of the Pauline Epistles in Light of Stylostatistical Analysis.* SBLDS 120. Atlanta: Scholars Press, 1990.

Osborne, Grant R. *The Hermeneutical Spiral: A Comprehensive Introduction to Biblical Interpretation.* Downers Grove, IL: InterVarsity, 1991.

Pao, David W. *Colossians and Philemon.* ZECNT. Grand Rapids: Eerdmans, 2012.

Piper, John. *The Future of Justification: A Response to N. T. Wright.* Wheaton, IL: Crossway, 2007.

Polhill, John B. *Paul and His Letters.* Nashville: Broadman & Holman, 1999.

Ramsay, William M. *The Cities of St. Paul: Their Influence on His Life and Thought.* London: Hodder & Stoughton, 1907.

Rapske, Brian M. "Citizenship, Roman." *DNTB* 216.

_____. *The Book of Acts and Paul in Roman Custody.* Grand Rapids: Eerdmans, 1994.

_____. "Travel and Trade." *DNTB* 1245–50.

Reasoner, Mark. "Citizenship, Roman and Heavenly." *DPL* 139–41.

Richards, E. Randolph. *Paul and First-Century Letter Writing: Secretaries, Composition, and Collection.* Downers Grove, IL: InterVarsity, 2004.

Ridderbos, Herman. *Paul: An Outline of His Theology.* Translated by John R. DeWitt. Grand Rapids: Eerdmans, 1975.

Rupprecht, Arthur A. "Slave, Slavery." *DPL* 881–83.

Sanders, E. P. *Paul and Palestinian Judaism.* Philadelphia: Fortress, 1977.

Schnabel, Eckhard J. *Jesus and the Twelve.* Vol. 1 of *Early Christian Mission.* Downers Grove, IL: InterVarsity; Leicester: Apollos, 2004.

_____. *Paul and the Early Church.* Vol. 2 of *Early Christian Mission.* Downers Grove, IL: InterVarsity; Leicester: Apollos, 2004.

_____. "The Muratorian Fragment: The State of Research." *JETS* 57 (2014): 231–64.

Schneemelcher, Wilhelm, ed. *New Testament Apocrypha: Revised Edition of the Collection Initiated by Edward Hennecke.* Translated by R. McL. Wilson. Louisville: Westminster John Knox, 1991–1992.

Schnelle, Udo. *Apostle Paul: His Life and Theology.* Translated by M. Eugene Boring. Grand Rapids: Baker, 2003.

Schreiner, Thomas R. *Paul, Apostle of God's Glory in Christ.* Downers Grove, IL: InterVarsity; Leicester, Apollos, 2001.

Shogren, Gary S. *1 & 2 Thessalonians.* ZECNT. Grand Rapids: Zondervan, 2012.

Silva, Moisés. "Galatians." *CNTUOT* 785–812.

_____. *Philippians.* 2nd ed. BECNT. Grand Rapids: Baker, 2005.

Smith, Jay E. "Sentence Diagramming, Clausal Layouts, and Exegetical Outlining." Pages 73–134 in *Interpreting the New Testament Text: Introduction to the Art and Science of Exegesis.* Edited by Darrell L. Bock and Buist M. Fanning. Wheaton, IL: Crossway, 2006.

_____. "Slogans in 1 Corinthians." *BibSac* 167 (2010): 68–88.

Stein, Robert H. "The Benefits of an Author-Oriented Approach to Hermeneutics." *JETS* 44 (2001): 451–66.

Stendahl, Krister. "The Apostle Paul and the Introspective Conscience of the West." *HTR* 56 (1963): 199–215.

Stowers, Stanley Kent. *The Diatribe and Paul's Letter to the Romans.* SBLDS 57. Chico, : Scholars Press, 1981.

Strickland, Wayne G., ed. *Five Views on the Law and the Gospel.* Grand Rapids: Zondervan, 1996.

Swinson, L. Timothy. "Πιστὸς ὁ λόγος: An Alternative Analysis." *STR* 7 (2016): 57–76.

Thiselton, Anthony C. *The Living Paul: An Introduction to the Apostle's Life and Thought.* Downers Grove, IL: IVP Academic, 2009.

Towner, Philip H. "1–2 Timothy and Titus." *CNTUOT* 891–918.

_____. *The Letters to Timothy and Titus.* NICNT. Grand Rapids: Eerdmans, 2006.

Trebilco, Paul. "Itineraries, Travel Plans, Journeys, Apostolic Parousia." *DPL* 446–56.

Vanhoozer, Kevin J. *Is There a Meaning in This Text? The Bible, the Reader, and the Morality of Literary Knowledge.* Grand Rapids: Zondervan, 1998.

Wallace, Daniel B. *Greek Grammar beyond the Basics: An Exegetical Syntax of the New Testament.* Grand Rapids: Zondervan, 1996.

_____. "Medieval Manuscripts and Modern Evangelicals: Lessons from the Past, Guidance for the Future." *JETS* 60 (2017): 5–34.

Wanamaker, Charles A. *The Epistles to the Thessalonians: A Commentary on the Greek Text.* Grand Rapids: Eerdmans; Exeter: Paternoster, 1990.

Ward, Timothy. *Words of Life: Scripture as the Living and Active Word of God.* Downers Grove, IL: IVP Academic, 2009.

Watson, Duane F. "Cities, Greco-Roman." *DNTB* 212–15.

Weima, Jeffrey A. D. *1–2 Thessalonians.* BECNT. Grand Rapids: Eerdmans, 2014.

Wenham, David. *Paul: Follower of Jesus or Founder of Christianity?* Grand Rapids: Eerdmans, 1995.

Westerholm, Stephen. *Perspectives Old and New on Paul: The Lutheran Paul and His Critics.* Grand Rapids: Eerdmans, 2004.

_____. "Righteousness, Cosmic and Microcosmic." Pages 21–38 in *Apocalyptic Paul: Cosmos and Anthropos in Romans 5–8.* Edited by Beverly Roberts Gaventa. Waco, TX: Baylor University Press, 2013.

Witherington, Ben, III. *The Acts of the Apostles: A Socio-Rhetorical Commentary.* Grand Rapids: Eerdmans; Carlisle: Paternoster, 1998.

Wolterstorff, Nicholas. *Divine Discourse: Philosophical Reflections on the Claim that God Speaks.* Cambridge: Cambridge University Press, 1995.

Wright, Christopher J. H. "Mission as a Matrix for Hermeneutics and Biblical Theology." Pages 102–43 in *Out of Egypt: Biblical Theology and Biblical Interpretation.* Edited by Craig Bartholomew, et al. Grand Rapids: Zondervan, 2004.